AN ANATOMY OF TRADE IN MEDIEVAL WRITING

AN ANATOMY OF TRADE IN MEDIEVAL WRITING

Value, Consent, and Community

LIANNA FARBER

Cornell University Press
Ithaca and London

First published 2006 by Cornell University Press

Printed in the United States of America

Library of Congress Cataloging-in-Publication Data

Farber, Lianna.
    An anatomy of trade in medieval writing : value, consent, and community / Lianna Farber.
        p. cm.
    Includes bibliographical references and index.
    ISBN-13: 978-0-8014-4412-8 (cloth : alk. paper)
    ISBN-10: 0-8014-4412-8 (cloth : alk. paper)
    1. Economics—History—To 1800.   2. Commerce—History—Medieval, 500–1500.   3. Europe—Commerce—History—To 1500.   4. Economics—Moral and ethical aspects—Europe—History.   5. Commerce in literature. I. Title.
HB79.F37 2006
381′.094′0902—dc22
                                                          2005023945

Cornell University Press strives to use environmentally responsible suppliers and materials to the fullest extent possible in the publishing of its books. Such materials include vegetable-based, low-VOC inks and acid-free papers that are recycled, totally chlorine-free, or partly composed of nonwood fibers. For further information, visit our website at www.cornellpress.cornell.edu.

Cloth printing   10   9   8   7   6   5   4   3   2   1

For Marilynn and Harvey Farber

CONTENTS

ACKNOWLEDGMENTS

I am delighted to acknowledge all the assistance I have received while writing this book. I am grateful for research support from the Andrew Mellon Foundation, the Newberry Library, and the Centre for History and Economics at King's College, Cambridge, where I was first encouraged to think seriously about the history of economic thought. The University of Minnesota provided me with a single semester leave, a McKnight Summer Research Fellowship, and a Faculty Summer Research Fellowship. The interlibrary loan department at the University of Minnesota's Wilson Library filled one request after another. I could not have completed this project without their help. A portion of chapter 4 is reprinted from my article, "The Creation of Consent in Chaucer's *Physician's Tale*," *Chaucer Review* 39, no. 2 (2004): 151–64, with kind permission from Pennsylvania State University Press. An earlier version of a portion of chapter 2 appeared in my "Roosters, Wolves, and the Limits of Allegory," *Essays in Medieval Studies* 17 (2001): 81–94. The illustrations of Ambrogio Lorenzetti's "The Effects of Good Government" are reproduced with permission of Scala/Art Resource in New York.

It is a pleasure to thank the teachers, friends, and colleagues who have helped me think about the relationship between texts and the past over the years, particularly Sacvan Bercovitch, Christopher Cannon, R. B. Dobson, Elizabeth Fowler, Richard Kieckhefer, Rebecca Krug, Jeffrey Masten, Cyrus Patell, the late Rosemary Pearsall, Susan Phillips, Miri Rubin, Elaine Scarry, Peter Spufford, Helen Vendler, Wendy Wall, and Claire Waters. I am especially grateful to Barbara Newman for a long and extraordinarily helpful conversation at a crucial point in this project, as well as for her learning and friendship. Derek Pearsall has helped me with my work on Chaucer for many years, and has patiently read my writing on much else besides. I have been a very lucky recipient of his knowledge, hospitality, and friendship. Andrew Elfenbein and Kathryn Reyerson both generously

read drafts of the entire manuscript and through their characteristically astute comments made it much better than it would otherwise have been.
John Watkins not only read a draft of the whole but read many parts before there was a whole, and discussed still more before they existed. He has
been superlative in his tripartite role of mentor, colleague, and friend. Joel
Kaye and the anonymous reader from Cornell University Press both provided comments that were of tremendous help in sharpening my argument. Bernhard Kendler has combined professionalism, kindness, and wit
in a way that has made this process a pleasure. Marilynn Farber helped with
the proofs with great care. My debts to Michael Lower are far larger than
even he will ever know. I would, finally, like to thank my parents for their
love and support. This book is dedicated to them with gratitude and love.

AN ANATOMY OF TRADE IN MEDIEVAL WRITING

Ambrogio Lorenzetti, *The Effects of Good Government in the City*. Palazzo Pubblico, Siena. (Reproduced by permission of Scala/Art Resource, N.Y.)

Ambrogio Lorenzetti, *The Effects of Good Government in the Countryside*. Palazzo Pubblico, Siena. (Reproduced by permission of Scala / Art Resource, N.Y.)

INTRODUCTION

Economics was not an intellectual category in the middle ages. When medieval authors considered topics we would call "economic" they wrote instead about ethics, about justice, about law, about theology. This simple fact of medieval intellectual life has forced scholars interested in medieval economic thought to search widely for sources. Combing through entire theological summae for an article or two about trade, looking through penitential manuals for the few lines devoted to advising merchants or usurers, reading small parts of Aristotelian commentaries, searching for a few sections in career-long compilations of quodlibetal questions that speak, however indirectly, to our idea of economics—this has been the necessary work of those who hope to recover medieval economic thought. After gathering these hard-found pieces, scholars have then had the further labor of putting them together into a coherent narrative.[1] It is only from the shoulders of those who have performed such painstaking work that it becomes possible, and I believe necessary, to ask what is lost when we move scraps of writing from their medieval contexts to a modern narrative in order to create a picture recognizable to us as "economics."

The subject of this book is the idea of trade as it appears in medieval writing from the middle of the twelfth to the early fifteenth century. I begin by asking what we find if we look carefully at the accounts of trade that scholars interested in "medieval economic thought" might study; what we find if we look, that is, at places where medieval authors explicitly mention the mechanism of trade, at however brief or great a length. Such accounts of trade, I argue, show that trade was not a single economic act, but that it had three component parts: value, consent, and community. Justifications of trade not only rely on these constituent parts, they rely on them as necessarily unproblematic and straightforward. The ensuing chapters turn away from accounts of trade to places where each element of trade is directly discussed in order to show that the picture of value, consent, and community presented in medieval justifications of trade is falsely reassuring. In fact, these ideas were not straightforward but deeply contested. By thus anatomizing the story of trade and trying to place its components back into their medieval contexts, we find that writing that has been understood as descriptive is actually argumentative and that ideas about what we see as the economy are much less unified than the canon of "medieval economic thought" would suggest. At the same time, however, these ideas were much more deeply integrated into medieval life, thought, and analytical forms than we have previously realized. It becomes apparent that trade was not a simple act but a construction that brings together a range of actions and ideas.

For all the far-flung places in which we find them, the medieval writings that treat trade explicitly do not vary much in their reliance on the ideas of value, consent, and community. For the sake of example we can look at Thomas Aquinas writing about trade in his commentary on Aristotle's *Nicomachean Ethics,* a classic locus for "economic" thought.[2] Aquinas, following Aristotle, posits a square with points A, B, G, and D at its corners, and then draws two diagonals through the square so that the points are related in every possible way: "Let A represent a builder, B a shoemaker, G a house that is the work of the builder, and D a sandal that is the work of a shoemaker." When the shoemaker needs a house and the builder needs sandals, the two will come together to trade. But rather than ending there, Aquinas explains that "first an equality according to proportionality" has to be found so that "a certain number of sandals be fixed as equal to one house." The trade will then take place according to this proportionate equality. The equality must be proportionate, rather than absolute, because of the difference between shoes and houses. If some form of proportionate equality, accepted by both sides, is not made, however, "there will not be an equality of things exchanged—and so men will not be able to live together."[3]

Aquinas here breaks down the process of trade. Once we have the four basic elements of two different people, each with a different commodity, they must agree on some form of proportionate reciprocity so that they can know how many sandals to trade for a house. That they do agree is crucial, since if they do not one of them will feel that there was not "an equality of things exchanged." And it is crucial that both believe that an equality of things was exchanged, not only because it would be unseemly to advocate that one person feel cheated in an *Ethics* commentary but because if both do not agree that the exchange was equal then "men will not be able to live together." It emerges, then, that what we tend to see as the single activity of trade has three stages. First, two people decide how to value goods in relation to each other, determining some form of proportionate reciprocity. Next, they both agree on this proportionate reciprocity. Finally, the first two steps enable them to "live together."

Not only for Thomas Aquinas but for almost all medieval writers who explained trade, trade itself had three constituent parts: value, consent, and community. In medieval accounts of trade, these parts are presented not only as necessary but as necessarily straightforward. To understand why this is so, we need only think about what would happen to Aquinas's account if we questioned people's ability to determine value: suddenly we would have no way of knowing whether "an equality of things exchanged" had been achieved. Without this knowledge the traders would have no way of determining whether to agree, or else they might agree without equality, which would compromise their ability to live together. Or we could instead think of what would happen to Aquinas's account if we questioned the consent each party gives to the trade: suddenly it might be possible to force one party into agreement, which would mean that there need not be proportionate equality at all. Or we could think of what would happen if we denied that trade enabled men to live together: it might turn out that trade was not so beneficial for one of them; or it might turn out that one would depart, leaving the other with no trading partner the next time he needed sandals (or grain, or oil, or wine). At each stage of the process, then, value, consent, and community must not only take place but be recognizable and straightforward so that we can distinguish between a trade that partakes of proportionate equality and one that does not, so that we can distinguish between coercion and exchange.

That an act we think of as single, an act constitutive in many ways not only of the economy but also of civic life, should in fact have these three necessary and necessarily unproblematic parts is interesting, but it is not in itself troubling. The trouble starts when we try to return these parts to their medieval contexts, away from the histories of economic thought that we have compiled. It turns out that justifications of trade paint a far more optimistic picture of value, consent, and community than do other medieval writings. In other places, value, consent, and community are not transparent, as justifications of trade demand, but disputed and uncertain. This is true not only as we move from author to author but even when we look at the writing of single authors, who often treat the ideas of value, consent, and community differently when they write about trade than they do when considering the same issues in discussing other topics.

In this book, I try to place the components of trade back into their medieval contexts in order to show how justifications of trade, if taken together as direct representations of "medieval economic thought," mislead us. These accounts do not describe trade as it took place but instead make a sophisticated argument about why trade should take place. In order to see how value, consent, and community are treated outside accounts of trade, I turn to texts where these ideas are explicitly discussed. This turn away from accounts of trade entails examining not only texts that deal with seemingly disparate subjects (the just price, marriage, craft guilds) but also texts that are written in a variety of forms (decretals, legal glosses, court cases, theological summae, scholastic commentaries, poetry, city records). I use these texts because I am interested in finding places where medieval authors think through ideas about value, consent, and community in ways that complicate the accounts of these concepts found in justifications of trade.

This method stands in contrast to traditional history of thought, which tends to be written along disciplinary lines. The traditional practice has many advantages. Chief among them, perhaps, is that it allows us to follow a genealogy of thought across generations. At the same time, however, it has weaknesses. It sometimes privileges our interests above what texts have to say. This point becomes clear, for example, in Peter Biller's demonstration that although Aristotle's *Politics* discusses government and demography, and although medieval writers commented on both, modern scholars were for many generations interested only in the parts on government.[4] Another limitation of history of thought that moves along disciplinary lines is that people do not think only along disciplinary lines—they do not, for example, necessarily stop thinking about justice in trade when they stop reading the *Nicomachean Ethics* 5.5 (one of the classic loci for its discussion) to eat dinner, or to go to the market, or to move on to *Ethics* 5.6.

As I try to demonstrate the necessity of looking across disciplinary lines to compile a snapshot of thought, I also strive to remain sensitive to the distinctions among different kinds of writing. Although poems and legal and theological texts may all treat the same idea, they do not treat it in the same way. Authors are bounded, in what they write, by the demands of the form in which they write. Form often has a determinative effect on the kinds of ideas that can be expressed and the kinds of arguments that can be made. The way in which form constrains writing becomes clear, for example, in medieval considerations of consent. In the *Physician's Tale*, one of Chaucer's interests lies in asking whether you truly agree when you think you agree to something, or whether external factors have instead led you to believe you are consenting even though that consent is against your best interests. When Aquinas writes about the formation of marriage, he ponders whether consent can ever be externally known and whether, therefore, any person can be certain of his or her own marriage. Chaucer and Aquinas ask questions that jurists simply do not have the luxury to ponder in writing. When Robert and Agnes appear before the court, and Agnes says that she and Robert spoke words that created their marriage, while Robert denies this claim, jurists cannot ask the judge to start questioning Agnes about why she thinks she wanted to agree to marry Robert: What had her friends told her about Robert? How about her family? Was she trying to escape from a different situation? Nor does the judge have any way of knowing, when William and Alice celebrate their marriage, whether both believe the consent they voice and therefore whether the sacrament of marriage has taken place. These are all questions that fall outside the purview of the court system.

Although the argument of this book is not primarily one about poetry, it is certainly an argument that could not be made without the evidence poetry provides. In the middle ages poetry was in a good position to ask questions that other kinds of writing could not because it had no institutional pressure to answer the questions it posed, despite its often institutional settings such as the court or the monastery. Those who write quodlibetal questions must present arguments on both sides of the question and must in the end provide an answer; those who judge the legality of actions must arrive at a decision. Although poetry has a host of conventions (fabliaux have cuckolds, ballads have refrains) it often does not demand any kind of result. So, for example, Robert Henryson's fable of the "Cock and the Jasp," must, by virtue of being an Aesopic fable, contain a moral. What a moral says, however, is not so determinate. In this case Henryson provides a moral that seems to contradict the lesson of his fable. Such a stance would not be possible in legal or scholastic writing. To state that poetry can express kinds of ideas that other forms of writing tend not to express, however, is not to say that poetry always does so. In fact, it seldom does. Rather, during the period I examine there were no formal constraints on the questions poetry could ask, as there were on most other forms of writing. Poetry could think through questions without worrying about these final ends, even though it usually did not.

The vagaries of form, impinged on or not by various institutional requirements, make it important, in this type of intellectual history, to compile texts in a variety of genres. Because it is only by doing so that we can view what happens to a single idea when it is subject to the constraints of numerous kinds of writing, I have adopted this approach in searching for different ways that ideas that appear stable in justifications of trade were understood. In working on these texts I have tried not to treat them all as so much writing, leveling form, but instead to emphasize the importance of form. Exploiting the possibilities that open up when we bring together various genres, with their different imperatives and teleologies, is by no means a new approach. Barbara Newman and Paul Freedman, for example, have in different ways made excellent use of the possibilities of this

attention to form.[5] It is, however, something I consciously sought in analyzing how value, consent, and community were understood outside of
writing about the mechanism of trade.

This series of compilations is an effort to take seriously the idea that economics was not a category of thought in the middle ages. One result is a
different picture of medieval "economic" thought than the one usually
drawn. Because issues we consider economic were not confined to our notion of economic subjects, following medieval thought, rather than modern disciplines, brings out variations in thought that otherwise remain
invisible to us. Ideas about what we think of as the economy were, it turns
out, not as cohesive as the anachronistic canon would suggest. We see this
in terms of arguments about ideas we think of as economic: whereas writing that we consider part of economic thought is consistent in the way it
explains trade, once we look at the elements of trade we find far more variation and far less certainty. We also see the lack of unity in terms of sources:
people thought about "economic" issues when they wrote about a large
number of topics, not only those we consider economic. At the same time,
however, ideas we think of as economic were much more deeply integrated
into medieval life, thought, and analytical forms than we tend to realize.

Another advantage of taking seriously the truism that economics was
not an intellectual category in the middle ages is that it allows us new purchase on a problem that has long bothered students of medieval "economics": the discrepancy between the way medieval authors wrote about
trade, on the one hand, and the way we know medieval markets worked,
on the other. Medieval descriptions of trade used barter as a model for exchange. Nevertheless, we know that in neither ancient Athens nor medieval Paris did the builder who needed a new pair of shoes follow Aristotle
or scholastic authors' descriptions of trade by going to the market in search
of a shoemaker who happened to need a house that day. Instead the
builder went to the shoemaker, who may or may not have needed a house,
and offered him money in exchange for shoes.

This discrepancy between scholastic descriptions of trade and medieval
markets was for some years taken as a sign of medieval naïveté, a primitive
starting point from which those who cared about economics (Condorcet,
Adam Smith) had to advance.[6] Medievalists, also understanding these accounts of trade as descriptive, have asserted medieval sophistication in a
variety of ways. Some have concentrated on those aspects of medieval economic thought that are also present in modern economic thought, showing the continuity of economic thought and finding sophistication in those
ideas that anticipate or mirror our own.[7] Others have focused on aspects
of economic thought in which better claims to nuance and sophistication
might be made, such as usury or the just price, and have left direct ac-

counts of trade largely unmentioned.[8] Still others have examined the complex ways that people in the middle ages actually traded and manipulated currencies, leaving largely unmentioned the seemingly less sophisticated ways that money was presented in theoretical accounts of trade (as an auxiliary to barter, with value that derived primarily from its metallic content).[9] Still others have simply denied the discrepancy between description and reality, claiming, perhaps less plausibly, that scholastic authors did describe trade accurately and that, as Joel Kaye maintains, their texts show "the willingness of philosophers and theologians to reformulate economic conceptions in order to comprehend and accurately describe the changing realities of the monetized marketplace."[10]

By breaking trade into its constituent parts, however, and then placing these parts back into larger conversations, we can see that accounts of trade were not naive descriptions but complex arguments. As explanations rather than mirrors of trade, they prove remarkably astute at explaining an activity that religious writers traditionally found distasteful in a way that religious writers did not. Through a descriptive story of origins, these accounts show why trade was not only necessary but also salutary and natural. To state that scholastic accounts of trade were not descriptive, then, is not to return to a notion of medieval naïveté, but to recognize that sophistication wears many faces and mimesis is not her only guise. On the one hand, the accounts of trade that medieval writers posit and this book examines do not create accurate pictures of the exchanges taking place on a day-to-day basis. On the other hand, the fact that the authors do not necessarily describe the workings of the economy when they write about the mechanism of trade means neither that they do not understand the workings of the economy nor that what they do write lacks conceptual complexity. If we assume, as some scholars have, that the most complex way for medieval authors to write about trade is to describe it accurately, we institute a double standard: we modern writers do well to make arguments about the world, whereas medieval writers' highest form of sophistication lay in describing what they observed in a way consonant with our own modern understanding.[11] This is a form of condescension that I do not think Albert the Great, Thomas Aquinas, Henry of Ghent, and others, require.

Placing the components of trade back into their medieval contexts also makes more understandable a division in medieval thought long remarked on by those who study trade and merchants. There was a body of medieval writing that condemned trade. This writing went back to the idea that Jesus had thrown the moneylenders from the Temple, and it remained, in some forms, a current in medieval thought through the end of the middle ages. We see it, for example, in the need to explain why mercantile activity is acceptable, as well as in the avaricious merchant who becomes a stock figure of fabliaux and sermons. Alongside this current, scholars have noted a positive attitude toward trade and merchants, derived, in part, from the need for the Church to accept commerce if it were to thrive in an increasingly commercial society.[12] This more accepting attitude is one embodied in writing that has been understood as directly economic. Looking at the way that justifications of trade depend on the clarity of the ideas of value, consent, and community, however, and appreciating that these ideas were far from universally clear, shows us that those who distrusted trade may have had very good reasons for doing so, beyond nostalgia or deep conservatism. Even if those who wrote directly about the mechanism of exchange did not present it as problematic, their arguments rested on foundations that were. These arguments themselves, then, may not have reassured people who found the idea of merchants and trade troubling, however ingrained buying and selling were in daily life.

In examining different kinds of texts, about a variety of subjects, I never aim to offer a comprehensive account of value, consent, or community. Nor do I attempt to show every way or place that these ideas may have been debated. Instead I seek to identify some ways that these ideas troubled medieval writers, even if they did not trouble accounts of trade. By choosing to focus on trade, I do not consider many of the ideas that we think of as economic. Similarly, many works of imaginative literature that are often understood as making important "economic" points fall outside the purview of this book.[13] I omit them here not because they have little to say to our current notion of the economy but because I chose those texts that best illuminated the ways medieval writers thought about the constituent ideas of trade.

This book is divided into four parts. The first chapter, "The Story of Trade," establishes how a wide range of medieval accounts of trade tell the same story. These accounts not only depend on value, consent, and community but they depend on these elements to be stable and easily known. After looking at the way these ideas are present and necessarily straightforward in a large number of accounts of trade, I turn to Nicholas Oresme's *De moneta,* in which this account of trade is so deeply ingrained that Oresme does not argue for it, but uses it as the chief evidence for a different, more controversial, argument about money. The chapter thus shows the triumph of this account of trade if we look only at sources we regard as economic in the company of one another. The following chapters then move outward from this account of value, consent, and community to detail problems that occur when writers try to think directly about the ideas on which the writing about trade is based.

The second chapter, on value, begins by considering medieval accounts of value and the just price. It opens with the Augustinian distinction between natural value (the way we should value things) and human or economic value (the way we do value things). It then moves on to writing about economic value and the just price, showing that writers offered a plethora of suggestions that might retrospectively explain the way a given object was valued, but were unable to suggest how a person should determine value. It next turns to two of Geoffrey Chaucer's *Canterbury Tales,* examining how Chaucer plays upon our assumption that natural value is more stable than economic value. It turns finally to Robert Henryson's fable "The Cock and the Jasp," where Henryson questions our ability to distinguish in practice between natural and economic value, thus questioning the Augustinian foundation on which medieval accounts of value are based.

Justifications of trade often mention consent: if the parties do not agree to a trade it either will not take place or will not be trade. Rather than discussing what constitutes consent and how we might recognize it, however, justifications of trade assume that the trade itself indicates that consent was present. The third chapter, on consent, therefore has to look beyond conventional economic questions. The idea of consent is most fully considered in medieval writing in discussions of marriage. The chapter begins by tracing the way marriage came to be defined as the consent between the two partners and the wide dissemination of that view. It then examines a series of legal cases in which people articulated ideas about whether they had consented to marriage when marriages were challenged. The chapter moves next to the *Physician's Tale,* where Chaucer posits a case in which the heroine believes that she consents to her death, although the narrative suggests that such consent is against her own interest. The tale proposes ways in which her consent might have been constructed and questions whether we truly consent to any act even when we think we do. The chapter looks finally at Thomas Aquinas's writing on the formation of marriage, where Aquinas struggles with the differing ways that canon law and theology define consent. Because Aquinas finds the difference so troubling we come to see how even these close disciplines disagreed on the question of what constitutes consent, a question justifications of trade take for granted.

The final chapter, on community, posits the test case of London, which should, on paper, have been a community whose commonality and identity were largely formed through trade. By 1319, for example, the only avenue to citizenship for a noncitizen was through becoming a member of the craft guild.[14] The chapter begins with the alliterative poem *St. Erkenwald,* which posits an ideally united community of Londoners, past and present, from all stations of life, each one part of the whole while respecting a hierarchy that places the bishop at their head. From this point of idealized community, the chapter turns to the actual communities we find in London craft guild charters and ordinances and city records about the guilds. The guilds' charters and ordinances speak incessantly of the common good, the common profit, and the good of the community, which they use both as justification for their existence (the guilds should be allowed because they will benefit the community) and as their final aim (their purpose is to promote the common good). When we examine the records more closely, however, we find that the idea of community fractures into groups that are not only distinct from one another but fundamentally incompatible: one craft versus another; buyers versus sellers; members of a single guild versus one another. These divisions make it impossible to identify who might benefit from a "common" good, or who might be included in the idea of "community" at all. The chapter turns finally to the fifteenth-century ballad *London Lickpenny,* which presents London as a closed community. On one hand, all of the goods those who justify trade tout as its benefits seem available, and more: clothes and food and household goods, as well as legal help and advice. On the other hand, the speaker is excluded from this market by dint of having nothing to trade. It shows, as justifications of trade do not, what happens to those shut out of the communities that trade creates.

If, in gathering discussions about the components of trade, it seems somewhat far afield to turn to writing on value and the just price, marriage, and craft guilds, we need only to look at one of Ambrogio Lorenzetti's frescoes in the Palazzo Pubblico of Siena to see that it is not. The Council of Nine that governed Siena commissioned the work, variously known as "The Effects of Good Government" or "Good Government in the City and Country" or "The Well-Governed City and Countryside" or "The Effects of Virtuous Government in the City and Country" or sometimes simply "Peace."[15] Lorenzetti worked on it from 1337 to 1339. In 1425 Bernardino of Siena described it in a sermon:

> When I turn to peace, I see commercial activity; I see dances, I see houses being repaired; I see vineyards and fields being cultivated and sown, I see people going to the baths, on horses, I see girls going to marry, I see flocks of sheep. . . . And for this everyone lives in holy peace and concord.[16]

No viewer of Lorenzetti's fresco could argue with the order in which Bernardino describes the activities it portrays. The entire wall is covered with images of commerce: a tailor sewing, a goldsmith's workshop, a merchant looking at his ledgers, a cobbler's workshop, a shop selling wines and meats, people with a wide variety of goods to trade (a basket of eggs, a donkey laden with lumber, a chicken, a basket of various provisions, bales of wool) moving toward the various stores. Other figures seem to be traveling from the city back to the country. The countryside shows the production and cultivation of most of these goods, and the road between the city and countryside is filled with incipient commerce such as a man leading a piglet to the city and travelers going to and fro. From sheep to bales of wool for sale to a tailor sewing, we might reconstruct the history reified in each stage of commerce in front of us. These kinds of commercial activities take place across the span of the entire mural.

While Bernardino was certainly justified in naming commercial activity first on his list, by no means does the fresco portray commerce alone. Scattered among the various stages of trading are other acts of a thriving civic life: a wedding procession, people playing a board game, others leaving the city to hunt. There are magnificent permanent bridges across the rivers in the country. The architecture detailed throughout the city, against and in which the merchants and craftsmen work, is notably Sienese, portraying the kind of structures that the Nine promoted as public projects. Builders (presumably skilled) work on some of these buildings on a roof-top scaffolding. The labor of the countryside is also shown, producing the goods that will offer sustenance and be traded in the city: wheat, olives, and grapevines. The fresco depicts trade not as an isolated activity but as an activity that is bound inextricably with each part of the community, both holding together and creating civic life. Trade is at once that which allows the community to prosper and that which creates it. All of the activities, whether trade, those that lead to trade, or those activities, such as marriage, that seem to us outside of its purview, are equally part of the business of the community. Tracing the anatomy of trade outside of "economic" thought makes sense of such a picture, one that portrays not a trading community but a community whose cohesion depends on and is seen through trade.

1. THE STORY OF TRADE

When Nicholas Oresme (d. 1382), in turn canon and dean of Rouen cathedral, chaplain to and emissary of King Charles V of France, and translator of Aristotle, composed a treatise against currency debasement sometime between 1355 and 1360, he began not by discussing money but by looking all the way back to the first differentiation among peoples and the origins of trade itself:

> "When the Most High divided to the nations their inheritance, when he separated the sons of Adam, He set the bounds of the people" [Deut. 32.8]. Next, men were multiplied on the earth, and possessions were divided to the best advantage. The result of this was that one man had more than he needed of one commodity, while another had little or none of it, and of another commodity the converse was true: the shepherd had abundance of sheep and wanted bread, the farmer the contrary. One country abounded in one thing and lacked another. Men therefore began to trade by barter.[1]

Oresme draws a picture of initial isolation and abundance. His men face the problem not of need but of monotony. Each has "more than he needs" of his own commodity. Trade enables each man to help the other as he helps himself, the shepherd ridding himself of superfluous sheep while gaining bread, the farmer ridding himself of superfluous bread while gaining sheep. Oresme assumes rather than mentions two prerequisites for such trading: valuation and consent. Because the whole point of trade, in Oresme's tableau, consists of each person gaining what he lacks, trade necessarily consists of exchanging unlike objects for each other. Each party consequently must decide how to value what he has in relation to what he wants: how many loaves of bread should the shepherd receive for each sheep? The second prerequisite to trade that Oresme assumes is the consent of both parties, since without it the trade could not take place. If the farmer, for example, believed his loaves of bread so superior that one loaf should be worth two sheep, he might be entitled to his opinion, but he would not be having mutton for dinner any time soon.

Oresme assumes the consent of both parties due to the mutual benefits that result from trading. One of these benefits certainly must be the variety trade provides for both people who take part in it. But far from viewing trade only as a solution to the problem of uneven distribution (positive though that in itself might be), Oresme hints at even greater benefits when he asserts that "possessions were divided to the best advantage." The best advantage, we might suppose, would give each man enough of what he needs rather than too much of one thing and too little of another. Because farmers desire sheep and shepherds desire bread, the best advantage would seem that by which each had some of both: the solution that results from trade. In order for uneven distribution, which men must then rectify through trade, to constitute "the best advantage," trade itself must possess some positive value that compensates for the time and effort that each party spends trading. This advantage, present when the farmer goes to the time and trouble of finding the willing shepherd and conveying bread to him, must be even more pronounced when those of one country take the goods in which they abound to the country that lacks them but abounds in some other necessity. For Oresme, as he makes very clear in the remainder of his treatise, this value that trade promotes is the contact among people that results in community: the sharing of values that enables people to agree that a certain number of sheep are equivalent to a certain amount of bread, which confirms that although one is a farmer and one a shepherd, both alike value sheep and grain, and which allows each to live a bit better, as farmer and as shepherd, than he would without the other.

That trade should be described in such a way that it has these three constituent parts—value and consent, which must take place before it can happen, and community, which is simultaneously created and fostered by the trade itself—is not particularly surprising in the work of an Aristotelian writing in the second half of the fourteenth century. In fact, these elements figure implicitly in most Western considerations of trade at the time. That it should be described in such unreservedly positive, even enthusiastic terms might seem more surprising given the tradition of writing about trade that late medieval authors inherited from their theologically minded forebears.

In this chapter I trace the story of trade as it was told when medieval authors focused on exchange itself as a topic. These authors wrote primarily within a tradition of Christian theology, responding first to passages about buyers and sellers in the New Testament and then to the rediscovered *Politics* and *Nicomachean Ethics* of Aristotle. The history of the idea of trade has often been presented as one of religious suspicion toward commerce cleared away by the rediscovery of Aristotle. Accordingly it is not unusual for historians interested in economic ideas to begin with the Latin Aristotle or to focus on the medieval "Aristotelian tradition."[2] This genealogy is true but incomplete. Aristotle's writing in the *Politics* and *Nicomachean Ethics* did not present Christian writers with ideas about trade that were alien to them. On some points, such as the moral value of buying a good in order to sell it, many medieval theologians were in fact far less condemnatory toward commerce than Aristotle. The rediscovery of his texts did, however, provide a framework and a vocabulary for future discussions of trade. By the late thirteenth century the terms used to discuss exchange were largely Aristotle's terms. Value, consent, and community were all crucial for Aristotelian trade. Although they were often present in earlier discussions as elements of trade, after the rediscovery of Aristotle they became necessary components for the act of trade itself. In order to see how these terms might have sat so comfortably with medieval theologians and to understand how Oresme reached his rose-tinted picture of commerce, we must look back a number of centuries.

Church Fathers and Church Law

For Christian writers who commented on trade in the central middle ages it was axiomatic that trade involved moral peril, if not downright sin. Jesus had thrown buyers and sellers from the Temple, and church fathers had long insisted that all who engaged in commerce were suspect, wherever they happened to operate. In the third century Tertullian had asked, "Is trading fit for the service of God?" and had answered his own question, "Certainly, if greed is absent, which is the cause of acquisition. But if acquisition ceases, there will no longer be the necessity of trading."[3] It was a strong, but not very controversial, statement that avarice lay at the heart of trade. It hardly needed mentioning that avarice itself was the root of all evil. In the next century Ambrose asserted a necessary connection between trading and lying, depicting the merchant as one whose primary work was against integrity itself.[4] Others concurred that trade could not take place without lying and cheating, buttressing the conviction with the New Testament story of Ananias and Sapphira, who lie when they sell their land.[5] Ambrose also brought up the necessary cupidity of merchants when he remonstrated eloquently against the ways they controlled the supply of necessities, accusing them of "farming the farmers" and "producing scarcities" in order to satisfy their own greed.[6] Augustine sometimes concurred with Ambrose's connection between trade and deceit, stating at one point that business could not exist without fraud, as well as charging that merchants sought glory in their own works rather than peace in God.[7] In the sixth century Cassiodorus brought together these strands of invective by tying merchants' avaricious desires to their disregard for God and their blatant lies: "Merchants," he claimed, "are an abomination because they neglect the righteousness of God for an inordinate desire for money and burden their wares with lies even more than with prices."[8]

Pope Leo I (440–61), content with less spectacular rhetorical displays, commented simply that "it is difficult for buyers and sellers not to fall into sin." This conclusion was widely included in compilations of canons up to the time of Gratian's authoritative collection in the twelfth century, and Gratian, too, includes it in his *Decretum*.[9] Sometime before 1188 Augustine and Cassiodorus's negative views were incorporated into the *Decretum*, along with a homily, falsely attributed to John Chrysostom, on Jesus' expulsion of "all them that sold and bought in the Temple."[10] The pseudo-Chrysostom concludes that "thus no one can buy and sell without lying and cheating."[11] Deceit is at the very base of trade. Peter Lombard, writing around the same time that the *Decretum* was compiled, made a similar point in his *Sentences*, stating that merchants cannot perform their duties without sinning.[12] Sermon writers also followed suit, making the avaricious merchant into something of a stock figure.[13]

If the *Decretum*, however, does not construe trade positively (and Gratian certainly did not include any discordant texts extolling the benefits of commerce), the passages it incorporates from Augustine and the pseudo-Chrysostom nevertheless provide some leeway for those who trade. The pseudo-Chrysostom makes it clear that those expelled from the Temple were not craftsmen, who alter a good between the time they buy it and the time they sell it and whose activities are perfectly honorable. So not only the farmer who grows food before selling it and the shepherd who tends sheep before trading them but also the weaver who makes cloth, the smith who hammers horseshoes, and the baker who turns grain and water into bread, although involved in what we might call the "commercial economy," are not, for the pseudo-Chrysostom, engaged in commerce. Instead, he condemns only those few who sell the goods they buy unaltered save for the price. And the quotations from Augustine, while impugning covetous traders, remove the sin of greed from the act of trade itself, since "those failings are in the man and not in his trade, which can be carried on honestly. In all vocations, be it in those of shoemaking, tailoring, farming, sins are committed, but it is not the vocations that are at fault, it is the man who sins."[14] Any person who trades might commit a sin, but it does not follow that the sin inheres in trade itself. The passage also includes the idea that merchants deserve a profit for their labor.

Although the overall impact of these reservations may not be large within the framework of the *Decretum,* the reservations themselves are nevertheless important.[15] As many modern historians have pointed out, a Christian commercial society could not exist without Christian commerce.[16] The growing commercial economy in twelfth- and thirteenth-century Europe meant that there needed to be ways for Christians to engage in trade honorably. The picture of the wicked trader, reified as it was in foundational theological and legal texts and reinforced in popular literature, never disappears in the middle ages. But this picture was increasingly, and often enthusiastically, challenged by a different view of what exchange entailed.

Medieval Justifications of Trade before the Rediscovery of Aristotle

By the central middle ages, many writers, whatever their reservations, were willing to accept the idea that society depended on trade and that people lived better with trade than they could without it. In his late twelfth- or early thirteenth-century *Summa confessorum,* Thomas of Chobham not only provides the narrowest definition of who might count as a merchant, but goes further toward acknowledging the merchant's social utility. "Commerce," he advises,

> is to buy something cheaper for the sake of selling it dearer. And such activity is permitted to laymen, even if they do not improve the good that they bought earlier and afterwards sell. For otherwise there would have been great lack in many regions, because merchants carry what is plentiful in one place to another place where the same thing is scarce.[17]

Thomas begins, as the pseudo-Chrysostom had, by defining commerce in such a way that any alteration to the good becomes excluded and therefore free from blame. Thomas furthermore brings intention into the definition by proposing that only the person who buys with the express intention of making no changes to the goods before selling them again practices commerce. Thus the person who means to turn wood into a chair yet finds himself, through whatever circumstances, selling the wood unaltered escapes the taint of commerce. But even those few who do not alter the goods at all and never meant to do so, according to Thomas, do not engage in an activity inevitably marred by greed or lies. Instead they perform a necessary and useful service to the community. By carrying goods from where they are plentiful to where they are scarce, merchants allow people to have goods they need at times of scarcity while ridding themselves of those they do not need. The merchant here acts as the instrument for the kind of positive trade Oresme envisions, making it possible for the farmer with too much grain to obtain sheep in its place. Rather than directly disputing the position that merchants are greedy and must lie, then, Thomas looks to the results of commerce and, finding them positive, asserts that laymen may engage in it (presumably without sin, since this permission is granted in a confessional manual) because it aids people who would otherwise find themselves in great need.

Others, around the same time, tackle more explicitly the question whether the merchant must lie or act dishonestly to engage in trade. In his early thirteenth-century *Summa*, Roland of Cremona disputes Peter Lombard's conclusion that business cannot be conducted without sin, asserting that "business can be done without sin."[18] In Roland's formulation we see a hint of Augustine's distinction between a profession and a person. A merchant, like a baker, may sin, but that does not mean that either need do so because of his profession. In his *Summa de poenitentia*, first composed in the 1220s, Raymond of Peñafort similarly tries to delimit the ways trade may be conducted honestly and dishonestly. Buying and selling, he asserts, is not dishonest by its nature. There are, however, ways it may become dishonest: by intention (if one party means to cheat the other); by place (if the exchange takes place in a church, for example); by time (if business is conducted on holy days); and by person (clergy, for example, may not engage in trade).[19] Raymond's proscriptions essentially copy those of a contemporary Dominican confessional manual written by Conrad of Höxter.[20] Raymond, like Conrad, thus allows the lay merchant to buy and sell without intentional fraud in appropriate venues and at appropriate times. These restrictions were no more onerous than the restrictions placed on any other profession: bakers, smiths, and farmers could not deceive people without sin, either. If Raymond felt the need to spell out conditions for the honest merchant, those conditions acted to regularize the merchant's work within the community, disputing the blanket assertions about greed and dishonesty we find in the *Decretum* and the *Sentences*.

However light Raymond's restrictions may have been, it is perhaps more telling still that when William of Rennes glossed Raymond's *Summa* around 1245, he seems to have believed that Raymond's warnings struck too harsh a tone against the merchant. He goes to great lengths to tie the merchant's possible honesty to the good the merchant does for others, explaining that commerce is not only useful but also necessary, that merchants work not just for themselves but for everyone.[21] His protestations bring together the potential honesty of trade with Thomas of Chobham's emphasis on the way the greater community depends on the activity. Raymond's *Summa* circulated primarily with the gloss of William of Rennes (often incorrectly at-

tributed to John of Freiburg), which therefore worked to remind readers
of the good trade does for society even as it listed the ways traders might
act dishonestly. The same combination of emphasizing the importance of
trade while warning against the ways it might become dishonest appears in
the *Speculum doctrinale* of Vincent of Beauvais, Burchard of Strasbourg's
Summa casuum, and John of Freiburg's *Summa confessorum*, all of the thirteenth century.[22]

Alexander of Hales (d. 1245), an Englishman and first regent professor
of theology at the Franciscan convent in Paris (1231–38), looks both backward and in the direction that turns out to be forward in his *Summa theologica* of the first half of the thirteenth century, when he argues for the
lawfulness of trade. Alexander writes that trade is lawful when it is exercised without lying or perjury; when it is exercised for a necessary or pious
cause such as providing necessaries of life for oneself and one's family or
carrying out an act of charity; when it is exercised to provide for the public good; and when it is exercised to transport goods necessary for sustenance from other lands, particularly if merchants preserve them from
deterioration, theft, or fire.[23] Alexander here emphasizes the intention of
the merchant, just as Tertullian, Cassiodorus, and the pseudo-Chrysostom
had, but where they attributed vicious motives to him, Alexander ascribes
to the trader the intention of producing the beneficial effects that stand
as the result of trade. In making this point Alexander connects the good
the merchant does with the merchant's intention, revising the church fathers' assumption of vicious intent. Alexander explicitly looks back to Augustine, whom he quotes explaining that the failings of the covetous
merchant, like those of any other covetous man, "are in the man and not
in his trade."[24] He also looks back to Aristotle, whom he most likely knew
from a Latin translation of an Arabic commentary. Alexander explains that
"the Philosopher" says that since everyone needs more things for the necessities of life than he can produce himself, such as food, clothing, and
housing, there can be no life for man unless he joins together with other
men, each proficient in a different skill, to supply the needs of one another
through trade.[25] Aristotle's argument here is not, we can see, very different from Thomas of Chobham's argument. Both look on trade as not only
a fact of life in society but as an actual good for the life of society. The em-
phases in the two explanations are, however, slightly different. It is worth
examining Aristotle's arguments in detail not only because Alexander
quotes them but because he turned out to be prescient in looking to Aristotle, who in the decades after Alexander's *Summa* became the touchstone
for scholastic writing about the value of trade. Shortly before 1250, fewer
than five years after Alexander's death, Robert Grosseteste's Latin translation of the *Nicomachean Ethics* appeared; William of Moerbeke's Latin trans-

lation of the *Politics* appeared around 1260. In the first book of the *Politics,* as Alexander of Hales states, Aristotle considers the role of exchange within society; in the fifth book of the *Ethics* he considers justice within exchange itself.

Aristotle's Analysis of Trade in the *Politics*

In the *Politics,* Aristotle approaches the question of exchange through a discussion of household management. The head of the household must procure the goods necessary for that household, and these goods constitute genuine wealth.[26] Frequently, however, households do not possess all the goods necessary for life. The art of household management therefore demands that the manager acquire the necessary goods. Aristotle explains that to the extent that household management requires acquisitory skills, the art of household management is "one kind of acquisitive expertise," that "is by nature a part of expertise in household management."[27] But however important the skill of acquiring that which you do not have through trade, Aristotle holds no rosy view of trade or traders. Each possession, he explains, has two potential uses: the use of the object in itself, and the use of the object in trade. The first use he terms the "proper" and the second the "improper" use of the possession. He gives the example of shoes: the man "exchanging footwear with someone who needs it in return for money or sustenance uses footwear as footwear, but not in respect of its proper use; for it did not come to be for the sake of exchange."[28] The shoemaker uses his shoes as shoes—he does not use them for shelter or sustenance. But when he trades the shoes he has made for a house, or for food, he is not respecting the proper use of footwear. Although the specific pairs of shoes that he traded for bread may have "come to be" for the purpose of trade, footwear as a whole "came to be" to protect feet, rather than to gain bread.

In Aristotle's schema, every cobbler thus uses shoes improperly, as does anyone who creates in order to trade. Aristotle thus impugns the craftsman, whom even patristic writers exonerate, as well as the merchant proper. But we know that not only are cobblers (and butchers and bakers and candlestick makers) frequently heads of households, they are also members of the city. As members of the city, they have come together specifically to give each other the kind of help that a skilled shoemaker can offer to a skilled candlestick maker. Cities, according to Aristotle, arise when people form partnerships in order to help themselves live. This primary motivation of survival is soon satisfied, however, and "while coming into being for the sake of living, [the city] exists for the sake of living well."[29] The fact that the city does not continue long "for the sake of living" implies that once people have formed this union, they either see the potential for living well that the city offers or realize that in order to "live well" they must continue this union since each performs his own skill best, even though they have learned how to live from one another. Both alternatives highlight the fact that, once formed, communities continue not out of necessity but out of choice. The choice, furthermore, is not one of mere survival. There is no suggestion that people will perish if they leave the city, which makes the element of consent involved in living within the city even stronger and highlights the interdependence and mutual benefit that any such union entails: if any individual did not gain from it, he could leave (although he would not live as well, which is why he stays). Cities become, in effect, voluntary unions in which each member stays for his own continued benefit, and in which each member presumably furthers the extent to which all others can "live well." Part of "living well" clearly must entail trading what you have too much of for what you need.

In fact, for all his talk of "improper uses," Aristotle does not wholly condemn trade. Instead, he divides it into two, which he somewhat arbitrarily distinguishes as *chrēmatismos* or *chrēmatistikē* ("commerce" or "commercial expertise") and *kapêlikê* ("business").[30] "Commerce" here is the process of trading for what you need, which is a type of "expertise in exchange," and "arises in the first place from something that is according to nature—the fact that human beings have either more or fewer things than what is adequate. Thus it is also clear," Aristotle continues, "that expertise in commerce does not belong by nature to expertise in business; for it was necessary to make an exchange in order to obtain what was adequate for them."[31] Commerce therefore rests firmly on necessity and is an inevitable outcome of the uneven distribution of goods, which is "according to nature." "Commerce" is the name given here to exchange when it is used to procure sufficiency.

For Aristotle, however, commerce, with its positive function of procuring necessities, soon gave way to "business," or trade for the purpose of acquisition as an end in itself, rather than as a way to procure particular goods. The patristic writers highlight this tendency as greed, the tendency that for Tertullian stands as the only motive for trade. For Aristotle, the reification of the process of acquisition was a result of natural commerce, and it was enabled by the invention of money.

Aristotle explains that "the use of money was necessarily devised" because "the things necessary by nature are not in each case easily portable; hence with a view to exchanges [men] made a compact with one another to give and accept something."[32] In the form of its original use, money is positive: it helps men further the business of procuring sufficiency for their households.[33] By claiming that "the *use* of money," rather than money it-self, was necessarily devised, Aristotle emphasizes the fact that money's value lies in the way that men use it, rather than as an object in its own right. Problems start not with money but when men confuse the medium with the end. Aristotle accordingly turns his attention to "business," which, he explains, is the form of exchange that evolved into the art of making the greatest profit. This art of caring for the amount of profit rather than the goods traded (an art he labels "expertise in business") was made possible by a supply of money. "It is *on this account*," he continues, "that expertise in business is held to be particularly connected with money and to have *as its task* the ability to discern what will provide a given amount [of it]. . . . Indeed, they [experts in business] often define wealth as a given amount of money."[34] We know from earlier in the *Politics* that the amount of money possessed, the businessman's definition of wealth, is not the correct definition. Genuine wealth, we have been told, is made up of those goods that are "both necessary for life and useful for partnership in a city or a household."[35] Money is a useful intermediary in acquiring genuine wealth. Expertise in business confuses the instrument with the end, seeing the intermediary as the final goal. This process of misconstruing wealth has become the "art of business." While this (false) art would not be possible without a supply of money, it is not money itself that is to blame. Axes are instruments used by both woodcutters and axe murderers. The axe, however, is not bad because it can be used for bad ends. Instead, we must judge the use to which men put axes as moral or immoral. Similarly, it is not money itself, but the intention behind its use, that earns Aristotle's approbation or censure.

Aristotle distinguishes between types of trade, therefore, on the basis of whether they are used to procure sufficiency or to procure money, a materialization of the medium that should be a means to "genuine" wealth. He therefore puts forward barbarian nations, which do not use money, as an example of proper traders: "[T]hey exchange useful things for one another and nothing besides. . . . This sort of expertise in exchange is not contrary to nature, nor is it any kind of expertise in business, for it existed in order to support natural self-sufficiency."[36] This type of "natural" exchange can exist equally well without money. In fact, the "natural" exchange is so natural that people will naturally wish to make it easier. From this point of view, the invention of money seems a human inevitability. But for all its seeming inevitability, there are times, Aristotle tells us, when "money seems to be something nonsensical . . . because when changed by its users it is worth nothing and is not useful with a view to any of the necessary things; and it will often happen that one who is wealthy in money will go in want of necessary sustenance."[37] Aristotle here invokes the familiar story of King Midas. Money is not "true wealth" because on its own it cannot help people. It can only appear as wealth within the context of the compacts that men make, for only when men agree to let coins stand for genuine wealth can they (like Midas, like merchants) make this mistake. When we remove coins from the circle of communal compact, however, we know that they do not provide shelter or protection or comfort or sustenance. Their inability to help with any fundamental need for human survival makes it seem "nonsensical" to put any store in them at all.

Aristotle's denunciation of what we might call the "use value" of the materials that make up money is slightly disingenuous, however, since he himself provides a list of the practical considerations behind the invention of coinage. As we have already seen, Aristotle states that men invented money because they wanted to trade goods that were not "easily portable." Therefore,

> they made a compact with one another to give and accept something which was itself one of the useful things and could be used flexibly to suit the needs of life, such as iron and silver. . . . At first this was something [with its value] determined simply by size and weight, but eventually they impressed a mark on it in order to be relieved of having to measure it, the mark being put on as an indication of the amount.[38]

Far from nonsensical, iron and silver were chosen because they do possess inherent value, apart from their use as a medium of exchange. As King Midas learned, metals may not act like Shel Silverstein's "Giving Tree," providing apples to eat, a trunk to rest against, and leaves to take shelter under, but people who "live well" need metals for nails and horseshoes, swords and spearheads, plates and locks. But precisely because the metals used to signify value did not merely signify it (as paper money, for example, would) but were valuable in themselves, men should not have needed to "make a compact." Instead, silver should have been used like horses or grain or shoes or any other valuable good. Coins should have been a commodity among commodities, and their use construed as barter with silver or iron. The compact, however, creates another theoretical level to the use of silver and iron: coins not only have value, they also stand for value. These aspects of the metals coexist in coinage. This theory of value in money cannot be placed squarely in either literalist or symbolist camps. At the same time, the compact adds another layer to the relations among men, serving to cement the ties of those who enter into it, and to promote future exchange among them. Money therefore helps promote the positive ties of the community.

Aristotle's Analysis of Trade in the *Nicomachean Ethics*

Aristotle's suspicion of money itself and of business as an art of acquisition, on one hand, combined with admiration for the good trade can do, on the other, sat well with thirteenth- and fourteenth-century scholastic authors, who readily admitted the value of bringing grain from regions of plenty to those of bad harvests, but who distrusted the greed they habitually suspected of those who bought not for need but only to sell again. In the *Nicomachean Ethics,* Aristotle treated exchange not in terms of its larger utility, but as part of the virtue of justice. This analytic category for trade, although foreign to the church fathers, would have seemed familiar to anyone who knew William of Auxerre's *Summa aurea.* Writing around 1220, William had argued that questions of property were properly questions of justice, not of charity, as had been commonly held.[39] As with the question of the larger benefits of trade, then, Aristotle's argument about exchange as a kind of justice would not have seemed out of place to those who read it in the thirteenth century.

Aristotle treats the virtue of justice in the fifth book of the *Nicomachean Ethics,* explaining that there are two kinds of justice: distributive and rectificatory. Distributive justice has to do with the distribution of goods or honors, and "in these it is possible for one man to have a share either equal or unequal to that of another."[40] Distributive justice is not measured by amount: although you might, for example, be given much more land than I am, the distribution could nevertheless be just because you are more capable of cultivating it, or you have fought longer or harder to win it, or you have come from a more important family. Unlike distributive justice, rectificatory justice pays no heed to character, but rectifies a created inequality. These inequalities might be voluntary in origin (Aristotle suggests sale, purchase, loan for consumption, pledging, loan for use, depositing, and leasing) or they might be involuntary (inequality from theft, adultery, poisoning, procuring, enticement of slaves, assassination, false witness, assault, imprisonment, murder, robbery with violence, mutilation, abuse, or insult). In all these cases justice consists in reequalizing the conditions that held sway before one of these actions distorted the previous balance: if I steal something from you I must return enough to restore your property to its pretheft state. Purchase and sale, for Aristotle, are governed by rectificatory justice: if you sell something to me, I must give you enough goods or money in exchange to return our possessions to their presale levels. As in distributive justice, "the just is equal. . . . And since the equal is intermediate, the just will be an intermediate."[41]

The problem lies in determining how this "equality" or "intermediate" should be decided. Aristotle makes it clear that proportion must always be taken into account: "The just," he explains, "must be both intermediate and equal and relative." Accordingly, "the just involves four terms": the two people involved and the two objects over which equality must be decided. "The just," he concludes, "is a species of the proportionate."[42] This is true of both distributive and rectificatory justice, but in different ways. Distributive justice is geometric in its use of proportion, since the inequality itself is filled differently in proportion to the kind of person it affects. The offense of striking an official, Aristotle states, is more grave than that of striking a pauper, because the position of the official multiplies geometrically the offense committed. Rectificatory justice is instead arithmetic, because rather than taking into account the kind of person involved it considers only the kind of injury. "It makes no difference," Aristotle explains, "whether a good man has defrauded a bad man or a bad man a good one . . . the law looks only to the distinctive character of the injury and treats the parties as equal."[43] Precisely because the parties are treated as equal, the reciprocity itself must be "in accordance with a proportion and not on the basis of precisely equal return."[44] Justice in exchange, in other words, is based on proportionate reciprocity—it is not fair for a cobbler to give a builder one pair of shoes in exchange for one house; proportions must be taken into account. Aristotle is careful not to specify too explicitly how proportionate reciprocity should be measured, but he does state that without it exchange will not be maintained. On one level, this is strictly logical: if the trades that we make are not proportional, but heavily in my favor, then you will soon stop trading with me. At the same time, the possibility that trade might thus cease represents a grave threat to the community because, according to Aristotle, it is through exchange that "the city holds together."[45] We have already seen that cities form and continue for the purpose of living well.

Not only is exchange vital for the maintenance of the community, as Aristotle showed in the *Politics* and reiterates in the *Ethics,* it is essential that each person trades something he has for something he needs, since otherwise there would be no reason to trade at all. Aristotle is quite emphatic on this point: "[I]t is not two doctors that associate for exchange, but a doctor and a farmer, or in general people who are different and unequal."[46] Doctors have no reason to trade with doctors, because they both possess the same skill—that of healing. Doctors do not, however, grow wheat on the whole, so if they want bread and flour they must trade with farmers. Fair trade, in other words, demands not only that exchange be proportionate and reciprocal but also that the goods be different. If I gave you one pound of ordinary wheat in exchange for another pound of the same quality wheat, grown in the same location under the same circumstances, no question could arise about the justice of our exchange. It is a trade, however, that we would not make, because there would be no need for it.

In pointing out the necessary difference in trade Aristotle returns to the question of money. Money was introduced, Aristotle explains in the *Ethics*, to make different things comparable, since "it measures all things, and therefore the excess and the defect—how many shoes are equal to a house."[47] Here, too, scholastic authors would have found themselves on familiar ground. Peter of Tarentaise, the future Pope Innocent V, for example, had written in the middle of the thirteenth century in his commentary on the *Sentences* that money was a kind of measure, establishing equality between different things.[48] The *Ethics* speaks quite positively about the value of this measure: the number of shoes exchanged for a house must correspond to the proper ratio, since without it there would be "no exchange and no intercourse."[49] But "this proportion will not be effected unless the goods are somehow equal. All goods must therefore be measured by some one thing."[50] This thing, by convention, is money: "Money, then, acting as a measure, makes goods commensurate and equates them."[51] As in the *Politics*, money is instrumental in ensuring justice since it acts as a measure for all goods. The precise way in which people should measure these goods still remains unclear. At one point Aristotle, by way of example, shows how to work backward from prices to value, so that if one house is worth ten *minae* and one bed is worth two *minae* it must follow that one house is worth five beds.[52] Although this is not very helpful as a value theory, it provided the framework for thinking about exchange that would dominate scholastic thought for the centuries following the Latin translations.

Post-Aristotelian Analyses of Trade

Reading the *Politics* and the *Ethics* emphasized that money was a measure that enables trade, that society "holds together" through exchange, and that for exchange to continue it must be fair. It posited the necessity of valuation, since goods had to be different; of consent, since people had to agree; and of community, since this was the result of supplying the needs of another while yours were in turn supplied. These components, often explicit, remain always at least an implicit requirement in writing about trade after the rediscovery of Aristotle's work. In his commentaries on the *Ethics*, Albert the Great (d. 1280) pieces these elements together directly for the first time in the Latin middle ages. Exchange, he explains, takes place by proportion between the value of things. Determining value, then, stands as a preliminary step to any trade, since

in such exchanges one cannot exchange thing for thing, such as a house for
a bed or a measure of wheat for a pair of shoes, which are neither equivalent
nor always in equal demand. For the exchanger of grain does not always need
shoes so that he can exchange grain for shoes. For such exchange is not
made by the equality of the things exchanged, but rather according to a proportion of the value of one thing to the value of another thing, with this
proportion calculated with regard to the need that is the cause of the
exchange.[53]

In Albert's commentary we see the steps that must take place in any trade.
First there is valuation, since the goods exchanged must be different and
they are not equivalent on a one-to-one ratio (one house for one bed would
not be a viable trade in most cases). The proportions must therefore be determined by some assignation of the relative value of each good. There
must also be consent: whether the person who wants to exchange grain
needs shoes can only matter if he must agree to what he receives. If exchange could instead take place through coercion, the grain owner's need
for shoes would be immaterial since he would get shoes whether he wanted
them or not. Finally, the explicit reason for all of this trade is to satisfy the
needs of those who engage in it. This activity thus, as Albert had explained
before, best preserves society. Following Aristotle, Albert claims that society would fall apart without it.[54]

These elements of valuation, consent, and community reappear again
and again in scholastic descriptions of trade after the translation of the
Ethics and *Politics*. Henry of Ghent (ca. 1217–93), for example, explains
that the parties to a trade should be judges of whether the trade is fair, and
if they believe that they have received an unfair amount then their assessments of value should move "like arms of a scale" until balance has been
achieved.[55] The image shows the simultaneous importance of both valuation, in the scale comparing goods, and consent, in the need for those trading to judge the exchange themselves. Henry elsewhere breaks the process
down into a description of bargaining, whereby the seller places a higher
value on his object, the buyer a lower one, and each moves toward the
other until they reach agreement, all of which is lawful so long as the
process occurs "without any coercion or deceit."[56] The qualification is important because it appears in the specific context of possibly invalidating
the agreement of both parties. Not only is lying wrong because it is ipso
facto dishonest, it also negates the consent of the other party to the trade
and so invalidates the exchange itself. Giles of Lessines (d. after 1304), a
student of Albert the Great, combines the elements of consent and community when he explains that both buyer and seller benefit from the same
contract. Each, according to Giles, receives something he values more in

return for something he values less. The result is that both sides gain. Again we can see that this result requires first assigning value to what you have and what you want; next agreeing to the trade (which both sides do since the trade acts for the mutual benefit of both parties), and finally achieving benefits for both sides, because each gains, having helped the other (it was through trade that each received "that surplus that derives from a just exchange or sale"[57]).

In the thirteenth century these elements appear most fully in the writing of Richard of Middleton, who was the Franciscan regent master at Paris from 1284 to 1287. In his commentary on the *Sentences,* he, like Giles, explains that both sides must gain. In the process of this explanation he sketches the mechanism of trade:

> If in justice the mean of an object were always to be observed, then one who sells his good at a higher price than it is worth and one who buys at a lower price than the purchased good is worth, would have done so contrary to justice, and if such were the case no commercial transaction could be profitable without violating justice, which is false. . . . [T]here may be exchange which is profitable to the buyer just as much as to the seller.[58]

We will return to the question of how to determine "worth" and what it might mean to sell an object at a price above its worth or buy an object at a price below its worth. Here we can note that both buyer and seller determine what they are willing to pay or accept for the object, that both agree because each believes the determined value will be profitable to himself, and that the trade thus brings them together for their mutual benefit. Where Richard here seems to write from his experience of watching trades and a sense of traders' needs, in his second quodlibet he uses Aristotelian texts to work his way through the process much more deliberately.

Richard starts with the idea of natural law and, like Oresme after him, moves from the natural distribution of goods to the solution of trade:

> According to the right dictate of nature all men ought to come to one another's mutual assistance in their contracts, inasmuch as they are living under one sovereign, which sovereign is God. Now it is like this, that some parts of the world abound in some things of utility for human use, in which other countries are lacking, and vice versa. For example, this part of the world abounds in corn and is lacking in wine and another abounds in wine and is lacking in corn. Similarly, one part of the earth abounds in sheep and is lacking in horses, another abounds in horses and is lacking in sheep, and likewise in the case of other necessary things in use for human life, and therefore the right judgment of natural reason is that a country which abounds in one

thing suitable for human use should come to the aid of another part of the
earth which is lacking in this [thing], so that that [country] which abounds
in corn aids another country lacking in corn and also receives aid from that
one which abounds in wine, and in this way those who serve under one leader
in a military force will aid one another in their mutual needs.[59]

Richard thus begins with the observation of unequal distribution and the
dictate of helping those in need. It so happens, in Richard's picture, that
although distribution is unequal, the particular inequalities also differ
from place to place, which allows regions to aid each other mutually, rather
than having only one donor and one receiver (a case of charity rather than
of trade). This picture itself is not very controversial, as we have seen, because this idea of uneven distribution and the way regions may help each
other by properly trading resources is an old one. In the number of examples he provides, however, Richard suggests that this state of abounding
in some goods while lacking in others is not an exceptional case of famine
or a particular bad harvest but instead constitutes the normal and natural
distribution of resources throughout the world.

Richard moves on from this status quo of uneven resources and goods
to discuss how the mechanism of trade ought to work: "Now it is certain
that in a country which abounds in corn, corn ought to be less highly esteemed than in a country lacking in it, and I say the same of wine and of
other necessary things in use for human life."[60] Richard here explains the
ways a commodity can be valued differently, yet fairly, by two people if both
assign value based on supply. Although this explanation is not new, it is important because it provides a way for both parties to gain from trade while
maintaining the justice or balance of the exchange. It explains, in other
words, how one party can gain without the other party necessarily losing.
Richard continues by illustrating exactly how this principle might work:

When therefore a country deficient in corn and abounding in wine receives
a measure of corn from the other country which abounds in corn and is lacking in wine and supplies a cask of wine to the other country which is lacking
in wine and abounding in corn, the transaction is made according to the right
judgment of reason, and the service rendered is as great as the one received
and yet that transaction is profitable, for a measure of corn in the country
which abounds in wine is worth more than a cask of wine in that country, and
a cask of wine in the country deficient in wine and abundant in corn will be
worth more in that country than a measure of corn, and it may so happen
that a measure of corn in the country lacking in corn will be worth the same
as a cask of wine in the country lacking in wine. And thus you see that he who

has supplied the corn has received a thing of equal value for his corn, that is a cask of wine, and he who has supplied the wine has received an equal thing for his wine, that is a measure (of corn), and thereby both have profited, for to the supplier of corn a cask of wine has been worth more and to the supplier of wine the measure of corn has been worth more.[61]

We come to see in this detailed, if somewhat labored, picture how each party arrives at a different valuation for the same goods, why neither loses, and therefore why both agree to the exchange. The large answer for Richard lies in the fact that we value the same goods differently. He explains this fact through the idea of abundance and scarcity. Trade thus creates an equilibrium that is beneficial to all. Because all value this equilibrium above a lack of balance, everyone gains. We see also exactly how trade works to the benefit of both parties, striking a general mean while allowing both to profit.

After Richard thus makes clear how people might profitably exchange grain for wine in a way that accords with honesty and justice yet benefits both parties, he confronts the more troubling fact that people did not, in the late thirteenth century, commonly trade grain for wine. Instead they traded each one for money. It is with this more problematic insertion of money into the picture of mutual aid through exchange that Richard turns explicitly to Aristotle: "But since, according to the Philosopher in *Ethics*, V, it was difficult thus to convey thing for thing however much men were in need, especially because of long distances and danger on the roads, therefore a common measure of things for sale was invented, and that is money."[62] Richard, following Aristotle, thus presents money as a measure, a kind of poker chip of future materiality that reifies the value you gave, in turn allowing you to transform it into what you need. Aristotle does not write of danger on the roads, but such danger was real to Richard and he therefore mentions it because it explains, for him, one of the reasons money acts as a convenience.

Having established the usefulness of money as a lubricant to mutually beneficial exchange, the primary concern Richard faces lies not, as we might expect from a Franciscan, in the alluring nature of money, but in how, given this material measure, we might still believe that trade maintains its fairness for both parties. For it now turns out that you sell your grain for five dollars only if you believe that five dollars is worth more than the grain. But if that is the case, are you not overcharging the buyer? Richard asserts that this measure does not alter the general justice and mutual gain that takes place without it. In fact, it eases but does not change the nature of trade at all:

> Therefore you can see that if someone should receive corn in some given
> quantity in a country where there is a great abundance and bring it to an-
> other country which suffers a shortage of corn, and receive there much more
> money for his corn than he would have received in his own country which
> abounds in corn if he were to have sold it there, such a one profits, and the
> sale and the transaction are just, for he does not give more than he receives
> in the country in which he sells the corn, and the others also profit, who are
> aided in their need by this transaction. Thus, then, you see—which has been
> our first proposition—how just commercial transactions, in which the buyer
> gives as much as he receives, are profitable.[63]

Money does not change the profit that results from the fact that people
value differently, it merely converts the way they value into a standard measure, making that difference visible. When the person who receives money
continues the chain by turning the money into the good that he values
more than the one he sold, the act will become apparent as the same act
that occurred in barter. Money, far from changing the nature of the transaction, makes it easier for desirable transactions to take place.

Although Richard's analysis is not particularly concise, it shows a writer
thinking through not only the workings of trade but also why the move
from barter to money does not affect those mechanisms. For the early
church fathers the distinction held great significance, because the person
who bartered was more likely to have created his own goods and therefore
to have been something closer to an artisan than to a professional merchant. Richard of Middleton, however, asserts that once we accept the benefits of trade, the mechanism by which it takes place does not alter them.
If anything, the introduction of money increases the benefits of trade by
allowing the mutually beneficial processes to take place more frequently
and more easily than they could have otherwise. In delineating these
processes Richard moves again and again around the triangle of value, consent, and community. Trade takes place for the benefit of all, not just one.
It does this because people value goods differently. Because they value
goods differently each agrees to the trade because he finds it in his own
best interest. This sense of acting in one's best interest, however, does not
negate the justice or honesty in trade, because the exchange acts to the
benefit of all. And so we come back to where we began. The only prerequisite for this circle itself lies in an uneven distribution of goods. That prerequisite not only exists, it remains closed to question since it is the doing
of God rather than of man.

In the thirteenth and fourteenth centuries, these elements of value,
consent, and community appear over and over again in writing about
trade, even in the work of those not particularly taken with Aristotle's

analysis, like Bonaventure (d. 1274), an Italian professor of theology at Paris, minister general of the Franciscan order, and cardinal. Despite his general hostility to Aristotelian economic ideas, Bonaventure nevertheless counts exchange as one of the civil works necessary for society, alongside manual and spiritual work.[64] In so classifying trade, Bonaventure places it, even for professionals, with other honorable but unproductive professions such as governance. Walter of Bruges (fl. 1260s), too, points out that commercial activity is necessary for society, as do Giles of Lessines and Peter Olivi (1248–98).[65] Giles of Rome (1243/47–1316), the Augustinians' first regent master of theology at Paris, their minister general, and the archbishop of Bourges, puts it even more strongly. In *De ecclesiastica potestate* he treats trade specifically as a need of the Christian community, writing that "the Christian religion could not even survive, and could not have the necessaries of life, unless some Christians were anxious in relation to temporal concerns and so engaged in commerce." He uses this general need for Christian merchants as a prelude to discussing uneven distribution of goods, positing some who "abound in excellent wool but are deficient in fruitful vines, while the converse is true of others." He goes on to extend this parable from goods to skills, and posits finally a picture of the Christian community dependent on trade that he began by asserting.[66] John Duns Scotus (ca. 1265–1308), who taught in England, Paris, and Cologne, writes that merchants are so necessary for society that if enough people did not engage voluntarily in that profession the government would have to pay people to perform their functions for its own survival.[67] In the thirteenth century John of Bassolis similarly emphasizes the way trade enables communities to survive, as do Alexander of Alessandria (1268–1314), Remigio of Florence (d. 1319), and Durandus of Saint-Pourçain (1270–1334).[68]

These writers speak not only of the way trade helps the community but also of valuation and consent as crucial for beneficial commerce. Peter Olivi, for example, emphasizes the importance of consent when he explains that an exchange "is initiated and ratified by the free and full consent of both parties," that contracts of sale work only when they are "purely voluntary," and that a contract is valid only if the consent to it "cannot be considered involuntary" in any way, including through ignorance, inexperience, or compelling need.[69] Olivi, like Giles of Lessines, thus explicitly links the conditions for an honest sale with the fact that dishonest conditions violate the necessary consent of the other party. Francis of Meyronnes (ca. 1288–1328) also highlights this connection, stating that force, ignorance, or deception render contracts unlawful.[70] John of Bassolis makes the same point that "force and ignorance or deception" invalidate contracts, as does John Duns Scotus, who states that contracts are valid only when they are freely given and freely received.[71] Gerald Odonis also connects consent with justice, explaining that the fact of consent itself guarantees fairness. "No one," he writes, "is defrauded with knowledge and consent," also making the corollary point that ignorance and need invalidate a contract.[72] Although it is clear that ignorance keeps a person from fully knowing to what he or she consents, need represents a slightly more sophisticated concern about agreement because it shows Odonis's fear that true need might compel consent that would not otherwise be present.

The importance of these elements of value, consent, and community is both crucial and sometimes unstated for those who defend exchange because they come to define the act of trade itself. This definition takes place, by the fourteenth century, negatively as well as positively. Writers assume valuation, because if there were no valuation it would mean either that the goods were the same (a case of substitution, not trade) or that one of the parties had no choice (a case of coercion, not trade). They assume consent because without it the question of valuation itself is moot and the act again is one of coercion rather than exchange. They assume the benefit to both traders individually and to society in general because if both members individually did not benefit they would not have agreed to the trade and the community cannot help but benefit because goods are distributed unevenly throughout the world.

The Use of Trade in Oresme's *De moneta*

If we return to Nicholas Oresme's account of the phenomenon of trade at the beginning of the *De moneta,* we can see that it provides an elegant rendition of the story of trade widely told at the time. The most unusual aspect of Oresme's rendition lies in his insistence that an uneven distribution of goods constitutes the best advantage because it compels trade. Most writers were content to see trade as beneficial given that initial situation.[73] Oresme's insistence on the positive benefit of trade is crucial, however, because he uses the story of trade not to argue about trade itself but to argue about currency, which had been frequently debased in France during the reigns of Philip VI (1328–50) and John II (1350–64).[74] He contends that the currency must not be debased because money exists to facilitate trade, and trade exists to help the community. When the currency is debased, however, it harms the community and thus perverts the original purpose of trade. Oresme takes this as evidence of the evils of debasement.

Money, for Oresme as for others, is a measure that has been "artificially invented" to facilitate trade because "the exchange and transport of commodities gave rise to many inconveniences." Men, therefore, "devised the use of money to be the instrument for exchanging natural riches."[75] He emphasizes that money exists to help men trade, an activity they would perform even if it did not exist. Money makes it easier for the community to trade excess for necessity. It does not, in this explanation, possess any intrinsic value, "[f]or money does not directly relieve the necessities of life."[76] Rather than intrinsically valuable, money is in this sense intrinsically superfluous: it eases transactions that would happen without it. It is properly measured, therefore, in convenience. Its convenience also enables trade that might be too cumbersome without the medium of money. Money thus increases the number of (inherently positive) exchanges that take place.

By explaining the invention of money as an auxiliary to barter, a device that helps people trade, Oresme not only follows Aristotle, he keeps the community the focus of his argument. His emphasis in discussing coinage remains firmly on the human agency that creates and uses the coins and the ways coins help the community. Oresme reminds us over and again that the important stakes in the game of debasement are not revenue but the community and its rights. "[M]oney is the property of the commonwealth," he asserts; and again, "money is essentially established and devised for the good of the community"; and again, money is "very useful to the civil community"; and again, "money belongs to the community."[77]

Oresme follows Aristotle in his account of the use of money and its purposes, but moves away from Aristotle's conclusions about the form coins need to take. That markings should be on coins had become one of the standard criteria for money by the time Oresme was writing, although the list of the coins' necessary characteristics varied somewhat from author to author. Gerald of Abbeville, for example, thought that money needed certain weight, due material, and an official stamp; Giles of Rome asserted that the desirable properties of money were portability, the preciousness and utility of the material, and a sign to show the weight and value of the coin; and Guido Terreni required that money be made of metal, easily portable, and stamped with an image or mark to ascertain its value or weight.[78] When Oresme addresses this question his primary concern is not with the theoretically most desirable form money could take (as if he were creating a currency), but with the continuity of the currency already in existence. He explains first that form, including any markings, must not be changed, because such changes reduce the credibility and authority of both prince and coin by highlighting the ease with which money can be altered. Any change thus throws doubts on the security of the money. Any such doubts hamper the ability of the coinage to facilitate exchange, which should be its primary role.

Retaining the status quo is essential not only in the markings on the coins but also in what we call them. Oresme explains this argument in terms of proportion: he asks us to assume that there are three coins in circulation, respectively worth a penny, a shilling, and a pound. We could not, he asserts, alter the description of one without changing the description of the others, because then the proportions would be thrown off. In other words, if we suddenly changed the coin we call "penny" to be worth half a penny, and called the new coin "penny" and the old coin "two pence," then it would take twice as many new "pennies" to make a shilling. Thus making one change would necessitate a multitude of changes, including "for goods to be bought or priced at proportionately higher rates," and would result in the same loss of credibility that we have seen must always accompany change.[79]

Far more serious than even these charges, however, is an argument that is implicit in Oresme's example of changing the name. Changing the name of a coin is another way of describing debasement. If instead of calling a penny "two pence," we mix base metal into the copper of pennies, so that they contain only half the value, we have decreased the value of the penny to the point that the copper value we used to call "half-penny" we now call "penny." Debasement can thus be seen as a form of renaming, or changing names. This point returns more explicitly six chapters later, where Oresme explains that debasement is against nature, because it forces us to "call something which in truth is not a penny, a penny."[80] When coins are debased, the people in the community become liars, or have lies thrust on them, because they call things by false names. In order to keep the delicate balance in which coins both are valuable and represent value, we must not change the names that we give to them, because this name change is simply debasement from a different angle.

While a name change can thus be viewed as debasement, Oresme argues that the inscriptions on the coins themselves are as important as what we call them because the inscriptions can lead to perjury, treason, or blasphemy. The image on a coin, Oresme explains, serves as a guarantee of its authenticity. By viewing the marking as a guarantee (rather than an honor, for example, or memorial), Oresme brings out one more layer of significance that was latent in Aristotle's description of money: the inscription represents the "compact" among the community that conceptually distinguishes money from metal. The marking takes on significance only within the community that acknowledges the king, or the saint, or God, that is on that coin. Furthermore, the marking is made in the name of the person who gives this guarantee. When the name of God or a saint appears on a coin, therefore, they are invoked "as a witness of the genuineness of the money in material and weight," and altering this genuineness is therefore blasphemy.[81] When the name or image is instead that of the prince, the marking signals his assurance that the coin meets the standards it says it does.[82] If anyone forges a coin, he therefore lies in the name of the prince and commits treason. If the prince himself lies about the coin (by authorizing debasement, for example), he commits perjury.[83]

Whether the alteration is made by prince or citizen, the harm done is harm to the community. While on one level this should include the prince, in discussing the harm that the prince can wreak on the community, Oresme draws a line between the two. If the prince sanctions debasement, then "the amount of the prince's profit is necessarily that of the community's loss."[84] Oresme, in other words, posits an equilibrium between the community and the prince based on the complete ownership of the coin by the subjects and the complete separation of ownership between the prince and the people. Debasement destroys the balance of this equilibrium—the prince's gain is necessarily the community's loss.

Furthermore, the prince who debases the coinage, taking wealth from the community, loses the community's trust. Therefore Oresme emphasizes that debasement reduces the credibility of the prince—a price he should not be willing to pay.[85] Trust is particularly crucial in the circulation of money, moreover, because without it money cannot circulate at all. If each time the cobbler brings the baker a coin for bread, the baker must first weigh it and then melt it down to assure that it is pure, they are bartering with metal rather than using money. And if the baker does not trust the coins, but instead demands a pair of shoes for every ten loaves of bread, we are back where we began, before the invention of money. Oresme therefore emphasizes again and again the prince's need to maintain the trust of the community by visibly maintaining the quality of the coin and avoiding any steps that would make the coinage even appear suspicious. No Machiavelli, Oresme contends that the easiest way to make people believe that the coin is pure is for it to be pure in fact.

But because the primary requirement of coinage thus appears to be credibility, a question arises about why the prince needs to be involved in its production at all. According to Oresme, the prince does not, after all, have any right to or property in the coinage. Oresme answers that the prince's mark is not proprietary but merely convenient. "A king," Oresme asserts, "prefers the public good to his own and loves above all things, after God and his own soul, the good and public freedom of his subjects," and he quotes Cassiodorus not on the perfidy of trade, but on the aims of government: "The art of governing is to love the interests of the many."[86] The prince stamps the coins, then, to guarantee their authenticity for the community, because he structurally stands in the best position to guarantee the coin for the realm. Because "the prince is the most public person," his stamp will be most convenient.[87] As money was invented for its convenience, so the community uses the prince's guarantee for the same reason.

The prince thus puts his mark upon the coin to aid the exchanges that take place within his kingdom. The mark is not a proprietary sign, so for the prince to take advantage of his position by debasing the currency is to profit from the property of others. Any such gains are clearly unlawful, and shameful to the prince and his family.[88] These arguments are based on Oresme's contention that the prince does not own the coinage. But in discussing the properties of money, we must distinguish between the coinage, as a collective whole, and the individual coins that make up the coinage. Money, as the "balancing instrument for the exchange of natural wealth," is "the property of those who possess such wealth," when we conceive of money as particular coins. Money represents the grain the farmer sold and the cattle he will buy. The grain was his grain, not the prince's; the cattle will be his cattle, and will feed his household, not the prince's; and the money is similarly his property, not the prince's. As a collective unit, Oresme could not be more emphatic in declaring that "money is the property of the community" and that it belongs to the community as a natural right.[89] Money belongs to those who use it and whose use creates its efficacy. The collective nature of this property means that, unlike other property, it is not transferable—the rights to it cannot be traded or given away. So not only does the prince not have the right to alter the coinage, the community cannot give this right to him. In the first place, collectivity prohibits the transfer of property: I may want to trade away my own right, but I cannot trade away yours. And even if we all agree to trade away our joint rights, we cannot trade away the rights of our children and grandchildren, because those rights do not belong to us. The proper way to regard this property, in other words, is not so much as property but as a right that cannot be transferred.[90]

To illustrate his point about the nontransferability of the right to the coinage, Oresme compares coinage to wives: "[J]ust as the community cannot grant to the prince authority to misuse the wives of any of its citizens he will, it cannot give him such a privilege over the coinage as he can only misuse, by exacting a profit from changing it."[91] The analogy works with the two-punch logic of his argument about coinage. Whatever you want to do to your wife, you do not have the right to do to my wife. If we thus had a wife in common, as we have the coinage in common, you could not give her away. However, even if we both agreed to give her away, or that the prince could have his pick of either of our wives, husbands do not have the right to give or trade their wives away in any case. Even if husband and wife agree that the wife should be given away, the bond between husbands and wives, once created, cannot be thus dissolved.[92] Similarly, even if men want to give the right of the coinage to the prince, it is an inalienable right. To give it away is impossible; and if the prince seizes it, it is tyranny.

Oresme is quite explicit on this point about tyranny. Allowing debasement is, as we have seen, equivalent to allowing the prince arbitrary seizure of things that do not belong to him, a practice that, Oresme points out, is also known as tyranny. Oresme here skates on thin ice, arguing that debasement, a common practice in France as elsewhere, constituted tyranny. What is so remarkable about Oresme's explanation of trade at the beginning of the treatise, then, is not what it says about trade, but that he believed that his depiction would be so widely acknowledged that it could buttress an argument claiming that a common royal practice was tyrannical.

The exceptionality of Oresme's story of trade, in other words, lies not in the story he tells but in how he uses it. In the *De moneta* Oresme has no interest in justifying trade. His treatise is instead a prolonged argument against currency debasement. He invokes the story of trade not as justification for trade itself but as uncontroversial evidence for his larger, more controversial argument. Oresme reminds people that trade came into being to help the community so that when he points out the ways in which currency debasement hurts the community he can explain that debasement works against the principles of trade. By the second half of the fourteenth century these elements of trade were so firmly entrenched that they become the building blocks for other, newer points. Whether or not this foundation was as firm as it appeared, however, is the question to which the rest of this book will turn.

2. VALUE

Trade demands valuation because if people did not compare the value of goods they would never know whether to trade. Money, as we have seen, was explained as a measure, facilitating trade by being common and also therefore comparative. Since all things for sale could be compared to money, money could be used to compare each thing to any other. Determining the way valuation took place, then, should be a relatively simple matter of examining prices and how they were established. In fact, the matter is not so simple. In this chapter I examine the complications that set in once the need to determine value arises. One immediate problem stems from the fact that prices fluctuate. If, according to the scholastics, price measures value, but prices change, we might very well ask whether they believed that value fluctuates also. The scholastics recognized numerous scales of value, some of them seen sometimes as legitimate and at other times as illegitimate, some legal but sinful, some residing in the object, others in the user, some taking priority over others, some coexisting, and a few that would seem mutually exclusive. Historians have tended to try to regularize medieval accounts of value and price, variously creating a generalized medieval notion of price, categorizing the ideas of writers by whether they were theologians or jurists, or turning to individual writers to find a complete theory of price and value in each.[1] In this chapter I argue that accounts of value differ considerably among writers, even within the traditions of theological and legal writing that are often crucial to understanding medieval thought. The extreme variation, moreover, shows the incompleteness, in medieval terms, of each individual writer's account of value—an insufficiency we see only by juxtaposing a large number of accounts.

We find late medieval discussions about price and value primarily in writing about or indebted to the *Nicomachean Ethics,* in discussions about the just price, and in considerations of why merchants deserve a profit for selling items they do not materially improve. These discussions draw on three broad traditions of thought: medieval Aristotelianism; legal writing about price (notable for its intermingling of canon and Roman law); and scholastic ideas about the right to make a profit. In this chapter I begin by examining early examples of these three broad traditions as they exist in the central middle ages, looking at Albert the Great's conclusions about value in his commentaries on the *Nicomachean Ethics,* at Roman law about price, and at Robert of Courson and Thomas of Chobham's discussions of a merchant's right to his profits. By juxtaposing these examples it becomes apparent that although the traditions are indeed distinct, their conclusions about value are not. There are many different and even conflicting accounts of value accepted in each tradition, the accounts often overlap, and the particular tradition in which an author writes does not in itself determine the account of value he accepts. I then go on to catalog the primary ways medieval authors account for value, without regard to tradition, and to discuss the just price. These analyses highlight the proliferation of accounts of value, none strictly determinative nor prescriptive nor willing to say how value ought to be decided.

This uncertainty over the basis for valuation has troubled modern writers, who often look for absolute value in the just price and look to the middle ages for an account of objective value. When we want to combine the way people do value goods (economic or relative value) with the value the goods in some larger sense ought to have (absolute or objective value) we conflate two scales of value that Augustine of Hippo separated in the fifth century and that have remained largely distinct in discussions of value and price ever since. When we turn to the writings of Robert of Courson, Thomas Aquinas, Geoffrey Chaucer, and Robert Henryson, however, it becomes apparent that the pressure to reconnect these kinds of value is not only a modern one. In their work we see further complication of the straightforward process of valuation that justifications of trade depict.

Both Robert of Courson and Thomas Aquinas, in less and more detail, try to find ways to combine economic and absolute value. Chaucer's *Shipman's Tale* and *Franklin's Tale* do not so much seek to combine absolute and economic value as to suggest that our longing for a world of absolute values is misplaced. The *Shipman's Tale* teases us by presenting a world in which problems arise when a wife tries to keep economic value out of her more "natural" relations with her husband. A solution is achieved only when she accepts the congruity of economic and natural value. The *Franklin's Tale,* in contrast, presents the instability of absolute values when they are challenged by relative economic values. Robert Henryson's fable "The Cock and the Jasp" removes valuation from trade. In the fable and its moral Henryson suggests that determining value is something we do constantly.

He also suggests, however, that even attempting to draw a line between absolute and economic value, a line that is crucial for all thinkers from Augustine onward, is much harder than we are prepared to admit and perhaps, at any particular moment, not possible at all. Any account of medieval thought about value, however, needs to begin with Augustine of Hippo.

The Augustinian Foundation

In *De civitate dei,* Augustine draws a distinction between natural value, on one hand, and economic value, on the other:

> Now among those things which exist in any mode of being, and are distinct from God who made them, living things are ranked above inanimate objects. . . .
>
> This is the scale according to the order of nature; but there is another gradation which employs utility as the criterion of value. On this other scale we would put some inanimate things above some creatures of sense. . . . For instance, would not anyone prefer to have food in his house, rather than mice, or money rather than fleas? There is nothing surprising in this; for we find the same criterion operating in the value we place on human beings, for all the undoubted worth of a human creature. A higher price is often paid for a horse than for a slave, for a jewel than for a maidservant.[2]

Augustine here posits two ways of measuring, one by means of a scale of nature, the other by means of a scale of human utility. The two ways are unequal. The first way, the order of nature, is an absolute scale that works according to God's creation. The second way, utility, clearly flies in the face of God's creation, putting human expediency above questions of life and death. The idea that utility is the economic measure is one we will see again many times. Here, however, we can note that in the first pair of comparisons (food versus mice; money versus fleas) there exists no simple condemnation of those who choose to measure by utility, nor is there a straightforward call for us to change our measure. Augustine presents the measure of human utility as a natural scale of measurement for people— would not anyone prefer to have food rather than mice? His comment that "there is nothing surprising in this" works doubly, making us acknowledge that we would most certainly prefer food to mice (in part precisely because mice are alive), and then making us realize the far grosser violations of the scale according to nature that take place in the economy all the time. The realization of the problems of human measure becomes clearer in the phrase "for all the undoubted worth of a human creature," for although we may not doubt the worth of a human creature, neither do we value it when we measure using prices. The second set of comparisons thus places the way we know value should work against the way we do in fact value. When Augustine, in other words, presents two scales of valuation, one according to nature, the other according to utility, there is no question which is right, but neither is there any question that when it comes to paying prices the scale we use is not the one we would theoretically acknowledge. We do not, after all, value the maidservant more than the jewel, even though the worth of the human creature is "undoubted."

The sympathy for the economic scale of measurement at which Augustine hints in his first examples (who would not prefer money to fleas?) disappears in the conclusion to this discussion where reason becomes aligned with the scale of nature and the fleas:

> Thus there is a very wide difference between a rational consideration, in its free judgment, and the constraint of need, or the attraction of desire. Rational consideration decides on the position of each thing in the scale of importance, on its own merits, whereas need only thinks of its own interests. Reason looks for the truth as it is revealed to enlightened intelligence; desire has an eye for what allures by the promise of sensual enjoyment.[3]

The only exception Augustine permits is that good men may rank above evil angels by "the criterion of righteousness." Human need, which values food above mice, is not only contrary to the scale of nature, it is also selfish, and is here allied not only with need but also with pleasure and the promise of sensual enjoyment. The slide from needing food to needing jewels, from caring more for these objects than for mice to caring more for them than for people, is one that will disturb those who consider such scales for many centuries. Although utility may be the measure we use when we put prices on people and things, it is not, for Augustine, in accord with "rational consideration." We might find in this passage three ways of measuring value: a natural scale, which places the living above the inanimate, the sentient above the insentient, animals above plants, and the intelligent above the unthinking; a scale of human utility, which places food above mice; and a scale of pleasure, enjoyment, and desire, which places horses and jewels above people.[4] Augustine, however, explicitly calls upon us to see here only two scales of measurement, one natural, in accordance with God and reason, and the other human. The difference here between valuing food and valuing jewels disappears within the larger distinction between the right order from the perspective of nature and our own needs and desires. We are thus left with two scales, one natural, the other economic.

This distinction is crucial for medieval writing about price and value. In the first place, it is essential for understanding why prices fluctuate. Prices are measures of worth, which theoretically should remain constant. And, in fact, in the natural scale worth does remain constant. It is only economic worth that fluctuates. Augustine's distinction is also essential for understanding why, in medieval writing, the idea of a just price has nothing to do with theoretical justice or fairness. Although it has now been almost half a century since the idea that the just price meant a theoretically fair determination of value (whether a loaf of bread was "really" worth one penny or two) was thoroughly debunked, the idea that the just price should be just in this sense still persists.[5] But price itself, because it has to do with the way we value rather than with the natural scale of value, works inherently against such an absolute. If it did not we would value mice above food. So the very fact of discussing a market price means that we have left behind a notion of natural or absolute justice. Finally, Augustine's distinction is crucial because it is taken for granted in medieval Christian writing about value and price. When discussing what adds value to an object, medieval legists, canonists, and theologians do not consider any form of absolute or natural value but only economic value. This economic value is based on how people do measure value rather than how they should ideally measure it. The ideal, the thinkers already know, would be in accordance with the natural scale of worth. This is not, they also know, a scale used in economic valuation. The question that confronts them, then, in discussing value, is not one of how we should theoretically assign value in general (we should assign it according to a natural scale, although we do not), but instead one of what determines price or the way we judge economic value.

Three Models for Determining Value

In addressing this question medieval writers received little help from the sources to which they usually turned. The Bible provided little guidance.[6] Nor, perhaps more surprisingly, did Aristotle. As we have seen, in the *Nicomachean Ethics* Aristotle states that justice in exchange requires proportionate reciprocity. He gives the example that five beds may be worth a house, but provides no explanation of how he reached this ratio, or what creates this equivalency. Although there has been something of a modern side game in speculating on what combination of measures would allow such a proportion, medieval writers saw the example as an example rather than a prescription.[7] In commenting on the *Ethics,* they also, however, often felt the need to explain how value should be measured so that proportionate reciprocity could be determined. Albert the Great (d. 1280) laid the foundation for such explanations in his own commentaries, the first complete Latin commentaries on the *Ethics.*

In his first commentary (1248–52), discussing this idea of proportionate reciprocity, Albert states that we should measure proportionate reciprocity "with reference to *opus,* that is, with regard to the community's toil."[8] This explanation looks very much like a labor theory of value, with the value of the commodity coming from the work that goes into its creation. In his second commentary (1263–67), however, Albert provides a different explanation: commodities, he states, "ought to be taken in relation to use, that is, according to what they are worth in use to supply need."[9] This explanation looks very much like a utility theory of value, with the value of the commodity coming from how much others need to use it. The change from the first account to the second can prove surprising to modern students of economics, who see these accounts as opposing theories of value. Classical economic theory (such as that of Adam Smith) holds that the cost of producing a commodity, including rent for space and profit for the producer, determines the commodity's value. David Ricardo believed that he opposed this classical understanding when he advanced a labor theory of value. According to Ricardo, the value of a commodity depends on "the relative quantity of labor which is necessary for its production."[10] It is not hard to see why modern economists would hold these theories incompatible. The first defines value in terms of those who would consume the commodity: the value it holds for them. The second defines value in terms of those who produce the commodity: what it takes in order for them to continue production. Albert's commentaries, taken together, seem to advocate both of these positions. One way to explain these seemingly conflicting writings is simply to say that Albert changed his mind. Such indeed may be the case: the two commentaries were written over a decade apart by a man with an astoundingly fertile mind who continued to think through the *Ethics* and clearly could not have believed that his first commentary was his last word on it. At the same time, it is possible to see these ideas about value as complementary for Albert, even if they are not for contemporary economists.

In the first commentary, the one that explains price and value in terms of labor, Albert states that if buyers pay a lower price for a commodity than the work is worth, the craft of it will be destroyed.[11] In the second commentary, the one that explains price and value in terms of utility, Albert states again that "if the maker of beds does not obtain for a bed as much as he has paid in expenses, he will not make any more beds, and thus the craft of making beds is destroyed. And similarly in other crafts."[12] In both cases, in other words, Albert ties the idea of value to the idea of the market in terms of supply and demand: if the worker is not paid enough for his labor he will stop creating the commodity. This idea takes account of value as dependent on labor: if the labor is not appropriately rewarded the commodity will no longer be made. At the same time, it takes account of value as dependent on utility: if the commodity is not needed by others they will not be willing to purchase or trade for it at a price that will sustain the worker, and thus he will stop making it. These statements, which seem to see both the creator and the consumer of the object in terms of the market, are close to the way Alfred Marshall, at the turn of the twentieth century, tried to revise both classical and labor theories of value by giving up the search for intrinsic value and concentrating on supply and demand. Albert, of course, did not have to give up a search for intrinsic value because he never looked for intrinsic value in the act of economic valuation. The point in comparing the ideas of value Albert sets forth in his two commentaries to modern economic theories is not to suggest that Albert anticipates modern economics but to show the range of accounts of value that medieval thinkers inherited from this single author—they encompass the three most prominent accounts of value in modern economics: utility, labor, and supply and demand. Albert was the most quoted commentator on Aristotle in the middle ages.[13] Whether or not the accounts of value he provided were compatible, they were all passed down to medieval thinkers who sought to understand the basis of value in exchange within the Aristotelian tradition.

This tradition was not, however, the only one available to late medieval thinkers, despite the silence of scripture on the subject. In the twelfth-century compilation of canons that quickly became the basis for the systematic study of church law Gratian had declared that civil law should be respected when it did not contradict scripture or canon law, and in fact should be actively sought when scripture and canon law provided no grounds for ruling on a problem.[14] Pope Lucius III (1181–85) made this teaching official church law.[15] The *Corpus iuris civilis* did contain a number of laws and dicta about regulating price, and these became influential for Western medieval thought on the topic. One of these dicta stated that a thing is worth as much as it can be sold for, a saying that was a corollary to Roman law's recognition of the right of parties to bargain freely.[16] A contract of sale was considered fixed once the parties had agreed on a definite price. If the contract was to be oral, that was the end of the matter; if it was to be written, it had to be drawn up. The consent of both parties to the price itself was the crucial part of a sale. The price had to be certain. An agreement to buy an object at a price to be named later was not considered a contract of sale. If the parties wanted to leave the price to a later time they could agree that it would be what a third person would determine, but they were required to name the third party, and once he gave a price the parties could neither renegotiate nor disagree. If the third party could not decide on a price the sale was considered void. The sale would also be void if the seller tried to sell something that was not saleable, such as a public or religious place.[17]

At the same time that Roman law allowed this general freedom of negotiation for whatever price the parties agreed to pay, however, it imposed some limits on absolute freedom for any contract to which both parties consented. These limits could also, depending on one's point of view, be seen as protections for the people involved. The most important was the prohibition of any fraud within the bargaining. In fact, I would suggest, this prohibition follows from the idea of free bargaining, since it can be argued that the negotiation should not be seen as free if one party is permitted to lie or deceive the other. If, for example, William agrees to pay twenty dollars for a solid gold ring, but John has lied by claiming the ring is gold when it is really brass, then we might object that William did not agree to the price at all, since he consented to pay twenty dollars for a gold ring, not a brass one. At any rate, fraud was not permitted and invalidated any contract.

The second limitation that arose in Roman law was that of irregular or disproportionate injury. This idea developed in Justinian's *Code* as an addition to a general statement about the freedom of bargaining. If one man sold land at a price well below its market price, he was to have the right to repay the price and reclaim the land or to "receive the amount of the deficiency" from the buyer, bringing the purchase price up to the market price. The choice was to be the buyer's, not the seller's. The key elements of this provision are that it only takes effect in the most extreme instances, that in its original form it protects only the seller, and that it is nevertheless the buyer, not the seller, who has the choice of remedy. This law appears twice in Justinian's *Code* and was meant not as a way of rectifying any bad deal made by a seller but only as a way of correcting gross unfairness to a standard of having sold land for less than one-half of its market price. The law became known as that of *laesio enormis,* a term not used in classical Roman law.[18] The law was gradually expanded until, by Roman law of the later middle ages, it applied to buyers as well as to sellers and to all sorts of items of sale rather than just to land. The crucial issue, for our purposes, is how it determined that a good had been sold for 50 percent more or less than it was worth.

Roman law stipulated that the fair price be determined on the basis of prevalent prices at the time and place of the sale because "sometimes place or time brings a variation in value."[19] It gives the example of olive oil, which may have different values in Rome and Spain, or at times of harvest and scarcity. By tying the fair price to a notion of value that incorporates a particular time and place Roman law about fair prices clearly calls not for judgment about the inherent value of an object but for the market price. If the commodity in question was land, the fair price was to be determined by comparable properties in the area and by the income they generated from rents. If the sale involved another commodity, it was simply to be the prevalent price. The fair price was to be determined at the time of the sale, rather than the time the sale was challenged, again showing a clear awareness of the way that exchange value fluctuates over time. If grain was sold for a dollar a bushel at harvest, the seller obviously could not claim laesio enormis six months later at a time of famine, even if grain had quadrupled in price. In cases in which the value of the commodity at the time of sale was in question, the judge was supposed to consult *arbitrium boni viri*. Recourse to the judgment of a good man constituted a common remedy in Roman law when technical questions arose that might require specialized knowledge that a judge would not possess. The "good man" was a way of calling for the opinion of a respected and theoretically disinterested person who would know the price of rents or copper or whatever was being disputed at the time and place in question.

Roman law did use the term *justum pretium* in calling for a fair price. The term appears, however, not only in those places we would think of as appropriate to laws about the just price but throughout the *Corpus iuris civilis*. John Baldwin, who has examined the term's use most closely, concludes that "in most of these cases the meaning of the just price is a normal and customary price, which can be determined in commerce of free exchange which is regular and orderly. It is contrasted with an over-charged or trifling price or a price based on the prejudiced affections of one of the parties."[20] So an excessively small or large price compared to the just price might hide a gift, or usury. People could use the just price, that is, the normal market price, to reveal such dodges of the law.

The concepts of laesio enormis and the just price establish an important limit to the general idea of free bargaining, not only for the way they constrain or protect buyers and sellers but also for what they say about value. If the value of any object were whatever it could be sold for to any person, that would be a subjective theory of value. But if we accept these laws, then the fact that a buyer may be able to find a seller to sell him goods for much less than the market price does not mean that they are worth less than the market price. According to the idea of disproportionate injury, it means that the particular seller got it wrong. The idea that value, within a particular time and place, abides by a norm rather than remaining subjective and individualistic also forms part of the legacy of the *Digest,* which explains that "things acquire their value from their general usefulness not from the particular approach or utility of individuals."[21] Only within the context of this idea of common valuation can the law of disproportionate injury make sense. While providing a vague notion of utility, then, Roman law's firm stance on economic value is that it must be measured against a common norm.

There was, finally, a third general tradition of writing about value, and this comes from scholastic writing justifying the work of the merchant that seems directly indebted neither to Roman law nor to Aristotle. For example, Robert of Courson (d. 1219), an Englishman who taught theology at Paris from at least 1200 (he was a master at that date) until 1212, when Innocent III made him a cardinal, wrote a *Summa* around 1208 in which he explains that merchants need to consider the time, the place, and the labor they have expended on their goods. Merchants may sell their goods at a due price, which may be a higher price than that at which they bought them, according to Robert. The price should be calculated by adding together the cost of the wares and the merchant's labor. Robert goes on to warn against both fraud and greed. He does not explain how the merchant should calculate the cost of labor, nor does he explain what exactly the merchant may consider labor.[22] Whatever labor is, however, it made up part of the value of the object. At the same time, by explicitly mentioning the time and place of the sale in the due price of the goods, Robert suggests that the value of the goods is tied to the current local market for them. By warning against cupidity, Robert shows himself both conscious of traditional arguments against merchants and sensitive to the idea of excessive charges (presumably for labor, given that the merchant's expenses would have been whatever they had been). The idea of the value, or a fair price, the merchant may charge, then, is supposed to be tied to the cost of the object and the seller's work (both of which should be objective and measurable), but Robert clearly worries that such an objective set of criteria can give way to manipulation by emotion (greed), which would cause mismeasurement.

Thomas of Chobham, another Englishman, went into more detail about the circumstances that validate profit in sale, possibly because the intended audience of his *Summa confessorum,* which appeared around 1215, would need to know more precisely when merchants had sinned. According to Thomas, merchants may legitimately charge not only for the capital they expend purchasing goods in the first place and any improvements they may have added to them, but also for their own labor, for transport, and for expenses.[23] The higher price is justified, even if they do not change the goods, because they move goods from areas of abundance to areas of scarcity. The idea that a worker should be paid for his work is the same one we saw in Robert of Courson's *Summa* and is not in itself very surprising. In this section of the *Summa confessorum* Thomas explicitly compares the merchant and the craftsman. He states that some people

> buy the raw materials for things and add their workmanship and labor in or-
> der to make a new product. Thus some buy wood or stones or metal so that
> they might make utensils or tools necessary for human uses. . . . These are
> not called merchants but craftsmen and they are permitted to sell their
> works, and their skills, which they learned through great labor, provided that
> they do not practice fraud in their crafts.[24]

The craftsman's right to profit from the changes he makes in materials (Thomas gives the further example of hides and skins made into sandals and shoes) had never been questioned. By placing this unquestioned right of the craftsman to profit alongside the merchant, Thomas calls attention to the traditional distinction between the two: the craftsman transforms goods, the merchant sells them unaltered. At the same time, however, by drawing this distinction immediately after explaining that the merchant may charge for his labor, for transport, and for expenses, Thomas emphasizes the ways in which the merchant acts like the craftsman. Like the craftsman, the merchant works and deserves a reward for his work. Furthermore, because without merchants "there would have been great lack in many regions, because merchants carry what is plentiful in one place to another place where the same thing is scarce," the work of the merchant, like that of the craftsman, benefits the community.[25] Just as people need tools, utensils, sandals, and shoes, so people need grain at times of bad harvests, oil where it is scarce, horses from distant lands, and other goods that are not locally abundant. In enumerating transport alongside labor and expenses, Thomas might be suggesting that transport is separate from labor, or he might be trying to ensure that transport not be overlooked in the general work for which a merchant deserves compensation. Most likely, however, he is reiterating the way in which the merchant helps the community, a service that both adds value to the goods (the items are more scarce at their destination than at their origin) and that deserves compensation. Whatever the status of the transport, by expanding the items for which a merchant may legitimately claim profits Thomas simultaneously expands the list of qualities and actions that determine the value of an object.

Thomas, furthermore, explicitly links these factors that can add value or deserve reward to the idea of a just price. Merchants, in going about their work, are thieves if they tamper with merchandise so as to deceive the buyer and are sinners if they sell their goods for any amount above the just price, despite the fact that the law allows them to receive an amount above the just price so long as it is not more than one half above it. So the question of the actions for which the merchant may legitimately receive compensation becomes connected to the question of how much compensation he may receive. The distinction between law (which in this case allows compensation up to one half over the just price) and the stricter standards of morality (which in this case allow compensation of no more than the just price) is a familiar one in the middle ages. More significant, in this context, is the precision that such a standard seems to suggest. This precision is, of course, illusory. As Thomas's own list of factors for which a merchant may charge indicates, there is no single just price, above which every halfpence must be returned to the buyer. Instead, Thomas's injunction stands as a statement not about price per se but about intention as it relates to price. What the law allows is not so much a particular price as an attitude toward price: if you are able to get another person to agree to buy for more than the current price or sell for less than it, the law allows you to convince the person to do so, as long as you do not use outright fraud. What moral law requires is not conformity to a price list but an intention to sell for no more than a fair price, even if another party seems willing to pay above it. In Thomas's writing, then, intention comes to weigh as a factor in valuation.

By looking at simply the first Latin commentator on the entire *Nicomachean Ethics*, the Roman law on price, and two early theological writings about merchants, then, we can see a surprisingly large number of ways to understand the value of goods: the work that went into creating them; the expense of the goods themselves; their usefulness to others; the price people are willing to pay for them at a particular time and place; the work and cost of bringing them to the time and place where they are sold; and the intention behind naming a price. From the middle of the thirteenth century through the fifteenth century the factors for which people consciously account in valuation only multiply. It would be a mistake, however, to see these factors as related only to particular traditions of writing or as following any definite chronological order. In running through some of the more prominent reasons that medieval writers gave for bestowing and determining value, I will therefore turn to categories. These categories are ones of my own devising. I will consider in turn the way writers discuss first an object itself and changes that are made to it; second, changes in the circumstance of the object; third, the need for the object (its value to the buyer); and fourth, the activities of the seller that deserve reward. Although there are many ways to arrange the ideas about what gives value to an object, I use these categories (rather than chronology or discipline, for example) to present a large body of medieval writing about price and value, because it is the multiplicity of accounts of value in the later middle ages, rather than who said what, that is important here.

Foundations of Value

The Physical Commodity Itself and Changes Made to It

Some value, most writers agree, resides in a commodity itself. Certain expenses tend to be involved in acquiring an object. If a second person wants the commodity, the first person has the right to recoup his expenses. Thus, as we have seen, Robert of Courson and Thomas of Chobham discuss the merchant's right to recover his expenses in acquiring a commodity, and Albert the Great explains that the maker of beds needs to receive "as much for a bed as he has paid in expenses."[26] The canonists Rufinus, Huguccio, and Hostiensis, as well as the scholastics Alexander of Hales, Guy of l'Aumône, and Thomas Aquinas, also mention the merchant's justification in charging for his own expenses, such as transportation and materials, implying that these expenses form part of the object's value.[27] Thomas of Chobham and the Franciscan scholastic Peter Olivi go further, explaining that in some cases acquiring objects requires not only purchasing the object and/or the materials that constitute it, but also capital expenditures (establishing a mine in order to acquire silver or gold, or purchasing equipment in order to build ships, for example). Both therefore mention capital expenditure in their lists of expenses for which merchants may charge.[28] They thus recognize the capital expenditure needed to form or acquire a commodity as part of its value.

Medieval writers were also quick to recognize the value of material changes made to a commodity. Most take for granted the increase in value that results from material changes: as we have seen Thomas of Chobham assert, such changes are usually associated with a craftsman, and no one doubts the greater worth of the finished object. The Carmelite scholastic Guido Terreni agrees that the change in a product may increase its value, but he extends the notion of how a commodity may be changed by providing the example of the man who raises horses. The value of the grown horse, according to Terreni, does not consist only of the value of the foal plus the cost of keeping the horse as it develops (as would be the case if the value consisted solely of the materials and expenses). Instead, the value of the grown horse consists also of the fact that a grown horse in itself has more value than a foal. Although we here tread very close to the idea of utility, Terreni discusses the increased value in terms of the horse itself.[29] Others who join Thomas of Chobham and Guido Terreni in singling out material change as a source of value include Rufinus and his fellow canonist Stephen of Tournai, as well as Peter Olivi and his fellow scholastics Henry of Ghent, Francis of Meyronnes, and Bernardino of Siena.[30] All mention material change in terms of the greater value of the commodity itself, situating value in the commodity rather than (or in addition to) the work that goes into changing it.

Changes Made in the Circumstances of the Object

Medieval writers acknowledge that value depends not only on the object itself but also on its circumstance. The most obvious circumstances that affect value are time and place. As Richard of Middleton explains, "In a land that abounds in wheat, wheat ought to be less highly esteemed than in a land lacking in it."[31] Time similarly affects value, as Peter Olivi observes when he notes that "the same wheat is worth more at a time of dearth and famine or scarcity than at a time when all have enough of it."[32] The dependence of value on location had also, as we have seen, been noted in Justinian's *Digest*. The way time and place affected value was, in fact, often given as the very rationale behind trade, because it is only when a commodity has more value in one place than another that it makes sense to take it to the second place. Time and place were accordingly mentioned as constituents of the value of a commodity by the legists Azo, Placentinus, and Accursius, as well as the scholastics Peter the Chanter, Robert of Courson, Henry of Ghent, Giles of Lessines, John of Bassolis, Francis of Meyronnes, and Guido Terreni.[33] Pope Alexander III also recognized the principle that time affects value in *In civitate*.[34] Some writers also indicate the role time and place play in value by noting the effect that storage (postponing the time when an object will be evaluated) and transport (changing the place of valuation) have on an object's worth. Alexander of Hales, Thomas Aquinas, Giles of Lessines, Peter Olivi, Guido Terreni, and Bernardino of Siena, for example, all mention that storage and transport can increase a commodity's value.[35]

A second change in circumstance that might influence the value of a commodity is its scarcity or abundance, an idea summed up in the ancient adage that everything rare is dear (*omne rarum pretiosum*), quoted by Henry of Ghent, among others.[36] The saying suggests that abundance and scarcity are constitutive features of value since that which is abundant is not rare and thus should be less dear. This corollary may be implicit in the discussions of time and place, as it is, for example, in Richard of Middleton's comment that one country may value wheat more than another (a question of place) because it is more scarce in one place than another (a question of abundance). The reliance of value on abundance and scarcity is nevertheless mentioned explicitly by a number of writers, including some who also mention time and place as elements of value, including Richard of Middleton, Henry of Ghent, Giles of Lessines, Peter Olivi, and Guido Terreni.[37] Henry of Ghent singles out abundance and scarcity as determinants very clearly in his example of a port where a great number of ships carrying horses have just come in to harbor and all of the horses are being offered for sale. If someone buys a horse "at the just price according to the number of horses for sale at the present moment," but just after that single transaction "immediately all those having horses for sale take ship and depart with their horses," Henry writes that "because of scarcity that one horse is made more valuable, it is not unlawful to sell it right away for much more than it was purchased for."[38] Henry here goes out of his way to minimize all questions apart from abundance and scarcity: the place is the same, the time is only a moment or two distant, the need for horses has not changed, nor has the suitability of the place, nor has the horse undergone any sort of transformation. Only the supply of horses changes, but this difference alters the value of the single unaltered horse. Some writers, like the fourteenth-century Franciscan scholastic Gerald Odonis, point out that the scarcity of skills as well as the scarcity of commodities affects value.[39] Some, like Guido Terreni, tie the importance of scarcity to demand (an item or skill will not become expensive, no matter how scarce, if there is no demand for it), while others, like Richard of Middleton, use the concept of scarcity to moderate their ideas about the relationship between value and use (although water is very useful, it does not have a high economic value because of its abundance).[40]

The third change in circumstance that may add value to a commodity is when it is bought by a knowledgeable buyer. Henry of Ghent explains the reasoning behind this idea with recourse again to the example of horses. If an expert horse trader or horseman buys certain horses from a larger market because he thinks those particular horses are worth the price, the fact that the expert has chosen them increases their value for the nonexpert who needs a horse.[41] Peter Olivi and Guido Terreni also mention expertise as a factor in value.[42] The point here is not that the expert should be paid for his work or the time it took to gain his skills (a related but distinct idea that we will see when we turn to the ways that sellers should be compensated), but that the value of the object increases through the circumstance of having been chosen by an expert, even though the object itself remains unchanged.

Need for the Commodity (Value as Determined by the Buyer)

For many medieval writers need measured value. The need for a commodity not only influenced its value, it was its value. All of the other factors they discussed (the time and place, the expense of the materials, scarcity and abundance) had meaning only in so far as they explained need. So Thomas Aquinas states that "according to the truth of the thing need measures everything, it is evident that money was made for this"; Henry of Friemar writes that value is measured according to human need; Walter Burley explains that "need is truly the measure of all commutable things"; and Gerald Odonis argues that "according to fact and to nature, need holds everything together, that is, maintains everything in value."[43] Albert the Great (in his second commentary), Richard of Middleton, Durandus of Saint-Pourçain, Peter Olivi, Guido Terreni, and Antonino of Florence, among others, also mention need as the measure of value or a factor of value.[44] Refining this idea, many, including Accursius, Henry of Ghent, John Buridan, Godfrey of Fontaines, Peter Olivi, and John of Bassolis, explain that common or aggregate need, rather than individual need, should be taken as the measure of value.[45] So Henry of Friemar writes that human need (*indigentia humana*) "ought not to be taken partially with regard to this or that person, but universally with regard to the whole community," and John Buridan writes that "the need of this man or that man does not measure the value of a commutable thing, but the need all men in common have among them in common."[46] The impetus behind making this point for Henry of Friemar and John Buridan, as for the others who emphasize aggregate need over individual need, lies both in the nature of exchange and in a desire to prevent the exploitation of individuals. The nature of exchange ensures that although you trade five pair of shoes for one house, you personally value the house more, or you would not trade. Individual need should not, however, determine value, since that could result in taking advantage of the difficult circumstances of others. If, for example, John owns a medicine that Mary needs in order to live, but John does not need it at all, Mary may value the medicine above everything she owns. The economic value of the medicine, however, remains its common value, which is estimated by the general need for the medicine, the expense of the ingredients that go into it, the abundance of those materials and the skills necessary to concoct it, and all the other components of value we have seen, regardless of Mary's personal need. Although the question of value here comes very close to the question of the just price, the writers mentioned begin (and in some cases end) by making a connection between value and aggregate need, as distinct from individual need. Some writers do not, however, stipulate that need must be aggregate, and Richard of Middleton specifically refutes the idea, defining need instead as individual need, which, Richard asserts, allows fair trade among neighbors.[47] Because neighbors live in the same time and place, in order for them to trade, each must individually value what the other has more than what he has.

Writers think of need as a constituent element of value in yet another way, by finding value in a commodity's utility. For some writers, in fact, need and utility are the same. In his second commentary on the *Nicomachean Ethics*, where he speaks of need as the measure of value, Albert the Great writes that "need holds all exchangeable goods together—and need we said was use or utility or demand."[48] Albert here presents utility not as the use an object has theoretically but as our actual use for it, which allows him to equate it with need and demand. Although utility is certainly related to need, the tautology is far less certain in the writing of others, such as Giles of Lessines, who states that "a thing is justly estimated according to the utility that it brings to its possessor," and John of Bassolis, who believes that the value of goods should be calculated by "the need of things and their utility for human use according to the circumstances of time and place," suggesting a possible distinction between need and utility.[49] Such a distinction would presumably hold utility as possible use, a category that would remain distinct from actual need. So, for example, the utility of the Ginsu knife might be great (it slices, it dices) although my need for it is small. In addition to Giles and John, Richard of Middleton, Henry of Friemar, Peter Olivi, and Gerald Odonis all speak of both need (*indigentia*) and utility (*utilitas*) as components of value, although it is not always clear whether they mean the terms to be equivalent or distinct.[50]

Many writers further discuss the way need constitutes value by drawing distinct connections between scarcity (which we saw in the circumstances surrounding an object) and need, explaining that the more scarce a commodity is the greater the need for it and consequently the higher its value. We are here back to the old saying that all that is rare is dear, but from the other side. Gerald Odonis, for example, writes that "need holds everything together, that is, maintains everything in value, for we see that when things are in great demand they are worth more; for example, at time of harvest hired laborers are more dear, at time of sickness, doctors, at time of war, arms, and likewise in similar cases."[51] This particular observation is interesting for its explicit treatment of skills as commodities, subject to need and demand like any other. The link between demand and need as factors in value is nevertheless one made by many of the authors in the section on scarcity.

In thinking about the way value depends on the buyer, a few writers also mention the rather uneasy category of pleasure. We have already seen the link between economic value and pleasure in Augustine's statement that we often value jewels more than a person, and his combination of the allure of sensual enjoyment with human need. Although jewels may have practical uses, they also impress and delight, standing at times (in crowns and jewelry, for example) as material value and thus as signs of themselves.

Medieval writers, explaining and justifying economic trade, chose usually to describe the exchange of necessary commodities: grain, wine, horses, beds, shoes, tools. Although economic valuation thus represents a fallen state (placing grain above mice), it does not, if we stick to necessary commodities, represent an unreasonable one for most medieval writers. In this they seem to decide against Augustine.

The case for economic valuation becomes harder to make, however, once we include whims or pleasures. Nevertheless, Peter Olivi, Thomas Aquinas, and Antonino of Florence, seeking to explain why baubles could be valued more highly than food, include pleasure among the qualities that imbue commodities with value. Peter Olivi, after discussing how we value an object based on its use "for our purposes" and its difficulty to procure, moves on to explain that

> it is evaluated according to the greater or lesser pleasure to our will in possessing such things. Indeed, as understood here, to use an object is to take it for oneself or have it in the power of one's will, and thus a certain part of the value of usable things is judged by the will's enjoyment or by the greater or lesser pleasure that is taken in this or that thing and in having it at one's disposal.[52]

Although Olivi moves on to use this theory to explain individual preferences (one person prefers one horse while another prefers a different one) and disagreement over value, he here outlines value as stemming in part from pleasure in two senses. In the first place, there exists pleasure from a given object, which may be subjective—one person derives pleasure from lava lamps, another does not. The value resides not in the lamp itself, but in the pleasure one person takes from it. At the same time, Olivi writes clearly of the pleasure of possession. In this second sense the pleasure comes not from the object but from knowing that you own it. Thus one person may like the sparkle of diamonds while another does not. The first person values diamonds because of the pleasure of watching their sparkle, while the second does not. The second person may, nevertheless, take great pleasure in exercising the power of ownership over diamonds—not for their strength, not for the ease with which they can be traded, not because they are beautiful, but because he enjoys the knowledge of his own possession. This second kind of pleasure, like the first, stands for Olivi as one of the ways value works within the economic order. While Thomas Aquinas also lists pleasure as a constituent element of value (as does Bernardino of Siena, following him), Aquinas seems far less comfortable than Olivi in leaving a determinant of value so completely subjective.[53]

Seller's Activities That Increase an Object's Value (Value as Determined by the Seller)

Many writers thought that the work of the seller deserved a reward and in itself lent value to the commodity in question. So, as we have seen, Robert of Courson writes of "the labor expended on the wares" and Thomas of Chobham speaks of the value of the merchant's labor.[54] Similarly Huguccio, Hostiensis, Alexander of Hales, Thomas Aquinas, Giles of Lessines, Peter Olivi, and John Duns Scotus list the work of the seller as a factor that influences the value of an object and deserves recompense.[55] Some of these writers make clear that the value in labor does not lead to a simply arithmetical equality whereby one hour of any person's labor has as much value as one hour of any other person's labor. Gerald Odonis, for example, explains that the lawyer is a more expensive worker than the farmer, who, for a lawyer's brief, may trade grain that required a hundred times as much labor as the brief itself.[56] Peter Olivi points out that in a construction project the men who cut and move the stones receive less pay than the architect, which he connects to the greater skill and dignity of the architect's work.[57] The common idea that a person should be paid if he improves an object often also argues in favor of value in labor. Not all, however, agree. Durandus of Saint-Pourçain contends that "the labor that went into the product is never the object of sale, but only the product itself . . . ; because if a workman, for example a carpenter or a vineyard worker, could have produced his work without any labor at all, none the less he could have sold it," and maintains furthermore that buyers, who determine value, do it on the basis of the final project without regard to the labor at all.[58] In refuting the theory that labor does influence value, Durandus here demonstrates both that the idea of value in labor was common (or else he would feel no need to argue against it) and that it was not universal (or else he would believe it). Another aspect of the value of labor is the value of the skill of a worker, whether artisan, official, or merchant. Thomas of Chobham, Alexander of Hales, Henry of Ghent, Thomas Aquinas, Peter Olivi, and Guido Terreni all mention the value of a seller's skills.[59]

Some writers discuss the value of labor by asserting that merchants deserve living wages because they work and their work itself has value for the community. The value of this work should thus be reflected in the object itself because without it buyers would not have access to the objects at all. John Duns Scotus explains that "he who transports or stores goods honestly and usefully serves the state; therefore it is fitting that he live from his labor."[60] The work itself should allow a profit so that such a person may live, and the only place for this profit is in the sale of the goods. Because such sales result in general benefits (as we saw in discussions of the work of merchants), the work of providing an object for sale adds value to it. Laurentius Hispanus, Raymond of Peñafort, Godfrey of Trani, William of Rennes, and Hostiensis all join Scotus in writing that merchants should be paid for their work.[61]

Many writers also believe that sellers should be paid for the risks they take in bringing goods to market. Giles of Lessines, for example, explains that risk reduces the value of a commodity.[62] Thus if a merchant buys it when it still carries a risk, whether of loss at sea, bad weather that will not allow a good crop yield, or even a change in market conditions, it is worth less than it will be when he sells it to the buyer, who may buy what he needs without a risk. The fact that the seller, rather than the buyer, bears the risk increases the value of the commodity for the buyer. Because merchants never know what profit they will make, Giles states that merchants should make profits in order to balance out the risks they regularly take on all of the goods they sell.[63] John Duns Scotus describes the value of the risks taken by the person who "transports and stores goods" even more fulsomely: "for since he transports at his own peril if he is a transporter and stores at his own peril if he is a custodian, on account of such danger he may safely receive something back in recompense," because "a merchant involved in transport sometimes loses a ship filled with expensive goods, while another one sometimes loses in an accidental fire the most valuable things, which he stores for the state."[64] Although the value is thus, as always, measured by the price of the commodity, it is here conceived not in terms of the commodity but in terms of the seller, whose risk corresponds directly to the value of the commodity in question. In addition to Giles and Scotus, Alexander of Hales, Thomas Aquinas, and Peter Olivi specifically mention the risk the seller takes as a component of value.[65]

Finally, some writers believed that the value of an object increases if the sale causes the seller damage or deprivation. Gervais of Mont-Saint-Éloi, for example, explains that in estimating the value of a commodity "consideration may be had of the damage which the seller incurs by reason of his being deprived of it."[66] A common example was the nonstarving person who agrees to sell food to a starving person at a time of shortage. The well-fed person must not charge the starving person triple the usual price because of the starving person's extreme need. Or, since this could be interpreted as a matter of supply and demand, in order to understand what it has to do with sellers we can consider the negative case, which writers frequently expressed: a seller may not take advantage of a buyer's need. A seller may, however, value an object in order to cover his own loss—he may, in other words, take account of his own need or the damages that would result from the sale. So the hungry person, facing scarcity, may sell his food to the starving person at an increased price because the sale deprives the seller of food that would help stave off his own hunger. Although this case still clearly bears a relationship to demand (presumably if the good were available for more general sale the buyer could buy it from a seller who would not be damaged), the case as it is put emphasizes the relationship between the seller and the value of the object, which changes according to the damage its loss will do to him. It is in this case that we see the idea of need, and its role in value, as individual rather than aggregate. The point becomes perhaps most clear in the writing of John of Naples, who argues that if a seller would suffer a loss by selling a particular good, or if he needs it in a way not taken into account by the common value, or if he knows better how to use it than most men, he may charge more than the common value so that he will be compensated for having to part with it.[67] This discussion assumes that the buyer values the good not only more than it is commonly valued but more than the seller values it. John's idea of need and loss is here quite clearly individual rather than aggregate. This idea of individual need not only differs from the notion that communal need determines value, it also shifts the determinant factors in value itself to individual buyers and sellers, and most particularly, in John's writing, to sellers. Guido Terreni similarly looks to the seller's role in determining value when he writes that if a buyer's tremendous need induces him to sell, whereby he suffers a personal loss, he may raise the price to cover his loss, although if he suffers no extraordinary loss he should not sell it for more because of the buyer's need.[68] For Terreni, unlike for John of Naples, the damage a seller suffers from his sale stands as an exceptional, rather than normative, determinant of value. In this Terreni is more typical of the schoolmen, but he, too, imagines cases in which personal loss or need overcomes communal supply and demand as the constitutive element of value.

These discussions of value not only assume Augustine's distinction between natural value and economic value, many of them mention it explicitly. Thomas Aquinas, explaining the Aristotelian idea of proportionate reciprocity in exchange, specifies that "articles are not valued according to the dignity of their nature, otherwise a mouse, which is a sensible animal, would be of greater value than a pearl, which is an inanimate thing."[69] He thus uses Augustine's example in order to qualify the notions of value raised by the problem of justice in trade. Peter Olivi similarly begins his treatise on buying and selling by mentioning Augustine's distinction between the natural and the economic orders and making clear that his treatise deals only with the economic order.[70] John of Naples, too, makes the point that by natural valuation a fly is worth more than all the metal and precious stones in the world, but that economic value concerns itself with human use.[71] John Duns Scotus likewise begins his discussion of exchange with Augustine's caveat that in the natural order any living being is worth more than any inanimate object, although in economics value is instead determined "in relation to human use, on account of which exchange is made."[72] Francis of Meyronnes reiterates this causal link between exchange, use, and the economic order more explicitly in his commentary on the *Sentences* when he explains that justice in exchange not only accords with the economic order rather than the natural order but that it must accord with the economic order since the natural order itself would allow no trade at all.[73] Because the natural order is fixed rather than relative, the same at all times, in all places, and to all people, in the natural order there could never arise a disagreement about value, or a difference in valuation, or a situation in which one person might be willing to exchange something worth less for something worth more. It is only when we remove ourselves from the world of the natural order and absolute value to the world of human need and economic value that trade becomes feasible. If we were to apply the natural order to our world, all exchange and commerce would come to an immediate halt, because however much work, however much gold, however many shoes or houses a person had or offered, he would not be able to purchase a chicken or a cow. The idea of the natural order, Francis explains, is inimical to the idea of trade.

Pricing

The incompatibility between absolute value and human need is crucial to understanding discussions of economic value and price. It means that there can exist no single, invariable, theoretically fair price. As all of the explanations of value and prices discussed above indicate, economic value changes. These changes, as well as the multitude of factors that can play a role in determining value, make describing value complex, but they make setting a price even harder. If we accept that a price should measure need, which holds some relationship to, say, supply and demand, scarcity and abundance, skill, labor, and risk, to choose a few of the determinants we have seen mentioned, how should we go about declaring a fair price for a particular cow or horse or bushel of grain or pair of shoes? The multiplicity of variables that writers recognize as constituting value makes such a determination almost impossible. At the same time, in listing these variables, writers propose them as criteria that may go into a just price. In fact, many of them use language about a just price or fair price in considering the ideas about value listed above. So Giles of Lessines, for example, in explaining that the cost of materials and a reasonable reward for labor should go into calculating the price of an object, writes that these considerations

form part of a just price;[74] Gervais of Mont-Saint-Éloi, in explaining that
the circumstances of the buyer should not affect the just price of the object, declares that the just price should be determined by factors relating
to the thing sold and the loss the seller incurs;[75] and Guido Terreni, discussing the importance of abundance and scarcity in value, states that the
just price varies according to them.[76] The factors that legitimately constitute value, in other words, also determine the just price.

For medieval writers, then, the just price becomes something to be explained more than determined, a way of measuring not the price of a given
commodity against the commodity in general but a way of measuring the
price against other prices. It ensures not theoretical fairness about any natural value of an object, but some degree of fairness about the price you pay
for it in relation to the price others pay at the same place and time and in
the same circumstances. This fairness, however, can indeed be seen as ensuring a just economic value. Azo, Accursius, Odofredus, Alexander of
Hales, Albert the Great, Giles of Lessines, Henry of Ghent, Richard of Middleton, John Buridan, Antonino of Florence, and Alexander of Tartagni
all agree explicitly with the Roman maxim that a thing is worth as much as
it can be sold for, although they, like Roman law itself, often modify this
idea in order to protect against various kinds of fraud.[77] Alexander of
Tartagni, for example, adds that a thing is worth what it can be sold for so
long as the buyer knows and understands what he is buying.[78] This addition qualifies the price so that it cannot include fraud or coercion. Odofredus, in his *Lectura*, as well as Accursius, in his *Glossa ordinaria*, add that
a thing is worth as much as it can be sold for commonly.[79] They thus combine the popular idea that value must be determined by aggregate need
rather than individual need with the idea that this determination is the basis of the object's value. In doing so they not only tie the idea of economic
value to the market (a common strategy, as we have seen), they also use the
market to measure justice.

There thus exists no single or widely accepted means for calculating a
just price for any individual commodity. Instead there is all the chaos of
the legitimate means for determining value in general. John of Bassolis
warns that price should be "according to reason," a fine sentiment but one
that provides little direction.[80] But even the more ostensibly helpful lists,
such as the one from Thomas of Chobham, enumerate factors that may be
part of an object's just price but offer no actual means for determining
what that price should be. In fact, far from trying to dictate a particular
just price or formulation for a just price, writers often explain that the just
price cannot be calculated with any great exactness. John Duns Scotus
writes that it is impossible to agree on a precise point of just exchange, and
so we must allow great latitude;[81] Peter Olivi states that the just price can-

not be fixed with precision;[82] and John of Naples, even as he exhorts people neither to pay one penny less than the just price nor to accept one penny over it, acknowledges that economic valuation cannot be precise.[83] At the same time, it would be wrong to see in this acceptance of the common price a laissez-faire attitude toward however high a price a seller can finagle or however low a price a buyer can wheedle. Writers disagree, however, in where to draw the lines.

Gerald Odonis observes laconically that concealing minor defects in merchandise is common practice and that since merchants generally help society we should tolerate their ways. Although merchants often lie in order to sell goods for higher prices, he finds it difficult to condemn such a multitude. Odonis draws a distinction between the powerful, who mislead ordinary people, and common merchants, who exaggerate in predictable ways, condemning the first but tolerating the second.[84] Most writers, though, do not remain so sanguine in the face of fraud, however common it may have been. Most agree that fraud was wrong and in theory invalidated a sale. The particular action to be taken in the case of fraud, however, could vary. Laurentius Hispanus influentially distinguishes between a contract of sale that has come into being from fraud; fraud that affects the terms of the contract; and fraud that neither creates a contract nor has an incidental bearing on it.[85] Hostiensis illustrates these types of fraud.[86] In the first example, you want to buy my collection of the decretals, which I do not wish to sell. You tell me that another compilation will soon appear that will supersede mine. This is a conscious lie on your part. Believing you, I sell you my collection. In this case, the fraud that gave rise to the contract invalidates the sale entirely. In the second case, I am willing to sell the decretals, but because you tell me that they will soon be superseded I sell them to you at a lower price than I otherwise would have. In this case the contract remains valid because it did not depend on the fraud; however, harm caused by the fraud is subject to legal remedy. In the third case, you sell me a collection of the decretals at a price you unintentionally set above the just price. You do not mean to deceive me; I am simply wrong about the price a collection should cost, as are you. If the price nevertheless falls within the limits of one half of the just price there is no remedy.[87]

The invalidity of contracts based on fraud can also be seen, as I indicated above, as an invalidity based on the absence or falseness of consent. Most writers also held that contracts based on force or ignorance were invalid because they lacked consent. The extent of protection that consent itself offered, however, was subject to debate. The *Liber sextus* (1298) holds that no injury or deceit is done to the person who knows and consents.[88] John Duns Scotus similarly believed that the fact of free and full consent to a contract guaranteed its fairness.[89] Henry of Ghent agreed that in trade the two parties in question should be the judges of whether the contract was fair, and maintained that parties should be allowed to outwit each other up to one half of the just price, although this outwitting should be performed in good faith and without fraud.[90] John of Erfurt maintained that deception up to one half of the just price was acceptable in trade, while Hostiensis and Pope Innocent IV both supported freedom of bargaining.[91] Following principles outlined by Laurentius Hispanus, they drew the distinction between error, which might lead one party to sell for a price under or buy for a price over the going rate, on one hand, and fraud, on the other. Error was acceptable; fraud was not. Perhaps the greatest indication that some writers sought consent, rather than any particular price or range of prices, from the law of laesio enormis comes from the writers who found it acceptable for buyers and sellers to renounce any legal remedy for unfair pricing. Azo and other legists held that the right to seek remedy under the law of laesio enormis could be renounced by oath; Bernard Botone of Parma agreed in the *Glossa ordinaria* to the *Decretales* of Gregory IX; Sicard of Cremona, Larentius Hispanus, Tancredus, Vincentius Hispanus, and Johannes Teutonicus, among others, not only agreed but gave examples of the necessary oath.[92] If these writers had been concerned with the problem of setting or maintaining a price that was fair in terms of the goods being sold, the labor put into them, the norms of the market, or any of the other factors on the lists we have seen about value, then the renunciation would not have mattered, because selling for a price more than half over or buying for a price more than one half under the just price would have violated the determination of value. Instead, by allowing oaths to renounce the right to the remedies of the law of laesio enormis, these writers indicate that the primary concern in a contract is the knowledgeable consent of both parties.

Many writers, however, were not prepared to go so far. Although the law might allow deception and presume that consent ensured fairness, these writers tried to hold buyers and sellers to higher standards. The Franciscan confessional manual *Summa monaldina,* in a widespread formulation, stated that although human law allowed deception within one half of the just price, divine law allowed no deception at all.[93] William of Auxerre drew the common distinction between the civil courts, where a price could be unfair within one half of the just price, and the court of conscience, where buyers and sellers should make good any discrepancy.[94] As John Baldwin has shown, this distinction between civil law, in which deception and increments of unfairness might be allowed, and moral law, in which any deception or unfairness was sin, was drawn by many medieval writers, including Thomas of Chobham, Peter the Chanter, Robert of Courson, Stephen Langton, Radulphus Ardens, Alexander of Hales, Albert the Great, and Thomas Aquinas.[95] Although the law might not require remedy within the limits of laesio enormis, these writers thought that any discrepancy should be returned immediately.

A problem arose, however, when these writers tried to combine their injunction that a person who bought goods for any amount under the just price or sold goods for any amount over the just price return the difference, on one hand, with their knowledge of the imprecision of economic valuation, on the other. How could a person make correct restitution if she could not precisely determine what the just price was in the first place? This was not a question of simple error which, once discovered, could be rectified, but one of knowing that you had followed precisely an imprecise formulation. Because an imprecise and changing value clearly could not be followed precisely, some writers turned to intention as a measure of the justness of a price. The distinction we have already seen between error and fraud represents one way of talking about intention. If a loaf of bread is commonly worth one penny at the time and place that I want to buy one, but not knowing this I purchase a loaf of bread from a baker who has just arrived in town and who, also ignorant of the common price, sells me a loaf for a halfpenny, my underpayment would be an error, committed unintentionally. Although I should pay the baker another halfpenny if made aware of my mistake, I would not have sinned. If, on the other hand, I knew that loaves of bread commonly sold for one penny at the time and place in question but took advantage of a baker who just came to town by saying that I would give him the outstanding price of a halfpenny for a loaf, to which he agreed, then I would have sinned because my intention would have been to take advantage of the baker. Some writers also use intention to measure the validity of prices by considering the intention behind the profit. If the intention was to maintain the seller's household, according to Huguccio, Raymond of Peñafort, and William of Rennes, then the price was fair.[96] Similarly Laurentius Hispanus, Raymond of Peñafort, and Godfrey of Trani maintained that prices are fair if the seller intends only to make an honest living.[97] If motives of greed or avarice drive his sale instead, then his price is not fair regardless of the price.

Intention also becomes an important question in judging storage over time or sale for a certain price at a later date. This is, in fact, the problem Pope Alexander III (1159–81) faces in *In civitate*.[98] The decretal deals with people who buy goods now worth five pounds, promising to pay the sellers six pounds at a later date. Such contracts, according to the decretal, are common. The problem is whether the contracts are usurious. The question, according to Alexander, hinges on whether the future price is known. If the buyers and sellers know that in the future the goods will also be worth five pounds, then the sale is usurious because the seller charges six pounds for goods worth five. If the future price is uncertain, the sale is fair because both buyer and seller assume a risk (the goods may be worth five pounds at that time, but they may also be worth seven). The decretal, in other words, uses knowledge as a way to determine intention. Pope Gregory IX (1227–41) repeats this principle in the decretal *Navaganti*.[99] All who make distinctions based on intention realize that these matters cannot be determined by courts of law. Their idea of fairness or right or justice in price thus moves away from justice in an Aristotelian sense, which determines the outward relations. In these cases, price, which should have been according to justice, must instead be judged by the internal forum of the conscience because of the nature of economic valuation.

The case presented in *In civitate* also raises important questions about why a buyer would buy "pepper or cinnamon or other goods" worth five pounds and agree to pay six pounds for them later. The most straightforward answer would be that the buyer needs them now. As we have seen, for many writers need constitutes the only reason for sale, and for many need itself measures value, so the fact of need in sale hardly comes as a surprise. The difference, however, between the person who needs pepper (or bread or shelter) and pays five pounds now and the person who needs these goods and agrees to pay six pounds later is not only time (the very commodity that usurers sell, according to the theologians) but the economic situation of the buyer. The buyer who agrees to such a contract may well be in extreme need. In such a case, what is a seller to do? There are some common answers that deal with aspects of this problem. One is that sellers need not injure themselves by selling. You thus cannot be compelled to sell bread your family needs because I am hungry. At the same time, Peter Olivi reports, just because a person need not sell a good does not mean that she may charge any price she wishes if she does sell it: "[W]hen conducting a sale," he writes, "it is forbidden for me to put an unjust price on my good or accept it, because then I do not assign it to a thing as being simply mine but rather as something to be exchanged for another."[100] Sellers may not, in other words, price their goods according to the specific need of the buyers. To do so would be to charge for (or include in the value of the good) the individual need of the buyer. The individual need of the buyer, however, does not belong to the seller, and thus she should not be able to include it in the value of her goods. This is another reason it is so important to many writers that goods be valued commonly instead of individually. Gervais of Mont-Saint-Éloi makes this point when he explains that "when an object or service is offered for sale, . . . its just price is fully determined by factors relating to that object or service alone, regardless of circumstances affecting the buyer," and again that "valuation should not include anything which accrues to the buyer without damaging the seller, for such utility does not come from the seller but from the condition of the buyer."[101] The seller may take into account her own loss, but not that of the buyer. The circumstances affecting the buyer that Gervais mentions are clearly those that pertain to the individual buyer, rather than the common scarcity of the commodity. Godfrey of Fontaines, Giles of Lessines, John Duns Scotus, and Francis of Meyronnes, among others, make similar points.[102] This point that buyers may not take advantage of the particular needs of sellers is a potential corollary of another oft-stated principle: value in exchange must be without regard to person. The point itself is made forcefully in the *Nicomachean Ethics.* Exchange is a form of rectificatory justice, which operates without regard to person. The value of a bed does not change based on whether it is sold to a craftsman or a king.

In Francis of Meyronnes' formulation, exchange may be unjust by force, ignorance, deception, or usury.[103] It may also be unjust by taking advantage of individual need or deviating from the common or just price. There exists no single way to determine the just price—for the decretalists, the judgment of the single good man on whom Roman law relied often burgeons into the judgment of ten witnesses.[104] The value in exchange will always be economic value and therefore variable. The idea of the just price itself provides little help, explaining more how people do value a commodity at a given time and place than how it ought to be valued. The idea of the just price does not, however, therefore divorce itself from the idea of justice. In the most obvious sense, it tries to ensure that people do not cheat one another or lose goods or money due to ignorance. It thus can be seen as a fair price for each trade. At the same time, it is not only modern nostalgia, in the form of insisting that a just price be some sort of absolute price or valuation, that wants to find something fundamentally fair about the process of valuation. Some medieval writers seek more secure grounding for the just price as well. Robert of Courson and Thomas Aquinas each attempt to bring together the way people do value with the way they should value.

Justice in the Just Price

Scholars have long noticed that Thomas Aquinas never explicitly equates the just price with the market price. Robert of Courson, too, refuses such identification, but because of Aquinas's greater stature the question has come to revolve around him. The debate itself provides a salutary example of the dangers of taking Aquinas's thought as representative of all medieval thought. John Baldwin and Raymond De Roover both maintain that Aquinas did equate the just price with the market price, despite the lack of a statement directly identifying the two as coterminous.[105] Joel Kaye instead argues that the lack of a positive statement joining the just price to the market price was the result of "his recognition that such a linkage brought with it serious theological, ethical, and metaphysical difficulties."[106] The difficulties Kaye points out were real for Aquinas, as they were for Robert of Courson and perhaps others. Nevertheless, these difficulties do not mean that either Robert or Aquinas failed to accept that, according to the law, the current price was the just price. Rather, both sought a way around the problems Kaye suggests, not by rejecting the connection between justice and market price, but by trying to link the market price to a larger idea of what justice in pricing might require. Robert of Courson attempts this connection when he thinks about pricing; Aquinas brings together the two forms of valuation in a passage that is not directly about the just price at all but rather about the value of counterfeit goods.

Robert of Courson writes of the merchant whose wares are worth ten shillings. The merchant believes that his labor is worth another shilling. The merchant may then sell the wares for eleven shillings, according to Robert, "without oath and fraud."[107] The price, in other words, would be fair because it would take account of his expenses and his work. As we know, however, these factors do not cover the range of ways prices are determined in the market. We may easily imagine a case of a market glut, or lower than usual need for the merchant's wares, and then ask what the merchant should do if the common run of prices is less then eleven shillings for these wares. Robert recommends that the merchant not sell the wares immediately but wait until he finds a market favorable enough to sell the wares for eleven shillings, which would, Robert says, be the just price. When Robert speaks of the "just price" in this way, we can see that eleven shillings becomes the just price in a double sense: just in terms of what the buyer pays for the wares as compared to the market; and just in terms of the expenses and work the merchant put in to them. A merchant who could take Robert's advice would reconcile the "worth" of the goods in themselves with their market price. The seller would not be forced to lose money or labor, nor would he violate the principle of the wares being worth what they could be sold for commonly. The idea of the value within the wares themselves instead comes into equilibrium with their market value.

Thomas Aquinas also seems intent on bringing together the economic value of an object with its absolute value, at least as a possibility, in the *Summa theologiae* in the passage where he discusses not the just price but the immorality of counterfeit:

[G]old and silver are valuable, not only on account of the utility of vessels or similar things made of them, but also on account of the dignity and purity of their substance. Hence if gold and silver made by alchemists do not have the true substance of gold and silver, the sale is fraudulent and unjust, especially since there are some properties of gold and silver, in their natural action, which are not found in gold made by alchemy. Thus the true metal has the property of making people joyful, and is helpful medicinally in certain diseases; moreover true gold can also be utilized more frequently, and retains its purity longer than counterfeit gold.[108]

This discussion falls under the article "Whether a Sale Is Rendered Unlawful by a Defect in the Thing Sold" and thus immediately tells us that impure gold is not a separate substance from pure gold but is instead an imperfect form of the "real" substance. In other words, Aquinas measures all kinds of gold against gold as it should be. The phrase "not only on account of" simultaneously accepts the idea that value can reside in an object's utility and asserts that this is not the kind of debased value with which he is concerned. Instead, he will consider the value that arises from "the dignity and purity" of true gold and silver. If Aquinas assumed that the value of gold and silver came only from "the dignity and purity of their substance," from an intrinsic quality located in their essential purity, he could have stopped here. Claiming the impurity of alloyed metal is tautology, not argument. But Aquinas goes on to explain that the sale of impure gold and silver "is fraudulent and unjust" not only from the fact of the impurity but "especially" because this defect causes ascertainable changes in the metals' properties. He thus appeals to our perceptual abilities, to properties that we can observe, to signs that will make invisible alterations discernible. The first "property" he names, however, is "its property of making people joyful," or a purely subjective and evaluatory, invisible feature of the gold. He lists a property that is literally located in us rather than in the gold. We are "made joyful" to the extent that we value pure gold; if we know that the gold is pure it will make us joyful; and the power of making people joyful therefore stands as one of gold's properties. In making this leap from objective composition to subjective effect, Aquinas links the intrinsic value of an object and the value that we assign to it when we trade it as a commodity. When he delineates gold's "properties," he then lists this emotive effect of the value that we assign to gold alongside the utility that it contains for us and its chemical composition. All three become equally ascertainable, and equally signs of its purity.

Aquinas's assumption of intrinsic value works at yet another level: by placing value inside the object, he removes the problem of assigning value from both the community and from individuals. Or, by locating value (even to the extent of "making people joyful") in objects rather than in people, Aquinas can assume that all people will value a given object the same way. He eliminates the aspect of consensus from the process of valuation, or more accurately, renders consensus unproblematic. This double-edged process of circumscribing the limits of absolute value while retaining value as a communally, rather than individually, determined quantity enables Aquinas to bring together the vocabulary of intrinsic value with the communal workings of the market in a form that reconciles it with the way the market does in fact work. At the same time, by grounding the determination of value in the community, he staves off the chaos that could come from the idea of value as an entirely subjective assessment.

Aquinas's example of gold's "property of making people joyful," however, also stands as the paradigmatic example of a case in which absolute or natural worth does not matter, does not affect the market value of an object. If I possess alloyed gold coins that I believe are pure, they will make me as joyful as pure coins would because I will not know the difference. If other people also believe that my alloyed coins are real, they will exchange other objects or services for them as though they were real, and the coins will in effect contain the same value that they would if they were pure. Fake coins will lose their value, will not function like true gold, only when someone determines that they are alchemists' gold.[109] In this problem, we see most clearly why people have for so long wanted to find in the just price a measure of absolute value, why they might find the notion of subjective value, or economic value, threatening. Economic value depends, after all, on people, and as Augustine pointed out, people are often wrong. For Augustine this was unsurprising, a condition of being human. For medieval lawyers and theologians, it was also unsurprising, versed as they were in Augustine, even if some, such as Robert of Courson and Aquinas, raised the possibility that economic value need not necessarily diverge from natural value. This did not mean, however, that Robert and Aquinas were the only ones who might have found the divergence between the natural and the economic troubling. We see the same questions being asked by Geoffrey Chaucer in the *Shipman's Tale* and the *Franklin's Tale* and being used by Robert Henryson in his fable "The Cock and the Jasp."

Precarious Value in Chaucer's *Shipman's Tale* and *Franklin's Tale*

Geoffrey Chaucer's *Shipman's Tale* uses a motif folklorists call "the lover's gift regained."[110] The (unnamed) wife of the (unnamed) merchant accepts 100 francs from a monk, in exchange for a night of "mirth." The merchant independently agrees to loan the monk 100 francs. When it is time for the monk to repay the loan, he explains that he has already given the money to the merchant's wife. Readers of the *Shipman's Tale* have long no-

ticed the commercial terms and values that pervade the story, most particularly in the identification of sex with money that Albert Silverman detailed in 1953.[111] Since Silverman's article, critics have not only built upon
his analysis, they have often gone out of their way to express dismay at the
commercialized world the tale presents. E. Talbot Donaldson writes of the
"reduction of all human values to commercial ones," concluding that in
this world "sensitivity to other values besides cash has been submitted to
appraisal and, having been found nonconvertible, has been thrown away";
Paul Strohm finds the tale the "most unsparing in its exposure of the im-
pulse toward [personal] profit" and sees the tale as a repudiation of such
a world, petty and debased even in its failings; and Lee Patterson, who declares that the "argument of the Tale, in short, is that profit derives from
the commodification of the natural order," laments that in the tale the
"natural relations" between husband and wife, merchant and monk, and
even monk and wife, are "degraded—commodified—when they enter
into the exchange system."[112] While the tale certainly does posit a commodified world in which sex can be and is exchanged for money, the alarm
critics display at a "natural world" that has become "degraded—commodified" is somewhat out of place, both in its easy equation of commodification and degradation and also in its insistence that commodification is
something that happens to the natural world once we admit merchants
and a mercantile ethos into it. Instead, the tale works to blur the distinction between a "natural" world and a "commodified" one, suggesting that
the two work in much the same manner already. The wife's problems come
not because she commodifies her marriage, but because she, like Donaldson, Strohm, and Patterson, seeks first to keep the commodified world out
of the "natural" relationship between husband and wife. It is only when she
proposes an exchange of sex for money—an exchange she thought would
work only extramaritally—within her marriage itself that the tale regains
its balance. Had she paid more attention, however, she might have realized
that her world was structured in commercial terms already.

Her world is one in which the friendship and affection the characters
demonstrate for one another regularly operate on the basis of exchange.
The monk always brings gifts to the merchant's home, "*for which*," the narrator tells us, "they were glad of his comyng" (7.50).[113] In a technique often used in this tale, usually nebulous causality is asserted using "for" or
"for which," in this case making clear the causal connection between the
monk's gifts and the household's pleasure.[114] Chaucer provides a lavish in-
ventory of the feast that the monk brings on this occasion, ending with the
comment "as ay was his usage" (7.72), stressing the habitualness of his extravagance. Similarly the merchant, at the end of the tale, good-naturedly
accepts his wife's declaration that she will repay him "abedde" rather than

in francs (7.424), and both monk and merchant, invoking their sworn brotherhood and declaring that "my gold is youres" (7.284), are careful to stipulate that their financial transaction is a loan, dearly given and soon to be repaid.

The oaths the wife and the monk make in the garden are also structured like exchange. When the monk swears to the wife that he will never betray her counsel, she replies, "The same agayn to yow," continuing, "By God and by this portehors I swere, / Though men me wolde al into pieces tere, / Ne shal I nevere, for to goon to helle, / Biewreye a word of thyng that ye me telle" (7.134–38). Her reply is entirely out of place in terms of the conversation itself. The monk has been encouraging her to talk about her sexual relations with her husband. The wife, while hinting at the inadequacy of these relations, had somewhat disingenuously declared that "[d]ar I nat telle how that it stant with me" (7.120). She might have required not only encouragement to continue but assurances of the privacy of whatever revelations she would make. The monk's oath seems designed to reassure the wife on these points. The monk, however, proposed no such revelations; he had merely made an inappropriate joke about her sex life and then urged her to tell more. Because he was engaged in no secret-telling or confession, there were no confidences the wife might violate and certainly none she needed to swear to keep. Instead her reply "the same agayn to yow" works like a trade, in which something given (in this case an oath) requires equivalent reciprocity. In this case she returns precisely the equivalent promise. She thus performs the structure of exchange without having anything that actually needs to be traded. The monk repeats the call for the structure of reciprocity when, at the end of their conversation, he entreats the wife to "beeth as trewe as I shal be" (7.207). He calls for equivalency and thus uses the comparative to measure the amount of trueness (rather than simply telling her to be true). There exists, however, no need for the wife to be "true" about anything in particular, nor anything for her to be "true" about since he does not plan to give her the money in advance. The measure itself seems to nullify the request since the monk does not plan on being "true" at all.

The empty exchange of oaths between wife and monk gives way to the far more celebrated agreement to trade money for sex. This agreement comes about precisely as medieval writers thought that trade ought to work. The monk has made clear that sex is what he values. He seems to value it more than his relationship with the merchant, which he has forsworn ("He is na moore cosyn unto me" [7.149]) specifically so that he can assure the wife of his attraction to her ("I clepe hym so . . . / To have the moore cause of aqueyntaunce / Of yow, which I have loved specially / Aboven alle wommen" [7.151–54]). The wife, however she may have encouraged this revelation, makes clear that her largest complaint about her husband is not his performance in bed but his refusal to give her as much money as she wants. After telling the monk that her husband is not so active in bed as the monk hinted, she declares "but yet me greveth moost his nygardye" (7.172). The superlative here could not be more emphatic. The conjunction "but yet" furthermore makes clear that his miserliness, rather than his behavior in bed, upsets her most.[115] Her declaration that her husband's miserliness troubles her most comes as a way of explaining her general valuation of him: "[H]e is noght worth at al / In no degree the value of a flye" (7.170–71). The statement is proverbial, but also more than that. It is comparative: a valuation in terms of worth that demands that the husband be measured on a scale. It thus differs from a complaint that her husband is no good, vicious, bad, violent, or any other quality on its own. The statement also echoes Augustine's distinction between natural and economic scales of valuation. It works doubly as an insult in this context. In the first place, on a natural scale the husband, a person, should have more worth than a fly, which may be alive but is not sentient. In the second place, flies, although alive and thus worth more than riches on the natural scale, are worth nothing on an economic scale. The husband, who should be ahead of a fly on either scale, seems to fall behind on both according to his wife's assessment. The wife explains that the lack of money from her husband bothers her more than anything else by way of explaining this doubly negative valuation.

The wife furthermore makes clear that she cannot get the money she wants within her marriage. Her desire to keep the sphere of her marriage separate from other realms of experience extends not only to her protested scruples in telling the monk her troubles ("[S]ith I am a wyf, it sit nat me / To tellen no wight of oure privetee, / Neither abedde ne in noon oother place" [7. 163–65]) but also to her fear of what would happen if her husband found out about her need for money. Although she must pay a hundred francs by next Sunday, "or ellis I am lorn" (7.181), she explains the urgency of her situation and her desire to reach an agreement with the monk in terms of the importance of keeping the monetary problem from her husband: "[I]f myn housbonde eek it myghte espye, / I nere but lost; and therfore I yow preye, / Lene me this somme, or ellis moot I deye" (7.184–86). Although her idea of the consequence if her husband finds out seems somewhat overblown, she makes the logic of the trade she proposes very straightforward: because she cannot allow her husband to discover her debt of a hundred francs she asks the monk for the money. In return she promises that "at a certeyn day I wol yow paye, / And doon to yow what plesance and service / That I may doon" (7.190–93). The trade that so "degrades" natural relations, therefore, is based on the wife's desire to uphold those relations by keeping money separate from her dealings with her husband.

At this point, then, both monk and wife have made clear what they want: the monk wants sex, the wife wants money. They thus arrange a trade, summed up in the rhyme of "frankes" and "flankes" (7.201, 202). Although most critics write about the way this exchange converts sex into money, we might note that it not only equally turns money into sex, it does so in the same way that houses are turned into shoes. In other words, it works as an exchange, according to medieval writers, ought to work, giving each party something he or she values more in return for something he or she values less, at a rate on which both have agreed. There exists nothing in this account to suggest a particular affinity between sex and money, any more than between houses and shoes in the *Nicomachean Ethics*. The expert way in which the wife trades what she has and the monk wants with what the monk has and she wants shows the clear fallacy of the merchant's somewhat condescending speech when she calls him from his books. "'Wyf,' quod this man, 'litel kanstow devyne / The curious bisynesse that we have'" (7.224–25). She has, of course, not only guessed at and understood the merchant's business, but also just engaged in it herself.

Perhaps more important than any condescension it shows toward his wife, the merchant's speech to her about his business demonstrates his own attempt to keep separate the spheres of business and home. While the details about the merchant's work in the tale may indicate the kinds of business in which the merchant is involved, they also work spatially.[116] Chaucer separates the place where the merchant takes care of his financial affairs from the rest of the household, using words which he seems to invent— "countour-hous" (7.77), "countyng-bord" (7.83), "countour dore" (7.85) —to increase the sense of materiality of this space.[117] Within his large and hospitable home the merchant thus retreats to a place apart, full of its own specially designated objects, in order to pursue his business. His desire to place the world of business apart from his home and his other relations emerges not only in his speech to his wife but also in his attitude toward the monk. After he has loaned the monk a hundred francs, he stops by to see the monk. Chaucer makes clear that this visit has nothing to do with business or the hope that the monk might repay him:

> And whan that he was come into the toun,
> For greet chiertee and greet affeccioun,
> Unto daun John he first gooth hym to pley;
> Nat for to axe or borwe of hym moneye,
> But for to wite and seen of his welfare,

> And for to tellen hym of his chaffare,
> As freendes doon whan they been met yefeere. (7.335–41)

The causal connection "for," so common in the tale, here quadruples. The merchant sees the monk not from any motive of getting money but because of his affection for the monk, because he wants to see how the monk fares, because he wants to chat with the monk, in short, because he considers the monk his friend. The merchant could, of course, consider the monk his friend but still inquire about the loan. In this case, however, we are told quite clearly that these motives remain separate for the merchant, who, we here see, holds friendship apart from business.[118]

One problem, however, in trying to keep commerce "apart" or separate from other relations is the difficulty in being precise about what it must remain separate from. We can see how complicated such a determination may be if we return to the household's affection for the monk.

> Free was daun John, and manly of dispence,
> As in that hous, and ful of diligence
> To doon plesaunce, and also greet costage.
> He noght forgat to yeve the leeste page
> In al that hous, but after hir degree,
> He yaf the lord, and sitthe al his meynee,
> Whan that he cam, som manere honest thyng,
> For which they were as glad of his comyng
> As fowel is fayn whan that the sonne up riseth. (7.43–51)

The relationship could be described, as I described it above, as essentially commercial: the household's pleasure comes as a direct result of the costly gifts he brings. Such causality is, as I argued, difficult to dispute when the "for which" makes the reason for their pleasure so definite. At the same time, however, the relationship could be seen as considerably more old-fashioned. We might think of systems of traditional gift exchange. We might value generosity as a virtue and commend a man who tries to please others. We might also commend the thoughtfulness of a person who remembers not only the powerful but also "the leeste page." We might think that the desire to bring tokens of affection to those for whom we care is "natural," as is the pleasure recipients of such tokens derive from them. We would certainly be encouraged in these thoughts by the concluding simile that links the household's pleasure to the pleasure birds feel at the sun in the morning. While such a comparison, direct from nature and creatures who operate in no commercial system, could alert us to the corruption of the merchant's house, it could equally assert that the pleasure we take in generosity, gifts, and remembrance is as natural for people as the pleasure birds take in the sun.

We could similarly query the merchant's relations with his wife when he comes back successful from his business trips:

> His wyf ful redy mette hym atte gate,
> As she was wont of oold usage algate,
> And al that nyght in myrthe they bisette;
> For he was riche and cleerly out of dette. (7.373–76)

Thomas Hahn reads the causality of this "for" as a conversion of the merchant's "sexual drive" back from money to sex: the merchant, he asserts, has been "screwing society and from this deriving a deep sexual excitement."[119] If we interpret the passage in this way, the connection between money and sex becomes more than an expedient for a trade (like grain and cattle), but instead becomes a particular connection that could only exist in a culture that values money. The natural act of sex has thus become linked to mercantile activity, which uses money as a measure of value. At the same time, however, it is possible to read the passage less as a comment on the act of commerce than on the nature of pleasure within a marriage. Business, as the merchant explained to the monk, is his work. He has, the narrator tells us, worked hard and diligently. He has then come home, where his pleasure and relief takes the form of a night of mirth with his wife. This night of marital celebration, expressive of pleasure at a job completed and well done, could certainly fall within the realm of natural rather than commercial relations. The habitualness of the wife's meeting the husband when he returns home from business, moreover, whether or not it encompasses the night of mirth, bespeaks an intimacy between husband and wife that at the very least calls into question the account of their relationship that she has given to the monk.

In drawing relationships that lead so easily to double readings, Chaucer begs the question of whether we would term the relationships between the monk and the household and between the merchant and his wife ones of reciprocity (the proper base of natural relations) or exchange (the natural base of commodified ones). The *Shipman's Tale*, however, works to make these terms indistinguishable: it presents exchange as a form of reciprocity, and reciprocity as a form of exchange. In this world, "natural" relations can remain based on reciprocity only so long as they succeed. When they break down, they become problems of unequal trade, of creditors and debtors. "Reciprocity" is founded on a shared set of values: the activities, duties, and functions that the wife, for example, performs, are perceived by both husband and wife as equal in value to those that the husband can expect, based on his own activities, duties, and functions. The process of establishing a relationship between the very different worlds of husband and wife, of negotiating a balance between them, is the same process by which the valuation of commodities takes place, by which people determine how much grain, for example, should be equivalent to how many sheep. In the *Shipman's Tale,* domestic relations "become commodified" when the wife proposes to trade sex for money with the merchant because the "balance of trade" between the merchant and his wife has become unequal. In order to maintain "their station," the wife spends more money than her husband gives her. She therefore needs something to exchange, and uses her body. Through this set of problems and solutions we see the mechanism of the domestic world that remains invisible when reciprocal relations suffice: they show that "reciprocity" is exchange gone well, or equal exchange where both parties agree on the equivalency of what is given and received. The point is not that trade or merchants have commodified human relations but that these relations were structured like those of commodities already.[120] Once the wife realizes this, and accepts the erasure of boundaries between mercantile and domestic spheres, both sets of relations return to stability.

There is a perfectly good reason, however, that medieval authors who write about trade speak of trading grain, sheep, shoes, houses, oil, and wine, rather than sex. They, like the readers who seem distressed by the tale, cannot be comfortable with the notion that sex acts like any other commodity, part of an economic scale. This is, however, the way that Chaucer treats it, suggesting that only when the wife feels that trade should be kept out of marriage do her "natural" relations become adulterous. In teasing us with this smoothly working world of exchange, a world not immoral but amoral, Chaucer forces us to ask what happened to absolute or inviolable values. The fear of a world that works without these values spurs D. W. Robertson Jr., E. Talbot Donaldson, and Paul Strohm alike to find the tale an implicit commentary on the values in which Chaucer really believes.[121] This fear of a world that does not need inviolable values is also what Lee Patterson calls "the primary condition of economic man: when the worth of goods is determined solely by their exchange value, then value is radically contingent."[122] This fear also goes some way toward explaining modern scholars' continuing desire to find in the medieval just price some ideal of theoretical justice rather than accepting that the market price, however contingent, was itself considered just. It is also the fear we have seen Robert Courson, briefly, and Thomas Aquinas, in much more detail, address in their accounts of economic value that leave room for objective value. Because the *Shipman's Tale* poses the same question

about the possible links between subjective and objective value, it may clar-
ify the way Chaucer thinks through the question if we compare it to
Aquinas's analysis.

In thinking back to Aquinas's example of the value of true gold, superior to alchemical or counterfeit gold in its various properties including
that of "making people joyful," we can recall that on one hand placing this
property alongside others worked to objectify subjective valuation, while at
the same time it made the entire account of value vulnerable, since counterfeit gold makes one who does not realize that it is counterfeit as joyful
as real gold does. In the *Shipman's Tale,* the monk's money works as counterfeit gold does in Aquinas's example. At first it has, for the monk, all the
properties real gold might have. It quickly loses these properties, however,
once the wife finds out his trick. It seems a fairly safe bet, given her disgust
("Yvel thedam on his monkes snowte!" [7.405]) when she hears of the
monk's actions, that she will not sleep with the monk for money again. Perhaps the most important element of the transaction between the monk
and the wife, from this point of view, is the speed with which the wife finds
out that the money is fake in the sense that it is not, as the monk pretended,
given freely to her without the knowledge of her husband. The monk's
"counterfeit coin," if we continue the analogy with Aquinas's analysis, thus
gets taken out of circulation very quickly. In other words, in teasing us with
the possibility of natural relations that mirror the commercial and work,
Chaucer never allows the situation to get out of hand. He maintains this
control first by assuring us that the "trades" between wife and monk will
not continue, and second by suggesting that the wife wants extra money
for clothes, but neither needs money for routine household expenses nor
wants it for extraordinary luxuries that the merchant might not be able to
afford. The "transactions" between husband and wife only go so far as is
necessary to correct what had been a trade imbalance. By refusing to portray relations as completely arbitrary, and by carefully restabilizing this explicitly commodified world, Chaucer leaves open the possibility of ties to
other, more permanent values, even as he presents these values as con-
ceivably superfluous. Chaucer thus refuses to come down on any side at
all: he does not categorically reject Aquinas's suggestion of a tie between
price and a more absolute form of value. At the same time, he presents the
possibility (latent in Aquinas's writing) that money is just another commodity: in this case, the fluctuations in what and how much it can be traded
for, its worth, need be no more threatening to the notion of absolute value
than any other fluctuations in the way that we value any other commodities. Chaucer departs absolutely from Aquinas, however, in his explanation
of the purposes that trade serves.

Aquinas, following Aristotle, explains that people trade "for the common advantage of both parties, since one needs something that belongs to the other, and conversely."[123] There exists nothing remarkable in this description. As we have seen, it contains a close connection between exchange and community, a connection found in most medieval accounts of value. The process of trade—by which two people come to agree on a set of values, to agree that both sides of the transaction exist in proportion to each other, and to confirm their agreement through the act of material exchange—is the process that Chaucer makes manifest within the merchant's marriage. Once the wife is willing to engage explicitly in this act with her husband, she need no longer incur the loss that she did by trying to engage in it extramaritally. By locating the value of "true gold" in a variety of properties, including its ability to "make people joyful," Aquinas, as we have seen, claimed that in the process of exchange a community recognized the value of gold, and confirmed their evaluation. The process of bargaining was thus one that recognized the properties that inhere in gold, and which reconfirmed the community's ability to value, or to realize value. His conflation of subjective and objective value did not remove either type but implied that the value on which the community settles will be the same as the true, absolute value. Although the community obviously does not decide how to value the wife's sexual favors (which is part of both the joke and the discomfort of the *Shipman's Tale*), the place where Chaucer departs most significantly from these accounts is in the potential role of surplus.

The idea of surplus is crucial to those who write about trade because it allows them to postulate that in giving up one object for another, people who trade do not deprive themselves of necessities (as they would if they traded shelter for food, for example). Chaucer in effect eliminates the idea of surplus from trade. Surplus depends on our ability to be sated, to have had enough, and therefore to identify excess. But once everything is treated as a commodity, desire, too, becomes converted and convertible into any other object. Once all things become convertible to that which we want or need, however, and once we allow these needs or desires to extend to station, reputation, and sexual desire, we have come to accept the alchemists' gold as real, and surplus itself becomes superfluous. The merchant "riche was, for which men helde hym wys" (7.2), and the wife confirms the slip between appearance and essence when she buys clothes to serve as a sign of the station she has achieved, even as they help her achieve it. The *Shipman's Tale* works because no character's desire exceeds his or her station, because the wife does not decide that she needs new diamonds rather than a new dress; because the husband does not decide that she now must "pay" for every bite of food or kind word. The incongruity of decent, controlled characters in a system that flaunts its potential for indecency and wild excess makes us search for alternate bases of value. One place we might expect to find such values that the tale explicitly closes off, however, is in the traditional world of community, kinship, and oaths.

The monk and the merchant, the narrator tells us, were born in the same village and claim kinship with each other. Their affection is so close and reciprocal that in describing it the pronouns can become mixed up with no ill effect: "The monk hym claymeth as for cosynage, / And he agayn; he seith nat ones nay, / But was as glad therof as fowel of day" (7.36–38). Presumably the merchant is the one who never says nay, but the "he" could just as easily be the monk. Either way, the sentiment remains the same. Chaucer furthermore uses the simile of the bird that we have already seen as a sign of pleasure whose naturalness remains unquestionable. There can exist no suspicion that a bird's happiness at daybreak is in any way calculating. Moreover, after rehearsing these connections of community, claimed kinship, and pleasure in each other, we are told: "Thus been they knyt with eterne alliaunce, / And ech of hem gan oother for t'assure / Of bretherhede whil that hir lyf may dure" (7.40–42). The "thus" provides yet another of the causal claims that run throughout the tale. The monk and merchant's connections, the traditional ones of village, kinship, and friendship, knit them together eternally. In the final couplet their assurances to each other become definitely mixed, but our inability to distinguish one from the other is precisely the point. Each makes exactly the same promise to the other so that no distinction between them can be made. For all of these traditional reasons, then, as well as the eternal alliance the narrator claims, their ties to each other should be permanent.

Despite the seemingly eternal nature of these ties, the monk quite easily dismisses them, swearing that his swearing meant nothing ("[B]y God and Seint Martyn, / He is na moore cosyn unto me / Than is this leef that hangeth on the tree!" [7.148–50]), in the process using an analogy from nature to show that not everything must be related, a purpose quite different from the narrator's invocations of birds and the dawn. This swearing does not, however, prevent the monk from calling the merchant his cousin three more times in eight lines of speech (7.257–64) when he asks the merchant to loan him the money he will give to the merchant's wife. As oath multiplies upon oath, each proving the one that preceded or follows it false, it becomes clear that such bonds, far from eternally binding, are not necessarily even momentarily true. The wife has also sworn, not only the empty promise on the monk's prayer books but also the unnecessary promise to repay the monk's loan: "And but I do, God take on me vengeance / As foul as evere hadde Genylon of France" (7.193–94). Taking the measure of the proliferation of these oaths, Paul Strohm notes that "[t]he wife's Ganelon reference cuts with unintended irony, measuring the facility with which these glib oathtakers have debased the verbal currency in which they deal. It reminds the audience of a previous era in which the sacred bonds of vassalage were secure enough to permit spectacular and damnable transgression, and not simply cynical refashioning of the sort we encounter here."[124] While the reference may indeed call forth the kind of nostalgia Strohm evokes, it works also to show the ease with which oaths may be broken and the unlikelihood that anyone will be torn apart, Ganelon-like, by four horses for breaking them. These ties, in other words, the "natural" ties of place and kinship and swearing, are notable not because they are false (it is the monk who is false in this tale; there is no indication that the merchant breaks an oath) but because they are so fragile. Far from the permanence the narrator assures us they have, they need only bad intention to be broken. They certainly do not, in the *Shipman's Tale,* have the strength or resiliency we need to assure us of a more permanent base for value.

The fragility of traditional bases of value is a theme not only of the *Shipman's Tale,* which teases us with the picture of a world in which the most stable natural relations are those that mirror the commercial, but also in the *Franklin's Tale,* where Chaucer presents the precariousness of a world based on the stabilizing assumptions of absolute value. The *Franklin's Tale* belongs to the folklore group known as "the rash promise."[125] When Dorigen's husband, the knight Arveragus, sails off "to seke in armes worshipe and honour" (5.811), as a knight must, Dorigen is courted by the worthy squire Aurelius.[126] After telling Aurelius she will never love anyone except Arveragus, she rashly promises that if Aurelius can do away with the rocks of Brittany, which she fears above all else will kill her husband, she will grant Aurelius her love. She mentions a number of times the impossibility of meeting this condition. Aurelius's brother, however, digs up a magician who makes the rocks seem to disappear. Dorigen contemplates suicide before confessing to the just-arrived Arveragus, who tells her that she must go through with her promise because "[t]routhe is the hyeste thyng that man may kepe" (5.1479). Aurelius, moved by Arveragus's values, renounces his claim to Dorigen. The magician, who had demanded a ruinous price for the trick, hears what happened and, similarly impressed by Arveragus and now Aurelius's values, renounces his claim to the fee.

Whether we find the Franklin cynical or sincere, whether we find the relationship of Dorigen and Arveragus a sensible solution to the marriage debate or unworkable in "realistic" terms, there can be no question that the relationship is idealized and that the narrator goes out his way to convince us of the sincerity with which Dorigen believes in these ideals and loves her husband. Aurelius, pining with love for Dorigen, is similarly idealized as all that can or should be virtuous in a squire. This world, with its ideals, absolutes, and scruples, its careful mention of the free will with which characters swear oaths, the true love husband and wife hold for each other, and the respect each character holds for not only his or her own truth but also the "truth" others swear, would seem a complete respite from the relative values, calculation, and easy negotiation of the *Shipman's Tale*. The rejection of such a world becomes clear not only in the description of the reasons for which and ways in which Dorigen and Arveragus love each other but also in Dorigen's anger at the rocks. The narrator presents her anger as an explicit transference of her fear for Arveragus's safety: "[W]han she saugh the grisly rokkes blake, / For verray feere so wold hir herte quake" (5.859–60), we are told, before she states "wolde God that alle thise rokkes blake / Were sonken into helle for his sake!" (5.891–92). In her complaint she admits that "clerkes" would argue for the necessity of the rocks. She dismisses these arguments not due to their logical failings but because of her fear that they might harm Arveragus: for "his sake" she would have them gone. Such trepidation and resentment toward these inanimate objects is patently not calculated. Her offer to Aurelius—her love in return for his removal of the rocks—comes explicitly from her belief in its impossibility. In setting this condition Dorigen not only shows that she is thinking of Arveragus, not Aurelius, she also makes clear her own belief that trade, in this sense, can never happen. Furthermore, there is no other exchange she will offer, and she makes this proposal: she tells him because "wel I woot that it shal never bityde," adding, "What deyntee sholde a man han in his lyf / For to go love another mannes wyf" (5.1001, 1003–4). Dorigen thereby dismisses the possibilities on which the *Shipman's Tale* is based: that anything can become a proper object of exchange.

The *Franklin's Tale* also withstands commodification in its emphasis on the particular, the exceptional. Dorigen sees many ships go by, but wants only the one that will bring home Arveragus. Her resistance to creating the kinds of equations necessary for commerce also appears in her long list of women who have killed themselves rather than submitting to unwanted lovers. The list comes from Jerome, and although it does mention the stories of women whom he considered honorable, its links to Dorigen's particular situation become less and less clear as it continues. Donald Baker, for example, argues that the list moves from women who commit suicide to avoid rape to women who commit suicide after rape to particularly faithful wives.[127] None of these categories seems particularly applicable to Dorigen's situation. Although it may work to give her time or be rhetorically appropriate to her experience, as some have argued, the examples move from one to another by suggestion rather than by equivalence.[128] The cases she mentions not only fail to parallel her own, they also fail, in their scope, to parallel each other. The invoked community, too, seems to resist valuation based on the external signs that commodification would promote. Aurelius was "yong, strong, right vertuous, and riche, and wys / And wel biloved, and holden in greet prys" (5.933–34). The narrator presents his qualities as absolute rather than comparative: we have no idea, for example, whether he was stronger or more virtuous or richer than Arveragus, who himself "was of chivalrie the flour" (5.1088). Aurelius's general virtues make the community's regard plausible, while the parataxis refuses to allow his reputation more weight than any other of his long list of accomplishments. The description presents a stark contrast to the merchant "that riche was, for which men helde hym wys."

The story falls into trouble, however, not when Dorigen presents an impossible condition, but when Aurelius's brother turns out to be a Thomistic villain, content and even eager to manipulate appearances to achieve his (or his brother's) goals. Aurelius should not worry, he claims, because "with an apparence a clerk may make, / To mannes sighte, that all the rokkes blake / Of Britaigne were yvoyded everichon" (5.1157–59). He worries not that Aurelius should fulfill his promise, but that Dorigen should think it fulfilled, not that the rocks should be removed, but that people, upon looking at them, should not be able to see whether they remain present. His concern for appearances thus mirrors that of Aquinas's counterfeiter, who similarly cares only that people should think his coin is legitimate. It comes as no surprise, therefore, that the magician to whom the brother leads Aurelius should demand money for this trick: "He made it straunge, and swoor, so God hym save, / Lasse than a thousand pound he wolde nat have" (5.1223–24). The magician takes up a bargaining stance. His declaration that he would have nothing less than a thousand pounds is different in kind from Dorigen's insistence that she would have nothing other than a removal of the rocks. For Dorigen, the question is qualitative: a particular act, designed to increase Arveragus's safety, designated for its known impossibility. For the magician, the question is instead quantitative: how much money will be enough to make him perform the act he says he can perform. Aurelius, however, remains firmly in the world of absolute values in which the narrator placed him and so refuses to quantify or commodify his love. He does not, in other words, decide that Dorigen is indeed worth a thousand pounds, or that the magician's offer represents a bargain he should quickly seize since she is actually worth fifteen hundred pounds and he can now gain her for one thousand. Instead, he angrily retorts that she cannot be measured at all: "Fy on a thousand pound! / This wyde world, which that men seye is round, / I wolde it yeve, if I were lord of it" (5.1227–29). The extravagance of what he would give for her, combined with his hazy knowledge of what he promises (he cannot quite vouch for the shape of the world), removes him from the calculated and calculating world of the brother and magician.

The tale's happy ending depends on a string of renunciations of the kind of relations that commodification promotes. Despite his tears, Arveragus decides that the most valuable thing is truth: "Trouthe is the hyeste thyng that man may kepe" (5.1479).[129] Because it stands alone at the top of a scale of all things, there exists nothing worth trading for it. The statement also refuses subjective value since it would become meaningless if Arveragus found truth the highest only in this situation, or only for himself and Dorigen, or in any other way that might depend on circumstance. Instead, the statement makes sense only if it stands absolute. Aurelius, impressed by this display of absolute virtue, does not take his own opportunity to claim what he has traded for, but allows Dorigen to return to Arveragus: "Thus kan a squier doon a gentil dede / As wel as kan a knyght" (5.1543–44). Aurelius, in other words, imitates virtue rather than trading for it. Only with the renunciation of that for which he had traded with the magician does he seem to realize that he has jeopardized his ability to remain in a community that recognizes "gentle deeds": he will have to sell his inheritance, will bring shame on his relatives, and will go begging. His ability to remain within the community, however, is beside the point, because unlike the station sought by the merchant's wife in the *Shipman's Tale,* Aurelius believes in gentle deeds as valuable absolutely, in and of and for themselves. He thus belongs to a community that can recognize such value most completely in the moment when, in the service of these values, he shows himself willing to "shame his kin" by selling his inheritance and begging. Because of this resolution, his claims to himself, "my trouthe wol I kepe," and to the magician, "I failled nevere of my trouthe as yit" (5.1570, 1577), remain true. His act of self-debasement fortunately becomes unnecessary, however, when the magician, hearing his story, declares: "God forbede, for his blisful myght, / But if a clerk koude doon a gentil dede / As wel as any of yow" (5.1610–12). The romance can thus return to the world of romance because all have been persuaded to adopt its values. The resolution comes about through an act of community dramatically different from the one that takes place in exchange. Rather than deciding upon what he values and trading it for something another person values less but he values more, Aurelius comes to believe and imitate Arveragus's assertion of what value absolutely is. The clerk, rather than profiting through trade, then imitates the knight and the squire. The squire and clerk adopt the values of the knight, to make themselves like him, rather than trading for what he has and they want. In this romance world of stable values, community is thus achieved through faith and imitation, rather than through the negotiation that cemented the "radically contingent" world of the *Ship-man's Tale*. The contingencies on which the happy ending of the *Franklin's Tale* depends, however, demonstrate just how precarious absolute values can be.

The Problem of Value in Henryson's "The Cock and the Jasp"

Whereas the *Franklin's Tale* posits the instability of absolute value, Robert Henryson's fable "The Cock and the Jasp" goes one step further, questioning our ability to distinguish between economic and absolute value at all. The fable tells the story of a jaunty but poor rooster who sets out early one morning to look for food. As he pecks around in the ash he comes upon a fine jasper. After Henryson explains how a jewel came to be lying on a dung heap—it was tossed out by a careless servant girl, so eager to finish her sweeping that she little noticed what she threw away—and laments such carelessness, the rooster addresses the jewel. "O gentill Iasp, O riche and nobill thing," he exclaims, "[t]hocht I the find, thow ganis not for me" (79–80).[130] In the next five stanzas, the cock enumerates many ways the jewel could be valued. He observes that the jasper is fit for kings and lords, has glorious colors, and should make its home in a crown rather than in the mud. He, on the other hand, spends his days scraping in the dirt for food "to fill my tume intraill" (empty belly) (91). The cock reiterates again and again that his life is a search for basic sustenance and that fine though the jewel may be it has no use to him, "[f]or houngrie men may not weill leue on lukis" (104). The story ends as the rooster leaves the jasper on the ground and goes on his way to continue his search for food. The narrator has no idea what became of the jasper, but he will tell us the "inward sentence and intent" of the story, in accordance with the stated aim of the "Prologue" (117).

At this point, however, we might well pause to applaud this sensible rooster, who does not allow bright baubles or unsuitable riches to divert his hard work and search for basic sustenance. As the cock reflects, the jasper may be a handsome stone, appropriate for those who wish to possess or display riches, but it ill fits his own way of life. If this is not quite Augustine's distinction between the natural and the human, it at least tends that way. It also mirrors the distinction of need that writers employ when they suggest that need varies according to rank. We might also think of Christ's teachings that the poor will inherit the earth, and his warnings about the danger of clinging too fondly to earthly goods: it will be easier for a camel to pass through the eye of a needle than for those who possess jaspers to enter the kingdom of heaven. In his own version of this fable, written around the time of Henryson's birth, John Lydgate provides just such encomiums for the cock. Characteristically, Lydgate does not wait for the final moralizing "Envoy" to express his approval of the rooster, but presents him as an unabashed hero from the first: his red crest signifies courage and hardiness; every morning he praises the Trinity with a triple crow; he is the "prophete of all ioy and all gladnes" (85); his early morning digging for food provides a salutary example of diligence and honest labor as a means of procuring a livelihood; and he does not allow himself to be sidetracked from his straight path by the glitter of useless baubles that are not fit for his station in life.[131] In the "Envoy" to the fable, Lydgate reinforces the lessons of the story—or as Derek Pearsall has put it, "Lydgate labours the point already made."[132] The cock correctly understands that "to hym hit was more dew / Small simple grayne, þen stones of hygh renoun" (213–14) and that "[t]he vertuos man to auoyde all ydelnesse / With suffisaunce hold hymself content" (220–21). The lessons of the Bible, the scholastic writers, and Aristotle here come together in their emphasis on the value of and in labor, on the importance of station, and on the worth of household sufficiency. All of the rooster's honor and dignity that remain implicit in Henryson's version of the story are repeatedly pointed out in Lydgate's version, which (also characteristically) runs to 234 lines, as compared to the ninety-eight Henryson uses and the ten of Walter of England, their common source.

Lydgate's telling of this fable thus explicitly states the moral toward which Henryson's version points. Full of these sorts of congratulatory thoughts for the hard-headed but reflective rooster whom Henryson so vividly portrays, we can turn to the moral of his fable. But rather than praising the cock for the manifold virtues that Lydgate has so laboriously catalogued, Henryson's narrator does an about-face, scorning the cock whose ignorance and crass concern for food lead him to bypass that which "is sa nobill, so precious, and sa ding, / That it may with na eirdlie thing be bocht" (150–51). He enumerates many fine properties of the jasper (although not quite the full seven he promises), equating the jewel with honor, wisdom, and knowledge—"science" is the word he uses, the Thomistic "scientia," with its suggestion of religious knowledge and grace.[133] Because the cock cares only for lowly material needs, Henryson explains, he walks away from the true knowledge that the jasper represents.

One way of understanding the cock's mistake, in Henryson's version, is that he gets confused between what Kenneth Burke has called different realms of language.[134] When the cock saw the jasper, he assumed it was an actual jasper: a hard, bright stone valued by those who have the luxury of valuing such objects. Instead, it turned out to be a symbol for (probably religious) Knowledge. Henryson's fable thus plays upon the slipperiness inherent in metaphoric language, language that Burke would say "borrows" between realms—the image of a jewel is borrowed from the natural realm and used to stand for valuable nonmaterial qualities. Such borrowing is the property of all metaphoric language, and we usually depend on context to make the meaning clear: "Give thanks to the Lord!" means one thing if shouted after a serf has been given a large holiday bonus by the aristocrat landholder, but quite another if urged by a priest in church. By placing us within the world of a fable, Henryson points out just how precarious metaphoric language may be. You think a jewel is a jewel, and sensibly decide not to covet riches. Instead, it turns out you have given up wisdom. Henryson's version of the fable shows a diligent, prudent rooster, and implies a different lesson than the one that the moral provides, understandable though the moral becomes once we have learned it. Henryson uses the discrepancy between the two playfully to expose the instability of metaphoric borrowing.

Another way of understanding the cock's mistake, in Henryson's version, is that he becomes confused between scales of value as Augustine presents them. The cock, trying to adhere to a scale of natural rather than human value, places grain above baubles. Grain, after all, constitutes a necessary item for keeping him alive, even if it does not live itself. He cannot, however, consider the jewel something he might need rather than want. Even if he uses the rather looser definition of need that some writers offer, whereby it varies according to rank, his own rank cannot allow him to pretend any need for jewels. But two problems arise from this attempt. The first is that Augustine did not distinguish between food and jewels—both alike were signs of the human or animal world in which the rooster is mired. The second is that a system that ranks food and jewels by need or utility assumes a literalism that becomes apparent when the cock follows it. It does not allow a place for the symbolic nor perhaps, when actually followed, even for the spiritual. For what form can Knowledge take? Certainly, in Henryson's fable, not the form of a living creature like a flea that we could know we should value above grain.

In using his moral to teach what seems to be a different lesson than the telling of the story implies, Henryson exploits one of the possible interpretations of value inherent in his source, a collection of Latin fables by Walter of England.[135] In eight lines of Walter's fable, the cock looks for food, finds the jasper, tells the jasper that it is not suitable for him to keep because he cannot use it and he values only lowly things, and then leaves the jewel. The cock does not dwell on his hunger (which Henryson's rooster mentions in three separate places) and specifically reports that the more value an object has the less he values it. In the two-line moral Walter reproves the rooster ("Tu Gallo stolidum" he stenorously intones) for shunning the beautiful gift of wisdom and ascribes the rooster's behavior to stupidity. While witty, Walter's ending does not come as much of a shock and does not seem unjust. It brings together scales of need and economic value. Although it does not present them as the same, it does present each as a sign of the other, making the idea of need, and particularly its relationship to pleasure and desire, unproblematic. These differences from the effect of Henryson's ending arise in part from Henryson's superior portrait of the rooster, but even more from the system of valuation that Walter has established.

Our view of Walter's moral rests primarily on our interpretation of the claim with which the cock ends the story: the more precious a thing, the less he loves it. Walter seems to encourage us to see this as an assertion of absolute value: if a thing, whether a jewel or Knowledge, has value, then the cock does not care for it. In explaining his position, the cock acts like a vice character in a morality play or one of the seven deadly sins in *Piers Plowman,* boldly proclaiming what he is, however "psychologically" or "characterologically" implausible such a stance might be. Objects, in this system of absolute values, cannot stand as valuable to me but not to you, or good for me but bad for you; they are simply valuable or not, good or bad. On this scale, jewels and wisdom might very well stand for each other as species of the valuable, just as apples and oranges, whatever their differences, can stand as types of fruit. Walter encourages this absolute scale in his moral: What sort of stupid creature, he asks, would not value the valuable?

This interpretation of the cock's statement follows Walter's own sources, which emphatically demand an absolute system of value. The fable seems to originate in Phaedrus's first-century A.D. collection of Latin verse fables. In his own time, Phaedrus was either often mocked for writing such lowly, subliterary things as fables or was extremely sensitive about what he perceived as the unfavorable reception of his work. Whatever the actual case, he frequently complained about critics who asserted that his fables were not poetry. The story of the Cock and the Jewel originates as an attack on these critics.[136] The cock finds the jewel, cannot use it, and therefore walks away, leaving it in the dirt. Phaedrus offers no more explanation than a one-line moral that curtly states: "This tale is for those who do not appreciate me."[137] The tale thus begins its life as a straightforward attack on those who deprecate Phaedrus's fables. It asserts that fables are valuable, not just for me or for you, but absolutely. If you do not see their value, that is your limitation, rather than a difference of opinion or position.

Phaedrus's collection of fables was known to the middle ages through Romulus's sixth-century prose version of them, a version so faithful to Phaedrus that one scholar has remarked that the medieval tradition of Aesopic fables consisted primarily of "Phaedrus with trimmings."[138] Romulus does, however, broaden the moral of the fable of the Cock and the Jewel, explaining that it tells of those who despise wisdom.[139] Caxton, working from a French translation of Heinrich Steinhöwel's printed version of Romulus, combines the two implied morals, stating that the cock stands for those who reject wisdom, while the stone (the wisdom that the cock rejects) stands for the book of fables.[140] While the precise significance of the jewel shifts throughout these many versions, the system of valuation they impose never leaves room for variation. The rooster rejects that which is absolutely valuable, in and of itself, on an invariable scale of value.

In the statement of Walter's rooster that the more precious a thing the less he loves it, however, we could also see a claim about the relativity of value: an object that possesses great worth for a prince possesses little worth for a rooster, because princes find different objects valuable, or measure value differently, than roosters do. "More precious" would therefore refer to the love a prince, or even the world in general, bears the object, and the rooster's lesser love would refer to his own system of valuation. This is the same kind of subjectivity that medieval writers were quick to see as a prerequisite for trade, since, as Richard of Middleton states, if we did not value differently then there would be no trade at all.[141] Although Walter's sources do not admit the possibility of this interpretation, Walter gives it just enough play to make his moral witty. But this implication of relative value (for in Walter's version of the fable it could hardly be called more than an implication) is the one that Henryson picks up and uses to make his rooster's argument plausible and sympathetic: the rooster does not value the jewel because he must concentrate on his hunger; the jasper would look fine in a prince's crown but ridiculous on a rooster. In Walter's version, the rooster does not value the jewel because he (seemingly perversely) holds everything worthless that is valuable. Even had he known that the jewel represented wisdom, in other words, he would not have valued it. Henryson's rooster instead declares emphatically that he has no use for the jewel in particular, rather than rejecting the entire category of "the valuable."

This reading, in which Henryson knowingly manipulates the possible implications of the speech that Walter's rooster makes, creating a relative system of value in the story, contradicting it with an absolute system of value at the end, and pointing out the precariousness of scales of value, depends on the idea that Henryson is, in fact, setting us up to admire the rooster. Twice in print, however, Denton Fox, Henryson's best editor and most thorough student, has charged that any admiration we might feel for the rooster is anachronistic, that such a reading has been invented by that perennial scourge "modern critics," and that Henryson and his readers would have found such a response perverse at best, and more likely totally inexplicable.[142] Anachronism stands as a constant risk when we read poems that were written well over five hundred years ago, and the charge is a serious one. It is particularly important in this case because, if my reading is not anachronistic, it demonstrates that these ideas about value were not the exclusive preserve of elite schoolmen with access to the works of Aristotle, Augustine, and Aquinas. Lydgate's version of the fable is therefore salutary in showing us that admiration of the cock's diligence and satisfaction with his own status was, by the later middle ages, a perfectly plausible interpretation of the fable. So plausible, in fact, that Lydgate "fixed" the moral so that the story would make more sense. Lydgate and Henryson's versions of this fable make clear that, by the time they were writing, they assumed their readers would read the fable thinking in terms of a system of relative valuation, that it would "make sense" to them that a rooster should look for food and leave jewels to princes.

The rooster in Henryson's fable is not a trading animal: he does not, for example, try to negotiate with a prince who values jewels. In fact, although trade forces valuation, the moral of the fable would be deeply complicated if the rooster attempted a trade, because Knowledge is not alienable in the manner of a jewel or grain. The very difficulty of the scenario directs us back again to Henryson's point: before we can begin to value (and therefore before we can begin to trade), we must know the scale or realm within which we are working. This insistence on knowing the realm of valuation would be unproblematic for Augustine and for scholastic writers. As we have seen, they clearly separate economic value from other forms of value in a way that Henryson's rooster does not. Henryson's fable poses the difficulty of determining the scale of value we should use. As jurists and theologians find, however, even when the realms are clearly distinguished, and even if value is explicitly confined to economic value, it turns out that providing a means to determine value proves theoretically necessary but almost impossible.

When we think back to the easy valuation in descriptions of trade, whereby the shepherd values grain more than sheep while the farmer values sheep more than grain, and so they agree on an equality and trade, we can see that when it comes to thinking about value, this simple matter turns out to be very complex indeed. All later medieval accounts of value in trade rested on Augustine's distinction between natural and economic value, dealing only with economic value. Even with this distinction in place, scholastic authors suggested many ways an object might be valued (usefulness, the work that went into making it, the work that went into bringing it to the place it was to be sold, individual or communal need, to name a few). All of these suggestions, however, worked to justify the way valuation had been made after the fact (so this is the reason he traded one sheep for two bushels of grain); none explained how valuation of the sort trade assumes should be determined (in the following situation, how many sheep should one trade for two bushels of grain?). The different suggestions for what determines value, moreover, did not break down into accounts of value that varied by the training or religious order of the authors. Instead, most authors selected a number of possible means of valuation and listed them together, not as value theories, in the modern sense, but rather as ways of explaining the activity that happened every day. For those who wrote about the just price, market regulation, to the extent that it occurred, did not provide any ideas about what value was itself fair; instead, it tried to make certain that no single buyer or seller was taken advantage of disproportionately in relation to other buyers and sellers. The just price was just, in other words, not in terms of the value of the object, but in terms of the price that others paid and received for a similar object. In all of this writing, scholastic and legal authors not only maintained Augustine's division between natural and economic value, they depended on it, because if we valued according to the natural scale there would be no trade at all: a single sheep would always be worth more than all of the grain, oil, and wine in the world.

The imaginative literature we have seen, however, questions whether that distinction between natural and economic value always remains as firm as the scholastic authors suggest. Although fabliaux often show trades of sex and money, such trades are usually presented as the province of the base and vulgar, those who give no thought to ideas of natural value or anything more than their own physical desires. The wife in the *Shipman's Tale*, however, trades sex for money with the monk because of her desire to keep that "base" trade out of her marriage. Only when she realizes that her marriage is already structured like trade does her marriage regain its equilibrium. The fabliau thus questions the line between "natural" and "economic" relations.

Absolute, noneconomic values are the hallmark of romance. In romances, an ideal value, held by an ideal character, is proclaimed, challenged, and then seen to triumph. In one sense, the *Franklin's Tale* falls easily into this pattern. Arveragus proclaims that "truth is the highest thing," and by standing by that claim, even in the face of his wife's possible unwilling infidelity because of her rash promise, all of the characters prosper and grow: Arveragus's values are confirmed; Dorigen and Arveragus's marriage remains happy and strong; Aurelius and the magician both learn important lessons about value itself. In another sense, however, the *Franklin's Tale* does not confirm Arveragus's value as unreservedly as the story's ending might suggest. The threat to Arveragus's values comes not from another set of values but from another way of valuing. This way is based on trade rather than natural value. Arveragus's convictions do not triumph because they "defeat" the claims of trade. In fact, "truth" consists in upholding those trades once they are made, precisely because they are, as Aristotle explained, forms of justice. Arveragus's example instead persuades Aurelius and the magician to renounce the very claims that they might, by "justice," have made. Such renunciation is necessary for the romance to remain a romance. But the ease with which the romance, without such renunciation, might have slipped into a fabliau, suggests again a fine line between absolute and economic values, a line far more fragile than scholastic accounts of value would suggest.

In Henryson's fable "The Cock and the Jasp," the rooster has no way of knowing, when he stumbles across a jewel, that the jewel is in that instance a species of absolute rather than economic value. Furthermore, in concentrating on need and value that is economic, the cock forgets that another scale of value might exist. Economic value, the kind of value that theoretically remains secondary, in practice becomes the only scale of valuation we use. In these ways, Henryson, too, asks how firm the line between economic and absolute value, the line uncrossable in scholastic writing, really is.

If this imaginative literature questions how well the Augustinian distinction between economic and natural value holds up in the world and whether it is really so easy to tell how "rational consideration, in its free judgment" would judge, the *Shipman's Tale* and "The Cock and the Jasp" also reinstitute Augustine's link between need and desire, a link that largely disappears in scholastic accounts of economic value. For Augustine, as we have seen, both need and desire are equally opposed to natural value and rational consideration; both are equally myopic in looking only to their own interests rather than to the larger order of the world. In trade, especially, it would seem that Augustine should be right. A person must either need or desire that which she does not have in order to go to the time and trouble of trading. Whether it is need or desire that compels the potential trader, moreover, becomes particularly hard to know in the case of exchange: What precisely is the distinction between needing and desiring spices, or faster horses rather than slower horses, or new clothes? Nevertheless, as we have seen, the element of desire drops out of most scholastic accounts of value, even as need plays an extremely prominent role. Goods are valued by need, most authors tell us, while very few (Thomas Aquinas, Peter Olivi, and Antonino of Florence, following Aquinas) even mention the possibility of pleasure or desire that for Augustine was inseparable from need. This silence about desire exists despite the fact that many of these same authors directly invoke the passage from *De civitate dei* in which Augustine explains the way both are species of the same form of value.

The way in which desire drops away from need as a category in value represents another way of understanding that scholastic accounts of trade were argumentative rather than descriptive: despite Augustine's equation, it would have been far more difficult to justify trade in terms of desire than in terms of need. The fact that desire drops out of most accounts of trade and economic valuation, however, does not mean that it drops out of medieval thought about value. The *Shipman's Tale* and "The Cock and the Jasp" both suggest the connection between need and desire that Augustine makes clear and most scholastic authors ignore. As we have seen, the *Shipman's Tale* tends to make readers uneasy. If the discomfort comes in part, as I have suggested, from the desire to maintain a difference between "natural" and "economic" relations that the tale seems intent on collapsing, it also, I believe, stems from the specter of what might happen if an easy equation between money and sex were established: the merchant's wife, suddenly, could trade sex not only to pay off a single debt but for anything she desired. Chaucer, as we have seen, quickly contains this possibility, but the possibility itself underlies her trade with the monk. This trade, we should remember, was unsuccessful not because it was wrong, but because the monk did not act in accordance with justice in exchange.

In "The Cock and the Jasp," Henryson's rooster tries to maintain the implicit scholastic distinction between need and desire. The jewel is beautiful and fine, but he does not need it. Instead, he thinks, he needs food. He thus seems to understand the line between need and desire that should separate "legitimate" value from greed. It is, in fact, precisely because the cock understands this distinction so well that Lydgate congratulates him in his own version of the fable. But the moral of Henryson's fable returns us to the Augustinian world in which need and desire are not different from each other. Both are equally to be contrasted with absolute value, which the rooster completely ignores. The wit of the moral, however, depends on the idea that not only the rooster but the readers of the fable, too, will have forgotten this distinction. We all become, momentarily, the "stupid rooster" the moral condemns, having thought that it was better to concentrate on need than on baubles.

If we return to Henry of Ghent's depiction of the process of valuation that we saw in the first chapter, by which assessments of value move like arms of a scale until balance has been achieved, we thus come to see the difficulties behind this elegant fantasy. Weight is not only a measure because it is a common term between objects. Weight, as a way of describing the mass of an object and the pull of gravity, also has an external referent.

Two objects can be equal in weight, therefore, even before this equality is confirmed through measurement. Two items cannot be equal by the measure of money, however, until people decide that they should be. The suggestions about what criteria should determine valuation by money are, as we have seen, so diffuse as to provide almost no guidance in determining the value of a particular commodity. This again is different from weight, where a scale may be of great use in determining the weight of an object in pounds and ounces. The multiplicity of suggestions about the appropriate bases for value, moreover, take account only of economic value. Robert of Courson, Thomas Aquinas, Geoffrey Chaucer, and Robert Henryson, however, all evince a dissatisfaction with this conventional separation, whether because economic and absolute value should be combined, because they are combined, or because of the difficulty of distinguishing between them in practice.

3. CONSENT

Consent was, as we have seen, considered a necessary element of trade by medieval writers. It was not, however, one they analyzed explicitly. Because two parties had to agree to a trade before it took place, the material fact of the trade itself was understood to have proved that both had indeed agreed to it. When the imperative of consent was considered directly it was most often in negative cases: force, fraud, and coercion all invalidated a trade because they rendered it nonconsensual. Writing about trade thus tends to close off the possibility of examining the nature of consent because it makes the fact of consent appear stable and easily known. In order to see that the seeming stability of the idea of consent was a characteristic of writing about trade rather than a fact of late medieval thought we therefore need to look outside of writing that treats trade directly.

In this chapter I present three cases that explicitly consider the nature of consent. In the last chapter, the problems of valuation had to do with how to value and whether and how the Augustinian distinction between economic and natural value could be maintained in practice, but the difficulties that emerge in writing that treats consent are quite different. After discussing the extent to which consent is considered in writing about trade, I will examine the legal framework for determining consent that grew up in Church courts for deciding whether marriages had been formed. This body of writing grapples with the difficulty of determining whether consent had taken place when one party later denies it. Church teaching on the ways to verify consent was disseminated through a wide spectrum of medieval society. This broad dissemination points to a concomitantly broad awareness of the problems inherent in consenting (or believing that you have consented). I next turn to the *Physician's Tale,* where Chaucer considers, as legal courts could not, what mechanisms were at work in the creation of consent. In the tale Chaucer questions whether, when we think that we consent, our consent is really our own and freely given. Finally, I look at Thomas Aquinas's writing on the formation of marriage. This writing exposes the disjunction between the ways that different medieval institutions construed consent. In it we see the incompatibility, for Aquinas, of a legal system that demands proof as a protection for others and a theological system interested in internal (and thus unverifiable) sacramental truths.

I thus begin with considerations of consent made by those who had to determine whether consent had taken place, showing the broad awareness of these difficulties. I then move outward to a meditation on the difficulty of ever knowing whether even your own consent was truly consensual, and then outward again to the troubling consequences of this possibility. Where Chaucer wonders about the implications of the uncertainty of consent for what we would call ideology, Aquinas worries about the consequences of incomplete or compromised consent for the integrity of a sacrament and the health of souls.

Determining Consent in Trade

As we have seen, authors who write about trade posit consent as necessary for a valid exchange. Voluntariness is most often required in negative rather than positive terms: force, ignorance, and deception, many explain, invalidate contracts because they mean that one party does not necessarily agree to the trade.[1] For some the formulation is more positive. John Duns Scotus, for example, makes consent an explicit condition of trade by asserting that contracts are valid only if they are freely given and received.[2] Despite the frequent mention of voluntary agreement, however, these authors do not consider the nature of consent when they write about trade. Instead, the material fact of the completed exchange in the seeming absence of force or deception is understood to prove the presence of consent. Sometimes, as we have seen, even blatant deception is not enough to invalidate a contract if it nevertheless falls within one half of the current market price.

For all of the mentions of consent in discussions of trade, there is no sustained analysis of its nature. This lack of analysis becomes clear when we pause to examine the formulations of consent, even one so seemingly positive as Gerald Odonis's assertion that "no one is defrauded with knowledge and consent."[3] This statement echoes Aristotle's claim that no one voluntarily suffers injustice and Roman law dicta that hold that will precludes injustice.[4] Odonis's assertion, however, does not explain how we might know or recognize consent. It simply tells us that if this unexplained quality is present then a person has not been defrauded.

The way in which medieval authors understand voluntariness, moreover, sets the bar for the proof of force or deception very high. There were two traditions that came together to set standards for voluntariness in general: classical Roman law and the *Nicomachean Ethics.* Classical Roman law held that extraordinary force or deception had to be present to invalidate a contract. Medieval civil lawyers followed classic formulations in these high standards, holding that, in Accursius's words, "forced will is will." Although pure force or extreme fear or fraud might invalidate a contract, Baldus of Perugia explained that even the presence of these qualities that seem to make a contract involuntary do not in themselves necessarily invalidate a contract. Rather, he writes, "fraud or fear does not by the law itself render a contract null, but annullable." Odofredus tries to elucidate the criteria that might void a contract. He suggests, in Odd Langholm's paraphrase, "fear of death, as when someone holds a sword over your head, saying, unless you sell me this thing, you are dead." Rogerius is even more strict, claiming that any kind of will at all, even forced will, sufficed to make a contract binding.[5]

Aristotle considers the question of forced will in the third book of the *Nicomachean Ethics,* where he examines responsibility for actions. An action may be completely voluntary or it may be completely forced. People are responsible for voluntary actions but not for forced ones. There are other actions, however, that he places in a category of "mixed" voluntariness. The example most popular with medieval authors is that of the ship's captain who jettisons his cargo during a storm in hope of saving the ship. On one hand, the action goes against the captain's will: he has no desire to lose his cargo and certainly bears no responsibility for the storm.[6] At the same time, however, it does not go against his will: he decides that the best course of action in this situation is to throw his cargo overboard, and he is the one who orders or performs the action.

Scholastic authors did not hesitate to hold people responsible for actions of mixed will. This determination was imperative if people were to be held responsible for their sins, since sin is seldom completely knowing or completely free. For scholastic authors, moreover, the idea of mixed voluntariness was not one of a range of options for any action, but rather something that was central to their idea of fallen humanity. People never acted according to pure will, they believed, because people are by definition fallen and tied to their bodies. It was the desire to postulate what decisions we might make if pure will were available to us that led to the flourishing science of angelology. In the absence of such pure will, however, the fact that our actions are mixed in terms of voluntariness does not diminish our responsibility for them. The fact, then, that we might be forced by circumstance into a trade we would not make otherwise is a condition of having bodily needs and being subject to circumstances in general, rather than a sign of an invalid contract.

The "economic" locus in which these discussions take place most frequently, however, is not trade, where writers assume that the fact of the trade itself in the absence of notable force or fear or ignorance is a sign of consent. Rather, it is in discussions of usury. The question of the culpability for acts of mixed voluntariness arose when considering the position of the borrower of a usurious loan. On one hand, usury was clearly a sin. Scholastic authors held that anyone who aided the sin of another sinned herself. The borrower would seem, in this view, complicit in the usurer's sin, since without any borrowers the usurer could not practice usury. At the same time, however, scholastic authors were convinced that no one would pay usury voluntarily. Anyone, they wrote, would rather take a loan without usury than a loan with it. Even the borrower's word that he borrowed voluntarily was not enough to change their minds. Thomas of Chobham, for example, explained that even if a borrower says that he pays usury voluntarily, he does so with a comparative will rather than an absolute will. The distinction here is similar to that of agreeing in mixed rather than absolute terms: comparing this option to others, the borrower agrees.[7] William of Auxerre similarly distinguished between absolute and comparative will, as did Peter of Tarentaise, Alexander of Hales, Thomas Aquinas, and many other scholastic authors.[8] Nevertheless, these writers did not claim that usury was forced: usurious loans, they believed, were usually not the result of a lender placing a sword above the borrower's head and saying, "Unless you take this loan you will die." Instead, borrowers agreed to the lenders' terms. Gerald Odonis thus gave usury as an exception to Aristotle's statement that no one suffers injustice voluntarily.[9] Usury was unjust, but the agreement was real agreement, even if it was mixed or comparative rather than absolute. Scholastic authors understood borrowing with usury as necessarily mixed or comparative in terms of voluntariness.

Having established that people would rather not pay usury but agree to usurious loans nevertheless, the scholastic authors addressed the question of culpability by trying to assess need. William of Auxerre wrote that the person who would perish unless he borrowed money and could borrow money only with usury paid it against his right will and thus did not sin.[10] For William, as for later scholastics who followed his reasoning, compulsion made usury close enough to involuntary that it eliminated the borrower's culpability. These writers were clear, however, that volunteering to pay usury in order to secure a loan was different, and far worse, than trying to find a loan and being told that it would be available only if usury were paid.[11] The questions of how much need excused borrowing with usury and to what standard we should hold "compulsion" were seldom answered directly. Albert the Great, who seldom shied away from an intellectual problem, simply declared himself unwilling to determine the precise degree of need because it was too difficult.[12] Others gestured toward a scale of need. Aquinas wrote that the borrower who could manage without a loan but wants one for greater profit sins, but one who takes the loan for need does not.[13] By the fourteenth century, Durandus of Saint-Pourçain seems to have expanded the criteria for need, stating that a merchant may borrow with usury if he cannot live adequately from other sources.[14] Antonino of Florence, in the fifteenth century, agreed.[15] None of these writers, however, offered a standard as precise as the one of excessive force that we saw in considering contracts, as vague as that standard itself might appear to be.

The discussions of mixed voluntariness that we find in writing about usury, then, quickly turn into considerations of need rather than considerations of consent. Usury is necessarily mixed in terms of voluntariness because no one would prefer to pay it, just as no captain would prefer to throw his cargo overboard. Insofar as the borrower does, nevertheless, borrow the money, he agrees to pay usury, just as the captain agrees to lose his cargo. In both cases the agreement comes about from adverse situations, but in both cases the agreement itself nevertheless stands. The authors who write about the potential culpability of the borrower do not consider the nature of the borrower's consent because they already know that no one would consent to a usurious loan if a nonusurious loan were available. Even such a seemingly problematic example as the borrower's claim to pay usury voluntarily did not trouble their writing about usury, it simply served as another example of its mixed voluntariness. The scholastic authors moved on to think about the nature of the need that might lead to such agreement, but not to consider the nature of the agreement itself.

The Development of the Law on Marriage Formation

The most sustained consideration of the nature of consent in medieval thought was in the idea of the formation of marriage. To state that marriage offers our best opportunity to examine an articulation of ideas about consent is not to state that consent was uniquely important in marriage. Consent was crucial in a number of areas of medieval life: not only in trade and marriage, but also in conversion, for example. To understand why marriage provided such a fertile ground for this consideration, we can compare the difficulties consent posed in marriage to those it posed in conversion.

Conversion, like trade, depended on the consent of the actor to be valid.

Potential converts could be placed in situations that might hasten or even compel their agreement, but internal consent, however created, needed to be present. In trade, however, the fact of trade itself was a sign that consent had taken place. In conversion, baptism, the physical act that marked conversion, was not a certain sign that the supposed convert had actually or fully consented to the conversion internally. Although consent thus presented a theoretical difficulty in recognizing conversion, it did not constitute a significant practical problem. People who watched the convert's baptism had no way of knowing whether she had truly consented to the baptism, but at the same time they did not really need to know. If she were insincere, the fact of her insincerity would lead to the denial of the sacrament. Whether or not her consent to baptism constituted true consent was thus at some level not a concern for those who urged or even rewarded the conversion: others could treat her as though she were baptized, and if she were not it would be her sin, not theirs.

In marriage, however, the nature of consent had to be more closely examined because the bond was not only between one person and God (who could know the precise nature of the person's consent) but between two people. If, as the law held by the thirteenth century, consent created marriage, but one party had not truly consented, the lack of this agreement was not only a matter between the deceiver and God, it was also of the closest concern to the spouse who thought himself or herself married. It furthermore became the concern of the courts that found themselves in the position of ruling on whether a marriage had taken place. The fullest theory of consent in the middle ages thus came to be articulated around the subject of marriage. Because the question of marriage was of intimate concern to most members of Christendom, moreover, the teachings on consent became well disseminated and were demonstrably known at a local level by the unlettered, as well as argued over by some of the most erudite men of the middle ages.

To claim that marriage thus proves the best place to understand medieval thought about consent, however, is not to say that consent was the same in both marriage and trade. One difference lies in the fact that while trade was worldly (as we saw, it is determined on an economic rather than a natural scale), marriage was not only worldly but also sacramental. Where consent in trade, in other words, created a bond between two people, consent in marriage not only created a bond between two people but also one between those people and God. A second difference takes place purely on a worldly level. Although consent in trade led to a binding contract, it did not lead to an exclusive one. Marriage, on the other hand, was exclusive. The trader who did not like the person with whom she contracted could contract with a different person in the future; the unhappy spouse could not contract with a different person a month or year later (although, as we will see, some tried). Despite these differences, however, the question of consent in each case is of the same kind. Both need to determine how one person knows the consent of another. Where writers about trade rely on the fact of consent but are able to leave it unqueried, the high stakes of marriage mean that in that forum it must be discussed. The differences of scale make the question of consent in marriage a kind of magnifying glass, attracting attention and allowing us to view thought about consent that remains invisible when the stakes are lower.

We can see the way issues of consent came together around marriage in a suit brought before the Bishop's Court in York in 1382. Agnes Besete came to the court to sue Robert Peper for marriage.[16] Both admitted that they had engaged in carnal relations. One evening they were surprised in bed by one Alice, who asked the perhaps obvious question, "What are you doing here, Robert?" Robert, clearly startled, evaded the question, replying only "I am here now." Alice demanded that Robert take Agnes by the hand and swear marriage to her. When Robert suggested that he would do so the next day, Alice answered, "By God no, you will do it now!" Robert, seemingly cowed, took Agnes by the hand and said, "I will lead you as my wife." But Alice, still not content, gave him explicit orders: "You will say it in this fashion, 'I take you Agnes as my wife and to this I give you my faith.' " Robert did so and Agnes answered in similar fashion. The court, having been satisfied that Agnes meant the words she spoke, held that Robert and Agnes were man and wife.

The case encapsulates many important aspects of marriage law in late medieval England. First, marriage law was Church law. There was no question of turning to a local or king's court; marriage law was almost exclusively the preserve of the Church. Second, the marriage was held valid and binding even though no banns had been read, it did not happen in front of a church, and it was not blessed by a priest. Third, the examiner who recorded the depositions evinced a clear interest in not only what words were spoken but also in what Agnes thought they meant. He makes an explicit point of noting that Agnes had proven to him her intention of marrying Robert. Fourth, in trying to make Robert marry Agnes, Alice was quite insistent on the words he should use. In her insistence she shows a fine ear for distinguishing between a promise in the future tense (*ducam,* I will lead you) and one in the present tense (*accipio,* I take you). More significantly, her insistence demonstrates a clear knowledge of the importance of that distinction: according to canon law an exchange of consent in the present tense created a marriage, while an exchange of consent in the future tense was only a promise. Finally, in agreeing that Agnes and Robert were married, the court came to the conclusion that Robert's words of consent, although clearly reluctant, had not been produced under enough force or fear to move a constant man. Force or fear that met such a standard would have rendered Robert's words invalid. To understand how and why these laws came to be, to be widely known, and to be widely enforced in England by 1382, we need to go back to the middle of the twelfth century and to Gratian.

By turning to Gratian, we can see the process by which the diverse views on marriage that circulated in the middle of the twelfth century were synthesized into a consistent Church policy by the beginning of the thirteenth century. The consensus that emerged remained the official teaching until the Council of Trent (1545–63). Then we will turn to some of the ways these views were spread throughout Europe and particularly in England. Finally we will move to court cases in England that show both knowledge of the Church teachings and rulings that are consistent with them. However unproblematically consent is treated in writing about trade, this knowledge demonstrates a wide understanding of the potential problems of consent. I will present, then, the triumph of a consensual theory of marriage and an examination of what consent meant in medieval England in the arena in which it was most carefully articulated and widely understood. The various constitutive elements of marriage law in theory and practice have tended to be studied separately. What I hope emerges from this synthesis, in addition to a picture of the problems inherent in the idea of consent, is a stronger understanding of the stability and continuity of these ideas surrounding marriage in the later middle ages than has been previously made apparent. This continuity and the extent to which it was understood shows that awareness of the difficulties of consenting was not the purview of only a few writers but was a fact of marriage, an important element in medieval life.

When we speak of marriage law in the middle ages we are speaking of law that was practiced in and theorized for ecclesiastical courts. Although many areas of medieval law saw competition between the canon and common laws in the twelfth through fifteenth centuries, secular courts seemed quite content to leave the question of marriage to the Church.[17] The competition to regulate marriage in the later middle ages came not from common law but from local custom and a seeming belief by the laity who married that they were capable of regulating their own marital affairs without recourse to the Church or the courts.[18] Although local customs may have displayed more variety, when Gratian set about harmonizing discordant canons in the first half of the twelfth century there were three broad written theories current about the way marriage was formed. The consensual theory held that marriage was formed when the parties to the marriage exchanged words of consent to the marriage. The coital theory held that marriage was formed by its consummation. The third idea, taken from Roman law, was that marriage was created by a formal ceremony between the parties, usually a leading of the bride into the groom's house, or sometimes the transfer of a dower or other gift. Such were the written traditions Gratian tried to harmonize.

Gratian's *Concordia discordantium canonum* probably appeared close to 1140 in Bologna.[19] Better known as the *Decretum*, it was the first attempt to systematize ecclesiastical law, and some have even seen it as the beginning of legal science.[20] In it Gratian not only compiles authoritative texts from the scriptures and the church fathers, penitentials, Roman law, papal pronouncements, and canons from every kind of council, he also places these extracts in systematic order and, for the first time, comments on them, explaining how he believes they should be reconciled.

The *Decretum* first mentions marriage in the first distinction of its first part, which deals with the foundations and sources of canon law and its relationship to other types of law. Explaining that natural law "is common to all nations because it exists everywhere through natural instinct, not because of any enactment," Gratian gives marriage as an example of natural law.[21] He does not discuss the formation of marriage itself until the second book of the *Decretum*, in cases 27–36. On one hand, Gratian agrees with those who claim that marriage is made by consent and that coitus without consent to marry is no marriage at all. He thus uses the argument from those who advocate a consent theory to support a distinction between concubinage and marriage. At the same time, he agrees with those who claim that a union without coitus is no marriage, and that marriage therefore does not fully exist without consummation. He takes this argument from those who adhere to a coital theory of marriage. Gratian thus "harmonizes" the consensual and coital schools of marriage by explaining marriage as a two step process: consent initiates the process (*matrimonium initiatum*); consummation completes it (*matrimonium ratum* or *perfectum*). Consent without coitus, according to Gratian, is simply a promise; coitus without consent is fornication. Both parts are necessary to the formation of a marriage.[22]

By emphasizing marriage as a two-step process, however, Gratian's formulation can in some ways be seen as more in line with those who advocated the coital theory of marriage than with those who advocated the consensual theory of marriage. By requiring consummation for the marriage to become complete, Gratian makes the bond of marriage hinge on its consummation rather than the couple's agreement to it.[23] It is certainly true that Gratian, unlike those of the consent school, did not believe that consent alone formed a binding union. So, for example, Gratian explains that if a woman consents to one marriage but does not consummate the union and then later marries another man, consummating the second union is not adultery. Instead, she is married to the second man.[24] Similarly, a man who marries one woman through mutual consent and then marries a second woman is a bigamist only if he consummates both marriages. Otherwise he is married only to the woman with whom he had intercourse after the exchange of consent.[25] At the same time, Gratian, unlike those of the coital school, emphasized that consent of both parties to the marriage was an indispensable requirement for marriage. In one case Gratian considers whether a daughter may be given in marriage against her will. He concludes that even in cases in which her father has promised her in marriage, she can become married only by her own consent.[26] Gratian's formulation of marriage was widely influential, as we might expect from the work that almost immediately became the principal teaching text for law in the schools.

While Gratian's theory elegantly combined the two imperatives of consent and consummation, it did not entirely solve the problem of the way marriage was created, particularly for those who believed that copulation was an inappropriate requirement for a sacrament. Marriage had been called a sacrament in the New Testament.[27] In fact, it is the only sacrament identified as such in the Bible. While marriage was therefore referred to as a sacrament throughout the middle ages, the precise meaning placed on that label in the twelfth century is far from clear.[28] In the *Decretum,* for example, the word "sacrament" as it relates to marriage is used in at least three different ways. Sometimes, following Augustine, it designates the indissolubility of the bond; sometimes it designates the bond itself; and sometimes it refers to the sign of the union between Christ and the Church. But the view was increasingly advanced in the twelfth and thirteenth centuries that although marriage was unlike other sacraments in being self-administered, it was nevertheless a full sacrament. For those who advocated this view, it seemed somewhat inappropriate that the requirement for this sign of grace should be sexual intercourse. Understanding marriage in Gratian's terms, as a two-part process that was only perfected by intercourse, also posed problems for understanding Joseph and Mary's relationship. On one hand, it was unacceptable for Mary to have had carnal relations with her husband. On the other hand, it was equally unacceptable for Jesus' parents to have been unmarried.[29]

In his *Sententiae* (1155–58) Peter Lombard spoke to such concerns in advocating a purely consensual theory of marriage, as both Peter Abelard and Hugh of St. Victor had before him.[30] Peter Lombard, like Gratian, notes Isidore's saying that consent makes marriage, but unlike Gratian, Peter continues to compile similar sources before explicitly denying any essential role for intercourse in creating matrimony. Marriage, Peter explains, takes place whenever two people who are eligible to be married say that each consents to the marriage. This consent, he argues, forms a permanent and lasting bond. Although consent creates marriage, it does not serve as a continual requirement for the marriage. Instead, consent creates the marriage bond which, once created, is indissoluble. In this opinion he follows not only Isidore and the other church fathers and early authorities he cites but also Hugh of St. Victor, who had similarly explained that the efficient cause of marriage was present consent.[31] In the *Sentences* Peter explicitly denies that consummation is necessary for a marriage to be complete and binding. In emphasizing that present consent creates not only the bond of marriage but also a permanent and lasting bond, he differentiates his idea of the marital bond from that of the ancient Romans, for whom consent also constituted marriage, but for whom the consent had to be ongoing.[32] Because he places such emphasis on the act of consent, he carefully distinguishes between present consent and future consent. In order for a marriage to be immediately contracted, the consent must be expressed in present words (*verba de presenti*). If the consent is instead expressed in future terms (*verba de futuro*), the words constitute a betrothal, not a marriage.

These articulations by Gratian and Peter Lombard of the views that marriage was created either by consummation or by consent influenced most European writers in the decades after they were written. The *Decretum* became the basis for the instruction of canon lawyers almost immediately after it appeared. Similarly, the *Sentences* quickly became the primary text of the faculties of theology, and a commentary on the *Sentences* became, slightly later, the final and necessary step for a master's degree.[33] Alongside these two traditions, however, there was a third, also influential, theory that was perhaps even more widely followed in practice than those delineated by Gratian and Peter Lombard.

This third written tradition was preserved by medieval commentators on Roman civil law, known as legists or civilians.[34] The texts from the *Corpus iuris civilis* never state outright how a marriage is contracted. While intercourse was not necessary for a valid marriage, neither was consent alone sufficient. Charles Donahue, the closest student of the marriage passages in the *Corpus iuris civilis,* has concluded that in Roman law marriage required both consent and "some act . . . to indicate that the marriage has become something more than a promise and that something more than concubinage is involved."[35] This act tended to be a *deductio in domum,* or leading of the bride into the groom's house (usually referred to simply as a *deductio* or *ductio*). Consent was a necessary condition for marriage—a Roman law maxim had it that consent makes a marriage—but an insuffi-

cient one.[36] Not only did the legists hold that consent alone was insufficient, they construed consent itself in different terms than either Peter
Lombard or Gratian did. For both Peter and Gratian "consent" indicated
primarily the consent of the marriage partners: Peter even provided specific examples of words that the partners could say to express consent and
made clear that an expression of consent by the marriage partners alone
was all that was needed for a complete and binding union. For the legists,
however, "consent" was a much broader concept, often including the consent of all who had any power over the man and woman to be married, including parents and lords. The role of the prospective bride and groom
could be minimal. A daughter, for example, was generally presumed to
consent to her father's choice of a marriage partner unless she explicitly
opposed him; and in one place the *Digest* states that she may oppose her
father's choice only if the father chooses someone unworthy. Although a
son could not be similarly compelled to acquiesce to his father's choice,
his consent was assumed if he contracted a marriage he explicitly would
not have chosen but for his father's insistent urging. The father's consent,
on the other hand, was clearly necessary for the marriage of his children
(with the possible exception of an emancipated son). A father could sin-
gle-handedly dissolve a daughter's espousals, and even compel her divorce
from her husband, if he had "great and just cause." In fact, the only rule
in Justinian's *Institutes* about how marriages must be formed insists on the
necessity of parental consent for underage children.[37] The legists seem to
have supported this broader understanding of consent as well as the idea
that marriage was formed through such consent followed by a ductio.[38]

The written tradition was thus clear in its three basic arguments when
the bishop of Pavia wrote to Pope Alexander III (1159–81) requesting his
assistance. Alexander answered his inquiry in the decretal *Veniens ad nos*.
One G., it seems, had, while spending the night at someone's house, been
surprised in bed with his host's daughter. The agitated host insisted that
G. and his daughter wed each other then and there with words of present
consent, which they did. G., however, lived with a different woman, with
whom he had a child and to whom he had promised marriage at some future date. He had made this promise in front of many witnesses. To whom,
the bishop wanted to know, was G. married? (Or more vividly, if less collo-
quially, to whom ought G. adhere?)[39] In making a decision, as in the many
marriage decretals he issued over the course of his pontificate, Alexander
had a choice. There was the Roman tradition, by which G. would be married to the first woman if she had been led into his house formally or if
some sort of property or gift had been exchanged; to the second woman
if there had been some sort of formal ceremony after the promise in front
of her father; and to no one if no formal marker of the marriage had taken

place for either woman. There was the tradition from the *Decretum,* by which a matrimonium initiatum certainly existed with the woman in his own house and possibly a matrimonium ratum, but only a matrimonium initiatum with his host's daughter, making it possible that G. was married to the first woman but almost certain that he was not indissolubly tied to the second. There was also the consensual tradition, by which he was married to the first woman if he had ever expressed his consent to marriage with her in present terms, but, if not, had only been betrothed to her when he married the second woman, which he certainly had even if no further carnal relations with the host's daughter had ensued after being caught and exchanging marriage vows.

The choice, in this case as in the others on which Alexander ruled, was whether to favor the tradition as espoused by Gratian, which required coitus to form a complete and binding marriage; the tradition as espoused by Peter Lombard, which held that consent alone formed a complete and binding marriage; or the Roman law tradition as espoused by the legists, which required a ductio or other formal ceremony to create a complete and lasting union.[40] The decision with which Alexander was faced can thus be seen as a confrontation among the disciplines of canon law, theology, and civil law. On the whole Alexander, who had himself taught both canon law and theology at Bologna prior to becoming a cardinal in 1150, chose theology. Alexander believed that the bishop needed to make more inquiries. If G. had carnal relations with the first woman after the verba de futuro, he was married to her. If he did not, he was married to the host's daughter, unless he uttered the verba de presenti under enough force or fear to move a constant man. We will return to the question of this constant man, but here we should note that Alexander chose Peter's distinction over Gratian's. The distinction he applied in all of his decretals was that between verba de presenti, which resulted in immediate and binding marriage between eligible parties, and verba de futuro, which was only a promise of marriage (also referred to as a betrothal). Alexander added to this idea of betrothal the condition that if a future promise of marriage were followed by subsequent carnal relations the marriage immediately took effect unless one of the parties had made himself or herself ineligible through other means (contracting a different marriage, for example, or taking monastic vows).[41] By engaging in sexual intercourse, in other words, the couple removed the conditionality that the future consent imposed. Consent to intercourse following consent to a future marriage, according to this logic, constitutes consent to creating a present marriage. Alexander never mentions Gratian's distinction between matrimonium initiatum and matrimonium ratum.[42]

In the series of decretals on marriage that he issued, Alexander's decisions all work to increase the importance of the consent of both parties while decreasing the significance of other factors. "Consent" is very clearly understood as only the consent of the marriage parties, not the consent of the families, a possible interpretation of some of Gratian's writing; and not the consent of either slaves' masters or of lords, an exclusion that flew in the face of customary law in many parts of Christendom.[43] If a daughter were abducted from her father's house, the marriage between her and her abductor would be perfectly binding if she consented to it, even if her father did not.[44] In cases where there were doubts about whether a marriage had taken place and it could be feared that the girl's family would compel her to marry a different suitor while the case was being settled, Alexander recommended sequestering the girl.[45] Excessive force or threats used to compel words of consent invalidated the union.[46] The blessing of a priest and the publication of marriage banns were a good idea, and to be encouraged, but not necessary.[47] Whatever Alexander's intention, the effect of his writings as a whole was indisputably to decrease the importance of family and community while elevating the standing of the consent of the marriage parties to almost the only consideration.[48]

We do not know the precise dating of Alexander's marriage decretals, but we do know that the consent theory of marriage he advocated was not universally accepted at the time he promulgated these rulings. Each of the three broad theories about the formation of marriage (consensual, coital, and requiring some public ceremony, usually a ductio) had its advocates, even if they did not slavishly support the way the theory had been formulated in the *Decretum* or *Sentences* or the *Corpus iuris civilis*. In the half-century after the completion of the *Decretum,* most canonists followed Gratian's lead in advocating definitions of marriage that included consummation as a necessary part of a complete union. So around 1148 Paucapalea wrote that a consensual union without intercourse could be terminated for a good cause, while intercourse made marriage binding;[49] a few years later Rolandus emphasized the incompleteness of a union that lacked either consent or intercourse, insisting that each was an equal element in the initiation of a marriage;[50] around the same time the anonymous author of *In primis hominibus,* in a gesture of inclusivity or compromise, construed this equality of consent and intercourse differently, insisting that a marriage could be contracted *either* by an exchange of consent *or* by intercourse between two people capable of marrying each other;[51] and sometime between 1157 and 1159 Rufinus, trying to give some structure to the still largely unconsidered idea that marriage was a sacrament, explained that marriage was in fact two sacraments, the first conferred when a couple exchanged consent to marry, the second conferred when they consummated the union. The two sacraments taken together formed a marriage.[52] All of these writers can thus be seen trying to refine Gratian's idea that both consent and coitus were necessary to a marriage.

At the same time, those who studied Roman law held to the idea that marriage became indissoluble only with the leading of the wife into the husband's house, or occasionally another formal public acknowledgement of the consent, such as the exchange of rings. Vacarius, for example, writing in the 1150s, probably from England, dismisses Gratian's idea that marriage becomes complete upon intercourse and advocates the old Roman law position.[53] Bulgarus, in the middle of the twelfth century, similarly agrees that "marriage is made by affection following a leading [*ductio*]."[54] Johannes Bassianus, around 1180, seems, like Gratian, to have adopted a two-part scheme, but for Bassianus the elements come from Roman law: nuptials are made by consent, he claims, but perfected when the espoused woman is led.[55] Similarly both Martinus Gosia, one of the "Four Doctors" of the law, and the Gosian writings in the *Summa codicis,* which were generally more receptive to canonical positions than Bulgarus and Bassianus, require an outward manifestation of the change in status, again usually a ductio.[56] Not only did other legists dictate rules for marriage along these lines, their position seems to have been followed by Bishop Henry of Winchester around the middle of the twelfth century, as well as to have been the preferred opinion among decretists in the Rhineland.[57]

In the decade after the *Sentences* we see Peter Lombard's ideas acknowledged—but not advocated—by a number of canonists who state that some people believe that marriage is initiated by consent but ratified through intercourse, while other people believe that words of present consent form a complete and indissoluble marriage.[58] By the 1170s, however, some support for the consensual theory seems to have emerged among the canonists. Joannes Faventinus, for example, in 1171 notes and approves of Gratian's distinction between matrimonium initiatum and matrimonium ratum yet maintains that the marriage bond is created by mutual assent. By the 1180s Sicard of Cremona presents Peter's definition and distinction without noting any alternatives.[59] By the last decade of the twelfth century Huguccio, the influential decretist who later became bishop of Ferrara, advocates a completely consensual theory of marriage. Huguccio explicitly rejects both Gratian's idea that coitus was necessary to a complete union and the legists' idea that a ductio or ceremony of any sort was needed to supplement the consent of the marriage partners. Instead, Huguccio writes, present consent alone exchanged between a man and woman capable of marrying one another creates an instantaneous perfect and lasting union. All other forms and ceremonies, including intercourse, were for him extraneous to this basic bond.[60] It is not clear whether Huguccio was following the lead of Peter Lombard or of Pope Alexander III, who would have written *Veniens ad nos* somewhere between seven and thirty-one years before Huguccio's writing, but whatever the precise genealogy a more influential advocate for the consent theory of marriage could hardly have been found in these years.

The Triumph of the Consent Theory of Marriage Formation

Perhaps the most remarkable aspect of Alexander III's marriage policy is the extent to which all parties writing about marriage seemed to acquiesce in following it by the last decade of the twelfth century. The tradition of the schools is one of challenge, debate, and conflicting opinions. Peter Abelard famously set these conflicting opinions side by side in *Sic et non,* trusting his readers to draw conclusions; Gratian tried to create harmony from the discord; Peter Lombard attempted to show how the correct answers could be reached through proper reason. All through this time and beyond a standard method of instruction was the debate. Students made their own reputations as masters by successfully challenging the masters who came before them. Nor was there hesitation about correcting authorities. Gratian, for example, was criticized for his reasoning as well as for his Latin.[61] But even as the preferred forms of written discourse moved from the gloss and apparatus to the summa and then to the commentary, treatise, and *consilium,* Alexander's marriage doctrines held firm. It is, perhaps, less remarkable that papal rulings should remain unchallenged than that glosses or summae should go unchallenged, but even papal rulings were often disputed by noting that a pope's writing in a particular case should be applied only narrowly, and that everywhere else something different should be understood, or that common opinion and intelligence held that a pope actually meant something other than what might appear at first glance. Even within this world of frequent reinterpretations, the basic ideas surrounding marriage that Alexander laid out created a Church policy on marriage that remained in place until the Council of Trent.[62]

We can see this consensus of opinion in the writings of later popes, whose decisions about marriage cases increased the extent to which the consent of the parties to the marriage was the determining factor in marriage rather than allowing the importance of other considerations. The most important modification of Alexander's rulings in terms of the way consent was understood was Innocent III's amendment of the logic behind the idea that verba de futuro followed by intercourse created a marriage. Where Alexander seems to place consent in the act of intercourse itself, Innocent makes clear that it is not the act of intercourse that makes the marriage (as it was for Gratian, for example). Instead, Innocent explains, the act of intercourse is taken as a sign that the future consent has already become present.[63] The marriage does not become present and binding in the moment of intercourse; rather, intercourse serves as an outward manifestation of the inward change from future to present consent. This ruling strengthened the force of consent in creating the marriage. Innocent III further fortified the emphasis on consent rather than coitus in Alexander III's marriage doctrines when he ruled that if a man who promised marriage to two different women through verba de presenti had sexual relations with the second before the first, the man was nevertheless married to the first woman rather than the one with whom he had consummated the union.[64]

Changes made by the Fourth Lateran Council in 1215 tend also in this direction. They required that future marriages be announced in church by a priest sufficiently before the marriage itself for those who wished to bring forth impediments: the custom that came to be known as the reading of banns. They also required that marriages take place in front of a church.[65] But although clandestine marriages (i.e., any marriages that were not conducted in the presence of the church following a prior announcement in the church by a priest) were forbidden, the punishment for clandestine marriage was to be "a suitable penance" (*condigna poenitentia*), indicating that such marriages were indeed considered binding even if not strictly legal. There was certainly no hint that the marriage itself would be invalid. At the same time this canon expressly forbid priests to be present at clandestine marriages, which suggests that marriages away from the church but with a priest present were seen as something of a threat to ecclesiastical authority.[66] The Fourth Lateran Council also made marriage easier by reducing the number of impediments, particularly unwieldy degrees of consanguinity.[67] English synodal legislation seems to have universally supported these changes, particularly in its insistence on the validity of clandestine marriages.[68] A common solution to these laws and the high practical incidence of clandestine marriage seems to have been for priests to urge those who married clandestinely to regularize their unions later at a church.[69]

We can see the consensus of opinion too in the writings of the canonists, who by the late 1180s accept Alexander's definitions of the way marriages are formed without mention of the distinction between matrimonium initiatum and matrimonium ratum that had been popular only a few decades earlier.[70] Furthermore, the canonists became explicit in their adherence to the condition mentioned in *Veniens ad nos* that consent to marriage by the parties being married had to be free and uncoerced. Force used to secure consent, whether by parents or lords or another party, would invalidate the union. These laws were further ratified and disseminated in diocesan synods, which, even as they encouraged ceremonies such as publication of banns, vows at the church door, priestly blessings, and postnuptial masses, always admitted that words of present consent alone were enough to make a valid marriage.[71]

The marriage laws were also circulated through handbooks for confessors, such as Robert of Flamborough's *Liber poenitentialis* and Thomas of Chobham's *Summa confessorum.*[72] Robert of Flamborough was a Yorkshireman who was canon-penitentiary of the priory of St. Victor at Paris by 1205. His *Liber poenitentialis* (1208–15) seems to have been the first penitential committed to making canon law accessible to priests and confessors. Its four books take the form of a dialogue between a fictional penitent (who has had the widest possible range of experiences) and a priest, who takes the opportunity of hearing about the penitent's activities to instruct him in Church doctrine. Robert carefully explains that this dialogue is not meant to replicate an actual confession but to teach his reader. His concern with transmitting Church teaching is so great, in fact, that in the four books of the *Liber poenitentialis* as they survive he never quite makes it so far as listing what penances a priest should impose for each infraction.[73] He devotes the second book of his work to marriage, explicating recent decretals and conciliar rulings on the subject. Robert's book is notable both because it devotes an enormous amount of space to establishing the positive requirements of marriage in general and because it seems to have been used throughout the later middle ages. It continued to be copied throughout the thirteenth and fourteenth centuries; at least forty-seven manuscripts survive or are known to have existed in Europe.[74] It therefore continued to disseminate twelfth- and early thirteenth-century conciliar rulings over the following centuries.

The trend toward using the confessional manual to educate priests can also be seen in Thomas of Chobham's enormously popular *Summa confessorum,* which we have already encountered in its teachings on merchants and trade. Thomas had no certain training in the law. While he believed that priests must know conciliar rulings, his teaching was more theological and less legal in bent than Robert's (indeed F. Broomfield believes that the readability and popularity of Thomas's work stems from the fact that he was neither lawyer nor academic). Thomas, a subdeacon and ecclesiastical judge of Salisbury and rector of Chobham, Surrey, began work on his treatise around 1210 and probably finished it by 1216. Like Robert, Thomas typically devotes at least half of his attention to explaining the underlying rules and logic of the question under discussion before moving on to advice about what confessors should tell penitents guilty of any particular act. When he turns to marriage, Thomas briefly places matrimony among the other sacraments before stating plainly that only consent makes a marriage (*solus consensus facit matrimonium*).[75] In fact, Thomas goes on to explain with teacherly care that it takes not just one consent to make a marriage, but two: the consent of the man and the consent of the woman. These two consents, when given at the same time, join the parties in the perpetual bond of marriage.[76] Like others, Thomas finds it preferable for future marriages to be announced three times in the church before taking place, and then to be conducted at the church with a sacred blessing from the priest and a mass. Nevertheless, he, like others, also feels compelled to explain that "it is clear that a man and a woman can contract a marriage by themselves without a priest and without anyone else, in any place, so long as they consent in a perpetual way of life."[77] The *Summa confessorum* exists in over one hundred surviving manuscripts, many of which were used in priories and colleges where they would have been available to large numbers of readers. Moreover, at least two copies of the work printed in the 1480s still exist, which demonstrates its continuing popularity and influence. As Broomfield shows, it was also used extensively by the authors of later penitential manuals popular in England, such as the author of the *Speculum iuniorum,* the author of the *Signaculum apostolatus mei,* Ranulph Higden in his *Speculum curatorum,* and William of Pagula in his *Oculus sacerdotis.*[78]

Consent similarly trumps other considerations in Richard of Wetheringsett's *Summa "Qui bene presunt presbiteri"* (1215–30), which, echoing the fourth book of Peter Lombard's *Sentences,* explains that mutual consent is the efficient cause of matrimony.[79] Roger also urges priests to find ways of expressing to the laity the idea that marriage is made by words of present consent or words of future consent followed by carnal relations.[80] Similarly, in a passage that may or may not be taken from Thomas of Chobham, William of Pagula's *Oculus sacerdotis* (1319–22) also confirms that marriage is contracted through consent alone (*contrahitur matrimonium solo consensus per verba de presenti*).[81] In the middle of the fourteenth century, Johannes Andreae, one of Bologna's most important teachers, wrote a treatise on betrothal and marriage that seems designed for relatively popular consumption. In it he, too, explains from the beginning that marriage could only be contracted by consent.[82] The treatise was printed as late as 1485.

Even the legists came around to the idea that consent, rather than a ductio or other formal ceremony, created a binding marriage. Trained in legal disputation and with their own firm legal tradition, the legists are the group from whom we might expect the most formal disagreement. As Charles Donahue, who has most closely studied their views on marriage, understands their dilemma, in the face of the Alexandrine decretals they had three options.[83] They could disagree with the pope, arguing that his rulings construed marriage incorrectly. As we have seen, an old legal maxim held that only consent makes a marriage, but they could claim that this did not obviate the necessity for a more formal marking of the occasion, as they had in their earlier writings. Or they could comply with Alexander's decretals, accepting them wholesale. Or they could agree with parts of Alexander's interpretations while disagreeing with other aspects of them. The legists chose the third option, agreeing that consent alone could create a permanent union but disagreeing about whose "consent" this formulation required. They agreed that marriage could not be made by force, and agreed that the consent of the principals was required, but they tended to maintain that consent should be broader than just the man and woman being married. They also believed that marriage concerned larger communities of people—at the very least the families involved on either side. They therefore fought to keep the idea of consent itself more expansive than that specified in Alexander's interpretation and reaffirmed by subsequent popes and later Church councils until the mid-sixteenth century.

Just as remarkable as the general consensus surrounding Alexander's rulings on marriage is the extent to which the clergy in England tried to teach and implement them. Surviving marriage liturgies from the twelfth to the fourteenth centuries begin by questioning the parties about whether they agree to the marriage. This element of the liturgy seems to have grown in importance. For example, one note in a thirteenth-century hand added to a twelfth-century pontifical next to the questions to be asked about whether the parties consent to the marriage explains, "According to the law, their consent alone suffices; if it happens that it is lacking in a marriage, all the rest, even the public celebration, is void."[84] Future instructions became even more specific. For example, the Magdalen College Pontifical specifically scripts the questions the priest must ask the prospective bride and groom (by name) and the answers he must receive if the marriage is to proceed. Michael Sheehan, who has most carefully studied these liturgies, gives many such examples and concludes that "at each stage of the series of inquiries by which freedom from impediment and consent to the marriage were established, the *ordines* indicate that, if the answers of those involved revealed a situation not in accord with the Church's teaching obtained, proceedings were to be stopped."[85]

Furthermore, it seems that English priests followed these instructions. Thomas of Chobham, for example, while recommending that serfs obtain the approval of their lords before marrying, insists that they have the right to marry whomever they chose, even without the lord's approval, and urges priests to preside at these marriages. Thomas points out that priests should act this way because a lord could not control his serf's consent.[86] In a similar, if less socially daring, spirit, Richard of Wetheringsett approves of the clergy's implied tendency to stand up for men's and women's rights to choose and agree to their own marriage partners even when they go against the wishes of their parents or lords. Priests seem to have been coming under pressure from the unhappy parents and lords, but Richard urges them to remain firm in the face of this pressure.[87] Furthermore, evidence collected from Norfolk shows that such encouragement seems to have worked. Elaine Clark has found that despite lords' efforts to control the marriage choices of those who held land under them, the lords were almost entirely unsuccessful. By the fourteenth century they seem to have given up trying in all cases except those under their direct guardianship, instead accepting a fee to allow marriage at will.[88]

It seems likely, then, that efforts to instruct priests in Church doctrines about marriage met with success. Instruction was explicit in vernacular English works such as John Mirk's *Instruction for Parish Priests,* much of which may have been a loose translation of the *Oculus sacerdotis.*[89] Mirk, who probably wrote at the end of the fourteenth century, made clear at the outset that he wrote for priests who were not "grete clerks."[90] They should trust this book, he explained, which contained what they needed to know to fulfill their duties. In somewhat clumsy rhyming couplets (which may have aided those trying to remember them) he set out the fact that once words of consent have been spoken ("Here I take þe to my weddyd wyfe") the marriage is binding ("For þof he or scho another take, / þat worde wyll a domed man make").[91] Mirk also encouraged public rather than private weddings and advocated the presence of seven witnesses, although whether he believed seven was an appropriately poetic number, in keeping with the seven sacraments about which he was writing, or merely a prudent number, in case of later disputes, is never made clear.

John of Thoresby, archbishop of York, may have meant his *Lay Folks' Catechism* to reach the same audience of little-educated parish priests at which Mirk explicitly aimed, but the title of his work proclaims an intended audience even beyond the clergy. He published the *Lay Folks' Catechism* in both Latin and English. The English translation (which its editors characterize as "rude verse") was undertaken by John of Taystek, a monk at St. Mary's Abbey at York, presumably at Thoresby's request.[92] The English version is not a literal translation of the Latin but an elaboration of the more succinct Latin. The expansion was presumably also at Thoresby's request and complied with the theory that someone who could not read Latin would need more explanation and teaching than someone who could.

Both Latin and English versions were approved by the Council or Convocation of York in 1357.[93] The *Lay Folks' Catechism,* following what had, by this time, become convention, explains marriage as the seventh sacrament:

> The sevent sacrement is Matirmonye,
> That is, a lawefull festenyng betwixt man and woman,
> At thair bother assent for to lyve samen
> Withouten ony lousyng to thair life lastes (342–45)

The text emphasizes both that assent creates the bond or "fastening" of matrimony and that this assent must be mutual ("at thair *bother* assent") in order for the lawful fastening to take place ("*at* thair bother assent"). The marital bond, it explains, comes from and is made permanent by the mutual assent. At the same time, it stresses the permanence of the act—in the image of fastening that will admit no loosening throughout life we can almost see the marriage knot metamorphosing into marriage noose.

Determining Consent in Marriage Law

Perhaps the best evidence that Alexander's marriage theory was known and enforced in England comes from marriage cases brought before ecclesiastical courts.[94] And there is a great deal of such evidence, because despite the longevity of Alexander's marriage decretals and the consensus surrounding them, whether they made good legal policy is open to question. Frederic William Maitland famously wrote that this policy "was certainly no masterpiece of human wisdom. Of all people in the world lovers are the least likely to distinguish precisely between the present and future tenses."[95] This reservation, made with the benefit of both hindsight and Maitland's inimitable prose, is certainly borne out in court. It is perhaps in those judges who persisted in trying to follow the decretals despite the practical difficulties they encountered that we see the strongest testament to their use and transmission as a matter of practical life in England.[96] It is worth pausing to note, however, that even if lovers are not careful with their tenses, the distinction advocated by Gratian between matrimonium initiatum and matrimonium ratum would not necessarily have been any easier to enforce. If lovers do not distinguish well between present and future tenses when they make their vows, at least their vows are often made in the presence of witnesses. Intercourse is a more definite act, but also one more likely to take place out of the purview of others who might testify about it.[97] The problem with consent, as we shall see, was that it was a difficult requirement not because it was philosophically inappropriate to want consent from the parties of marriage, nor even because of lovers' grammatical sloppiness, but because as a practical matter it was very difficult for the law to determine and implement. The most eloquent and persuasive testimony to the way lawyers, judges, and priests tried to follow the Alexandrine decretals comes in the cases in which marriage was, for one reason or another, contested, and the law found itself trying to determine whether there had been previous consent.

These cases, naturally enough, generally derive from instances of secret or private marriages. Such marriages were, we should remember, discouraged and illegal but still binding. From the marriage litigation that survives it looks as though such private marriages were widespread, but it is difficult to know.[98] It could be that less problematic private marriages left no record, or were later celebrated publicly. It could also be that public church celebrations were the norm and did not lend themselves to the kinds of disputes that appear in the records. Records about English marriages in the middle ages have been most extensively investigated by Michael Sheehan (looking at evidence from the consistory court register at Ely from 1374 to 1382), Richard Helmholz (using evidence from a wide range of sources including act books, cause papers, formularies, and bishops' registers primarily from York, Canterbury, Ely, Lichfield, and Rochester from the second half of the thirteenth century through the fifteenth century), and Charles Donahue (adding evidence from surviving York marriage cause papers from 1300 to 1350). Helmholz's study includes an appendix of transcribed cases. Shannon McSheffrey has translated and edited a selection of otherwise unpublished depositions from the London consistory court from 1467 to 1476 and from the London commissary court from 1489 to 1497. Because my concern is with the way consent was understood in marriage cases rather than with making any new claims about marriage patterns or court proceedings in England, my discussion of the cases relies for its evidence on this corpus of published work.

Those who have studied the records have found that the discovery (or "discovery") of impediments of consanguinity or affinity after a marriage has taken place, long imagined as the favored means for getting out of a marriage gone bad, belongs more to the imaginations of historians than to life in medieval England.[99] It seems that people tended to handle bad marriages by themselves simply by separating, and it was only when someone challenged the separation or it otherwise came to a court's attention that the matter was investigated.[100] The problem of impediments became an issue not so much in finding reasons to separate as when impediments were brought to the attention of the couple and of the priest when banns were read announcing the intention to marry. In other words, the problem with reading the banns was, in some sense, that it worked. Sheehan

has described the cases of a number of couples who apparently tried to cir-
cumvent this problem by traveling somewhere else to solemnize their
union before a church, hoping, it seems, that the objection to their marriage would be dropped or that the courts would be more likely to find in
their favor if presented with a fait accompli.[101] These couples received the
most serious punishment, often excommunication that was only absolved
once they admitted their sin and performed penance, because they were
viewed as trying to subvert a sacrament.

A far more common reason for a marriage to come before the courts
was purported disagreement over whether a marriage had in fact taken
place.[102] This disagreement might take the form of one party bringing suit
to have another recognize a union, as when Joan Braunche claimed that
she and John, son of Thomas Dellay, had exchanged verba de presenti before engaging in carnal relations, while John admitted the carnal relations
but denied the contract;[103] or when, as Maitland predicts, Tilla Taillor re-
membered that she and John Lovechild exchanged words of present consent, while John Lovechild recollected only words of future consent;[104] or
when William Holyngbourne satisfied Agnes Lynch that they had married
each other but was not himself so certain about it.[105] There were also cases
in which the disagreement was over not whether words of present consent
had been spoken but over how they had been spoken, as when a woman
claimed that she had spoken with her mouth but not her heart, or a man
explained that his words had been spoken in jest.[106] In all of these cases
(and many others like them), the parties seem well aware of the fact that
present consent alone created a marriage; their disagreements stem from
the question of whether that present consent had been expressed.

The disagreement over whether a marriage had been contracted could
also take the form of a third party asserting that a marriage between two
others was not or could not be valid because the third party had previously
married one of the parties to the marriage. Such was the case of Robert
Grene, who claimed that he had married Maude Knyff by words of present
consent despite Maude's denial of the bond and her later (witnessed) exchange of present consent with Thomas Torald;[107] the case of John Fisher,
who, when a priest read marriage banns between John Frost and Amy Bird,
stood up to announce that Amy Bird was in fact his wife;[108] the case of Joan
Gibbe, who opposed the banns between John Dany and Alice Lenton because John had, Joan claimed, already married her;[109] and of Agnes Du-
rant, who claimed that John Draper was her husband based on an
exchange of present consent, despite his belief that he had never entered
such a union and was in fact married to Alice Cakebred based on both his
exchange of present consent and subsequent sexual relations with Alice.[110] Agnes Pateshull claimed not only wrongdoing but devious and in-

tentional wrongdoing when she objected to the proclaimed marriage of
Hugh Candlesby and Alice, widow of James le Eyr, on the grounds that she
had already married Hugh, claiming also that Hugh had purposely had the
banns for the (second) marriage read when he knew the church would be
empty and then solemnized the (second) marriage immediately.[111] In a
twist on the situation of a second marriage vow after a first marriage, the
defendant, apparently believing he had never consented to a first marriage, sometimes tried not to marry again, but instead to enter religious
orders, as when William de Potton took orders, entering the hospital of St.
John, Cambridge, and receiving the subdeaconate, all after allegedly having exchanged present consent in front of witnesses with Agnes Knotte and
having carnal relations with her (the court declared that his religious orders were invalid and he had to return to Agnes), or when Alice Geffrey
claimed that John Myntemoor should not continue as priest and Austin
canon of Anglesey because he was her husband (her suit was successful).[112]
These cases sometimes seem to show a disagreement about whether consent had ever taken place for a first marriage, again with all parties understanding that consent itself was enough to have created an initial
marriage. Sometimes they seem rather to demonstrate a desire to escape
an unhappy marriage for a potentially happier one, and in this desire ex-
hibit at least one party's attempt to regulate marital life without recourse
to the court.

In a final common category, the confusion over whether a marriage was
valid might take the form not of an external challenge from a third party
but from a party to a marriage that otherwise seemed valid and intact. In
these cases one spouse of a seemingly legitimate marriage might decide
that his or her present marriage should not stand because of a prior marriage. This prior marriage might be one contracted before the recognized
union by the party bringing suit, or it might be one earlier contracted by
his or her spouse. In either case such a prior contract would render the
plaintiff's own recognized union false. Such was the case when Alice Bake-
whyt brought Hugh Mayheu, her recognized husband, to court with Isabel
Loot to claim that her own marriage to Hugh was invalid because Hugh
had married Isabel thirty years earlier;[113] and when William Kele claimed
that his marriage to his wife Helen was invalid because he had previously
contracted a marriage with Alice Burgoyne;[114] and when Margaret claimed
that her marriage to her husband John Malyn Sr. was invalid because not
one but both of them had contracted previous marriages.[115] The most as-
tounding case of this sort is perhaps the one that Richard Helmholz describes, in which Joan Ingoly claims a marriage to Robert Esyngwald
twenty-one years after the fact. Not only had they never lived together as
husband and wife, at the time of Joan's claim Robert had for nineteen years

been married to and living with Elena Wright, while Joan herself had been married to and living with John Midelton for twelve years.[116] These cases might have arisen from conscience, or they might have resulted from trying to use the ecclesiastical courts to end (present) unhappy marriages legally.

Whatever the form of the dispute, however, and these are only the most common, the question on which the cases hinged was whether the parties in question had given their present consent to a particular union (or their future consent and subsequently had sexual relations). The possibility of changing one's status by lying or manipulating the reading of banns, as specifically charged by Agnes Pateshull, was always present in a system that recognized the binding moment between two people as an exchange of consent and that needed no witnesses to be valid. This potential for manipulation has been much decried by those who study medieval marriage law.[117] The courts did show some awareness of this threat and took steps to ensure at least that an otherwise legitimate union could not be declared invalid at the word of one person. As was the case in other matters, two witnesses had to swear to the same event in order for the court to consider it valid evidence. Collusion was still always a possibility, however, and in at least a few cases a certainty. Agnes Brignall, for example, produced witnesses who swore they had seen John Smyth marry her in York on the Wednesday before Palm Sunday. John Smyth, however, denied the claim and produced witnesses who swore that he had spent almost the entire day eighteen miles away at Pontefract, before setting out for Doncaster where he spent the night.[118] There is no way both sets of witnesses could have been telling the truth. There are also cases of people who swore that they were bribed, thus demonstrating either attempted bribery or actual perjury, and other cases where there is clear evidence that two parties colluded in claiming that they had been married earlier in order to help one get out of an unhappy existing marriage.[119] In still other instances, it appears the court believed that witnesses were not telling the truth. In these cases the rulings follow the testimony as it was given but conclude by leaving the parties to their consciences.[120]

On the whole, however, canonists did not worry overly much about lying witnesses, and they most certainly did not worry as much about it as later scholars are wont to do. There may have been a number of reasons for this. First, evidentiary rules required two witnesses for any event to be taken into account in judgment.[121] This was seen as a sensible precaution. If more people were determined to perjure themselves, there was perhaps not much a judge could do. Second, there is evidence that while some people may have lied, others took vows of marriage very seriously. When Margery Paston privately married Richard Calle, the family's steward, to the distress and disapproval of her family, Margery's brother John suggested in a letter to their mother, Margaret, that the family pretend the marriage had never taken place: after all, there were no witnesses. Margaret Paston, entirely prepared to disown her daughter permanently, refusing even to see or speak to her again and ordering her turned away from the door when she came to call, was still outraged by her son's suggestion: "I suppose what ye meant, but I charge you upon my blessing that ye do not, nor cause no other to do, that should offend God and your conscience, for if ye do, or cause for to be done, God will take vengeance thereupon."[122] The reminder of God's vengeance was also enough to move William Gell, who had married Joan Serle in front of a few witnesses by verba de presenti. Afterward William heard "about certain evil and harmful conditions of the said Joan." Regretting that he had given his consent, he swore in court that there were no witnesses to the contract. The case was dismissed, leaving him free to marry anyone he chose. The case might have ended there had he not told his father about the marriage, the tales of Joan, his testimony, and the court's judgment. Rather than thinking him clever, his father reprimanded him, saying, "Son, may it never happen that you so rashly damn your soul. It will be less bad for you to put up with vexation and loathing in your life than after your death to be damnably tortured by the pains of Hell." William, apparently taking these words to heart, went back to the court and confessed his fraud.[123] In a society that took vows and sacraments seriously, a clergy that took them even more seriously seemed to trust the ecclesiastical courts to do what they could.

The final reason that the courts may not have been overly worried about whether parties perjured themselves has to do with the role of the courts in these cases. The court was not supposed to find the truth in general, it was merely supposed to determine whether a given claim could be supported.[124] The difference can be seen in the fact that defendants were allowed to provide contradictory defenses, if they liked. The burden of proof was on the plaintiff. So one man in York claimed that he could not have contracted the marriage in question because he was in a different place on the day claimed, and if he had not been he would only have spoken the words with a joking spirit.[125] Both defenses were allowed because the court was trying to mediate between two parties rather than determine the absolute truth of what happened on that given day. Their burden was not one of truth but of assessing competing claims.

A possibility the canonists took far more seriously than the one of false testimony was that the court might be forced into a ruling that went against natural law or sacramental bond. They were very concerned by the chance that the combination of evidentiary rules requiring two witnesses to an event, on one hand, and the legality of secret marriages, on the other, could lead judges to rule against valid marriages in favor of illegitimate ones. They posed the case of a man who contracted a first marriage with no witnesses, and then a second with witnesses. The standard way to handle a case of two marriages was straightforward: although it was wrong to contract two marriages, the first union was the valid one; the second union was invalid because being married was an insurmountable impediment to marrying another person. Even consummating the second union before the first did not alter this judgment, as we have seen.[126] In the case the canonists posed, however, this standard interpretation leading to the invalidity of the second marriage was complicated by the problem of witnesses. If, after the man correctly returned to his first wife, the second wife were to challenge him, the judge would necessarily rule that he was married to the second woman because no witnesses could be produced to swear to the first marriage. What should the man do? On the whole canonists answered that the man should live with the first wife, suffering earthly excommunication and knowing that he would be absolved in heaven. In a more practical vein, one fifteenth-century Scottish canonist suggested that the man take the first wife away to live in a town where they and the sentence of excommunication were unknown.[127]

When examining the ways that both canonists and courts dealt with these questions, we must remember that the issue before the courts was not whether the men and women of whom we read were telling the truth, but how to know if consent had taken place. The doctrine of marriage gave some answer to this problem by decreeing that words, indicating interior consent, had to be spoken. Although the courts did have to wonder at times whether witnesses were lying, very often the presence of consent was determined not by the veracity of the testimony but by an examination of precisely what words had been said.

In some respects the canonists were very clear about what needed to be said: both parties needed to consent to marriage in the present tense, or in the future tense and then have sexual relations. The consent to marriage, moreover, needed to be explicit rather than implied. So promising to make an honest woman of someone, or to do what was right, or to stand by a person, or even to act toward a woman as a husband would act toward his wife did not constitute a marriage, even if such claims were followed by sexual relations and even if they were designed to mislead.[128] They were not promises of marriage and thus could not be claimed as such. There were many cases, however, in which the words spoken or not spoken were far less clear-cut than this theory seemed to presume, and the canonists did not shirk the problems ambiguous words posed. Here, in terms of examining how the courts understood consent, I would like to focus on three kinds of cases: conditional marriages, vows that used the word *volo,* and mistakes of person.

Conditional marriages were permitted so long as the condition was allowable. So a woman might say "I will marry you if my father agrees" or a man might say "I will marry you if your father provides a dower of five marks."[129] Such a case was treated as a present statement that went into effect as soon as the condition was removed: if the father agreed, or the dower were provided, the couple were married and did not need to exchange further words. As with a future promise, however, the condition was considered to have been removed by sexual relations.[130] So the woman who said "I will marry you if my father agrees" and then had intercourse with the man in question and the man who said "I will marry you if your father provides a dower of five marks" and then had intercourse with the woman in question would find themselves married even with no words, or negative words, from the fathers. Impossible conditions ("I will marry you if you grow wings and fly") were simply disregarded, as were dishonest conditions ("I will marry you if you rob the innkeeper"), unless they went against the substance of marriage ("I will marry you if you avoid offspring"), in which case the marriage was declared invalid.[131] In normal conditional marriages the problem with determining consent lay in when and how the condition was declared. So when a woman entered into a marriage and then declared, over a month later, that her words were conditional on her friends' agreeing to the match, the court ruled that she was too late.[132] This makes sense if we remember that, unlike Roman law, Church law had declared that consent created a binding contract. Adding a condition a month later could not undo what had been done, and sounded very much like trying to get out of a union that was later regretted. On the other hand, when John Sharp and Joan Broke spoke words of present consent in a field in the presence of John's friends, Joan, as the men were walking away, called out to them, "Listen, if my master and friends are willing to agree, I will assent to that contract." The men replied that she was too late, but the court ruled that they were mistaken, she had registered the condition on time.[133] In this case the condition seemed to the judge close enough to the spoken words that the union was never made whole independent of Joan's condition (importantly, she refused to solemnize or consummate the marriage). In deciding these cases the courts show a marked tendency to take into account not so much what one speaker had meant, but rather what the other could reasonably be expected to know the first had meant. If a person was deceived by vague or even misleading wording (as in the example of "I will do what is right"), that was unfortunate, but did not make a marriage. On the other hand, no

one could reasonably be held responsible for knowing an unstated condition, and unstated conditions therefore could not be allowed as aspects of
consent.

   This trend toward examining what the listener could reasonably infer
when determining whether consent had been given becomes even
stronger when we consider the cases of mistakes of person. Error of person was a technical category: if John married Joan believing her to be Jane
the marriage did not stand.[134] The case for allowing this error was fairly
straightforward, if somehow precociously Shakespearean, if we admit the
possibility of arranged marriages between parties who did not know each
other and remember that names did not need to be spoken in order for
the marriage to be considered binding. The question arose, however, of
whether the contract was still binding if the "error" were not an honest mistake but a deliberate manipulation. In order to consider this case we need
not move ahead in time to Shakespeare's works (although they do provide
ample opportunity to contemplate this kind of ploy) but can turn instead
to a case the bishop of Brescia brought to the attention of Pope Innocent
III. The case, reported in the decretal *Tua nos duxit,* tells the story of a certain man who could not induce a certain woman to have carnal relations
with him unless he first promised her marriage.[135] The man therefore
promised, using the words "John promises you . . . ." The woman was satisfied by this promise and carnal intercourse ensued. Ordinarily this would
be a straightforward situation in which we would not need to question even
the tense of the promise because the sexual relations, which both admitted, would have made a future promise binding. The complication here,
however, was that, unbeknownst to the woman, the man's name was not
John. The man, therefore, later claimed that he had not contracted a marriage since he could not speak for John and did not speak for himself. The
case, furthermore, could not work itself out as a simple error of person. In
the first place, it was not that the woman had meant to marry a different
person named John and had mistakenly married the fellow who spoke on
John's behalf. Instead she meant to marry the person who spoke but did
not know that his name was not John (as the decretal put it, he spoke in
his own person but under an alien name).[136] So the error on her part
would have been not of person but of name. In the second place, and more
important, she did not want to get out of the marriage; she wanted to hold
the fellow she thought was John to the marriage. That, after all, had been
the point of her condition: she did not want carnal relations without subsequent marriage, and she stuck to that point. The bishop wanted to know
whether a marriage had been celebrated.

   Innocent III admitted the strong presumption for marriage but maintained that, given the facts as the bishop had related them, "neither the

substance of a marital contract, nor the form of contracting marriage" could be found.[137] He based this decision not on the fact that John had promised for someone else, which he could not do (as if he were to sell the Brooklyn Bridge), but on the fact that he had never consented for himself. Innocent's ruling, in other words, is concerned less with what the woman could know and more with the question of how an external forum such as an ecclesiastical court could determine the internal consent of another person. That the man in question had used an alias seemed a fair indication to Innocent that he never truly consented to the marriage.

Almost immediately, however, canonists were unanimous in their disagreement, and their arguments are instructive both because they held sway in future cases and because they show us how a papal ruling could be universally rejected without being directly challenged.[138] Innocent III, they claimed, had written in regard to the internal forum of the man's conscience. In his heart he had not married the woman. He had committed fornication and would ultimately be judged guilty of that sin. However, as with the woman who claimed that she had spoken her consent with her mouth but not her heart, in such a discrepancy between words and interior thought, the court had to enforce the words. The man who was not John might know himself not to have agreed to marriage, but his marriage was nevertheless enforceable. When Raymond of Peñafort collected the decretals into the *Liber extra*, he summarized *Tua nos duxit* by writing that when someone takes advantage of dubious words of contracting with the intent to deceive and then knows a woman carnally it will be judged a marriage in the judicial forum but not in the penitential forum. The man, in other words, is guilty of fornication but must be held married. This, according to Raymond, is the import of the decretal following both truth and common understanding.[139] Although the case thus posited a separation between what was said and what was intended (as though speaking with one's fingers crossed), the case was used to show the necessity of enforcing what the listener could be expected to infer. The speaker spoke in order to deceive; it was then required that having deceived successfully he had to live with the consequences of his action, just as the woman who added a condition with her heart could not be expected to have the condition hold.

If dubious words with intent to deceive could thus be enforced, we are still left with another group of dubious words where the intention is much less clear: those that accompanied the word *volo* in marriage agreements. *Volo* is a verb of wishing or willing, but in the case of marriage, contracted precisely by the wills of two people to enter into that bond, the difference can be significant. Spoken assent was considered the verbalization of assent of the will. Willing can be either for the present or the future. So if the question is posed "Will you marry me?" and the answer is "I will," an exchange of either present or future consent could have taken place. The problem in England was compounded by the procedure of the courts. When a marriage suit was brought, the relevant parties gave depositions (usually in English) to an examiner, who recorded the depositions in Latin. The judge then read the Latin record.[140] Because English tends to use the word "will" for the future tense, it is more than likely that a good number of future contracts appeared before the judges with the word "volo." Even without such translation difficulties, however, the canonists were quick to note the delicacy of declarations using the word. The solution about deciding whether the contract was present or future seems to have been to look to the verb that followed volo. If the word was *habere* (to have) or another verb indicating execution of a marriage the words were considered verba de presenti, since you could not have someone as a spouse whom you had not already married. If you wished to have someone, the logic went, you must have already wished to marry him or her. On the other hand, if the verb following volo was *accipere* (to take or accept) or another verb indicating initiation of the marriage, the phrase was considered verba de futuro since if you were willing or wishing to take someone as a spouse that initiation could not yet have taken place. William of Rennes's reasoning in this case was rather typical. He began by noting the imperative of trying to determine the intention of the contracting parties. Such intention took precedence over any grammar. When determining the parties' intentions proved impossible, he believed that a distinction had to be made: when volo was followed by an infinitive signifying action it denoted neither a present nor a future promise. William provided the example of *bibere*: saying "I wish to drink" constitutes neither a promise to drink in the future nor present drinking. When volo was instead followed by an infinitive that signified a relation (as would be the case with "volo habere") then it expressed a contemporaneous wish and thus created a marriage.[141] This led to the somewhat peculiar situation that two people who said "I will have you as my spouse" to each other were married while two people who said "I will take you as my spouse" to each other were not, but the courts seemed to follow the theoretical reasoning, even though, like William, most canonists went out of their way to say that if these rules contradicted local custom the judges should follow local custom instead since the object was, after all, to determine consent rather than to enforce rules. In this case Alexander's ruling that future consent followed by carnal relations created a marriage worked to mitigate the problem because the couple were married, whatever verb followed volo, if they had intercourse after the exchange of words. This provision no doubt kept many cases uncontestable on these grounds.[142]

The import of these distinctions lies in the lengths to which the canonists went to try to judge consent. Sometimes it seems that there could be no best way of knowing how to understand a speech. To take a relatively simple case, for example, what are we to make of the understanding between John Bedeman and Agnes Nicholas? William Prudmay, seemingly related to neither, "asked John Bedeman whether he could find in his heart to have Agnes, there present, as his wife," and after receiving an affirmative response "asked Agnes whether she could find it in her heart to have John as her husband."[143] John afterward believed that they were married, Agnes believed that they were not. Being capable of finding it in your heart to marry surely is not the same as marrying, we might think. Had a marriage then been promised—in other words, did Agnes and John effectively say that they would marry each other in the future? While the options before the court might here seem like a question of verba de futuro or no promise at all, Agnes's own father testified against her, believing that by affirming the ability to find it in her heart to marry she had in fact married John through verba de presenti.

Another problematic area was the case of the negative promise. In 1374, for example, Agnes Lynch claimed that William Holyngbourne was her husband, a claim William denied.[144] William did report that he told Agnes he wanted to have carnal relations with her, and that she replied that in that case he would have to marry her. He declared that he had told her, "If I will [*volo*] have any woman as a wife, I will [*volo*] have you." Whether the will expressed was present or future is here unimportant since William freely admitted that carnal relations followed this exchange. The question was whether William had promised to marry Agnes. The canonists divided over this kind of promise, which they treated the same way as the statement "I will not have any woman except you as wife." Some argued that these statements did indeed constitute a promise, just as "I will not have any food except bread" meant that the speaker would have bread. Some argued that they did not preclude the possibility of not marrying at all, just as "I will not journey anywhere except Paris" left open the possibility of staying home.[145] In this case the court decided that William was indeed married to Agnes. We do not know whether the proctors who argued the case before the judge made either of these arguments, but the judgment itself sidesteps the theoretical issue and notes simply that Agnes was justified in believing that William had married her. We see again, then, that the question the judge sought to answer was the one asked by commentators on *Tua nos duxit* of whether dubious words with the intention of deceiving had clearly deceived. We should also note, however, that in cases the judges must have considered less dubious, as in the cases where a promise had been implied but not made, or in cases of *volo accipere,* the judges did not hesitate in declaring against a marriage.[146]

Given the strong desire, evinced over and again by canonists, theolo-

gians, and judges, to make certain that words were interpreted correctly
and intentions were clear, we might wonder why the law did not simply impose a formula, telling couples that if they spoke the words "I take you as
my husband/wife," for example, they had married, and if they spoke different words they had not. In fact, people sometimes acted as though this
were indeed the case. Margery Paston, for example, was questioned by the
bishop of Norwich about exactly what words she had spoken to Richard
Calle to effect their secret marriage. The bishop clearly hoped to find that
she had not actually married him (according to the report of her mother,
Margaret Paston, this was the express purpose of the interrogation); a
future promise, for example, could be voided if she were to contract a
marriage through verba de presenti with a man of whom her family approved.[147] Margery, however, answered that if she for some reason had not
spoken the correct words the first time the bishop should tell her what they
were so that she could speak them immediately, clearly implying that her
intention had been firm and that if a problem existed it had to do with formula rather than intent or consent. Depositions from London also show
an eagerness to get the words right and a clear awareness of the importance attached to what particular words were spoken, sometimes with the
couple who wished to marry repeating after a third party who was seen to
understand what words needed to be said in order to make the marriage
valid.[148] The writing about marriage often provides examples of verba de
presenti and verba de futuro in explaining the two forms of speech. So Peter Lombard gives the example "accipio te in virum, et ego te in uxorem"
as present consent; Thomas of Chobham provides the example "accipio te
in meam" as words of present consent;[149] Johannes Andreae, too, gives the
example "accipio te in meam" and adds another, "volo te de cetero habere
in uxorem / virum," noting, as Peter Lombard did, that for couples who
are capable of speech signs alone are not enough;[150] Peter of Poitiers also
provides the popular example of "accipio te in meum";[151] and John Mirk
gives the somewhat fuller "Here I take the to my wedded wyf / And there-
to I plyghte þe my trowþe."[152] Raymond of Peñafort explains that marriage
can be contracted by the phrases "accipio te in meam" or "volo te de cetero
habere in uxorem/virum" or "whatever other words, or even signs, by
which consent is expressed."[153] Nowhere do any of these writers suggest
that the words are more than exemplary, and, as we have seen, the courts
bear them out in allowing a wide latitude of phrases.

The reason for not simply declaring that a couple had to speak the
words "accipio te in meum," for example, or any other particular words, is
important in understanding what consent meant in the context of marriage for the canonists. There was, as we have seen, unanimity in the idea
that consent created marriage. If there were an agreed upon formula, it

would be equivalent to declaring not that consent created a marriage but that particular words created it—the words would be akin to knowing the password that opened a door. In this area, however, canonists and theologians alike strove to maintain the idea that words did not create marriage; they were instead necessary as the outward manifestation of an inward agreement. It was the agreement itself, not the particular form it took, that created marriage. The bond of marriage came into being when two people agreed to marriage and communicated their agreement to each other. This had to be done through language if both could speak because of the even wider latitude for error and misunderstanding if signs alone were used, but even verbal language was not essential: in cases in which the parties were mute signs were acceptable. The point, in other words, was to be as clear as possible about the nature of interior consent. For those who could speak this meant using language. For those who used language, the language should be a manifestation of inward agreement. The job of the courts, in the cases of dispute, was to work backward from the language to determine whether the consent had been present, or whether one party to the union could have known whether consent was present for the other.

In many ways the real test of the commitment to consent, and to language only secondarily as a sign of the consent, was in cases of coercion, where parties argued not that the words they spoke did not imply consent but rather that the words were necessarily false. Here we return to a provision in *Veniens ad nos* mentioned earlier. Pope Alexander III, we will recall, declared that if G. were not married to the woman with whom he usually lived, he was married to the woman with whom he had exchanged words of present consent, *unless* he had been compelled to utter those words by enough force or fear to move a constant man.[154] The *vir constans,* who had made his initial appearance in Roman law, becomes a Zelig-like figure after this decretal, appearing in case after case of marriage law.[155] James Brundage jokes that the constant man "became almost as ubiquitous in canon law as his younger cousin, 'the reasonable man,' in the common law of torts," a witticism that points to their similar function as legal fictions.[156] The fact and ubiquity of the legal fiction is important here because it points again toward the preference for using circumstances to determine whether consent had really been given over using rules to determine whether words had been spoken. In fact, it points to the willingness of those considering these cases to ignore altogether the words they painstakingly analyzed when addressing other aspects of marriage law. So when a man knots a towel around a woman's neck and threatens to strangle her unless she marries him then and there;[157] when a man threatens to kill both a girl and her father unless she marries him;[158] when an angry father commands a reluctant man to marry his daughter at sword point;[159]

when a girl is beaten with staves to make her agree to marriage;[160] all these actions were considered sufficient to move a constant man and the resulting marriages were held not valid because the consent to the marriages was held as stemming from the strong actions of others rather than from agreement to the marriage itself. The language was deemed immaterial and discounted because of the circumstances that gave rise to it. When, on the other hand, a man is surprised in bed with a young woman and required through words alone to marry her;[161] when a father threatens to disinherit his daughter of a plot of land if she does not agree to the match he proposes;[162] when a woman is told she will be thrown by her ears into a pool of water if she does not agree to marriage, but is told this in the presence of others who might stop her from being so thrown or from drowning;[163] or when a woman says she agreed to marriage by force, but then lives peaceably with the man for over a year afterward, having sexual relations that both agree were not by force;[164] the resulting marriages were held valid and binding, not because it was believed that no force at all impelled them (for who was not subject to some sort of pressure in marriage?) but because the force involved was not sufficient to move the constant man intent on not marrying the person in question.

The constant man employed here is also significant because in these decisions the standard that the court chooses to hold and reiterate over and over again is fictional. The constant man thus differs considerably from the good man we met in discussions of the just price. The good man is a representative of the community who is knowledgeable about the goods in question and disinterested enough in the outcome of the dispute to provide an honest estimate of whether a given price is more than 50 percent higher or lower than the current market price of the goods. The good man is thus a man who can be found and queried: an actual man rather than an idea or a fiction. The current price is an actual standard; any given price can be measured against it in percentages. The good man is the real person who gives testimony about the standard at the time and place he is questioned. The constant man is a fiction. He exists only in a hypothetical sense, and even though we might give examples of constant men (Abraham, Thomas Aquinas asserts, was a constant man), the question is not whether Abraham would have promised marriage if beaten by staves.[165] The actions of the constant man are meant to set a standard, but they are never real and thus never measurable. Actual actions cannot conform to or oppose those of the constant man; instead actual actions are supposed or presumed to conform to those the constant man would perform if he did exist and were in the situation at hand. In these most vexing moments, then, when language is necessarily insufficient because it is language itself that is coerced, what the law turns to is not another measure of consent (hand gestures, or diaries, or words spoken to a friend), but fiction. The constant man thus in some ways shows the limits of a legal system built on resemblances between cases and precedents and measures. All can fail in the event of coercion, and the law, wishing to cover those cases, turns to storytelling.

The Creation of Consent in Chaucer's *Physician's Tale*

The law turns to fiction in cases when it cannot analyze words because they may have been produced by force or fear strong enough to move a constant man, but it does not, indeed cannot, consider either the internal will toward consent or what creates consent in other cases. Such issues are outside the purview of the law, and considering them would prevent the business of the law from being done. It is enough, in most cases, to determine that consent has taken place. The question of how consent that does not appear the result of fear or force comes to be, however, is a question that Geoffrey Chaucer pondered a number of times in his fiction, most spectacularly in the case of Virginia in the *Physician's Tale*. Chaucer changed the story he found in the tale's sources in order to emphasize how consent is created. In the *Physician's Tale* Chaucer deliberately questions Virginia's conclusion that she must die in order to consider how such a decision is reached.

In a remarkable moment of the *Physician's Tale* Virginia consents to her own death, asking her father, Virginius, to kill her: "Yif me my deeth, er that I have a shame," she implores him (6.249).[166] This moment, like all those when Virginia speaks, appears neither in Chaucer's stated source, Livy's history, which Chaucer may or may not have known, nor in his unstated source, Jean de Meun's *Roman de la rose*, which Chaucer most certainly did know.[167] This particular addition arises from Virginius's response to the evil judge Apius's demand that Virginia be handed into his custody. Virginius is, as he understands the situation, faced with a terrible choice: to hand his daughter over to Apius "in lecherie to lyven" (6.206), or to kill her, ending her life before Apius can take her virginity. What is remarkable about this moment in the *Physician's Tale* is not so much that Virginius decides it is better for his daughter to be dead than dishonored (taking her head to save her maidenhead, as some have explained the pun), but that Virginia herself agrees with this decision.[168] Virginia's consent to her own death, which Chaucer adds to the story, is only one improbable moment in a tale generally considered flawed, but it is a crucial moment. The primary question that drives this tale, I believe, is what might lead a young woman to decide that death is preferable to loss of virginity and to agree to her own death.

While some Chaucerians have simply condemned the *Physician's Tale* (it

is, one succinctly stated, "the faultiest" of the *Canterbury Tales*), many more
have analyzed the problems with the tale, providing a variety of diag-
noses.[169] Noting that the story as told in Livy's history and the *Roman de la
rose* is explicitly political, Sheila Delany has argued that in the *Physician's
Tale* Chaucer introduces political ideas but is subsequently unwilling or unable to treat them as the plot develops.[170] Angus Fletcher also sees the tale
as moving away from the question of explicitly political authority but contends that it takes up questions of writerly and historical authority.[171] Linda
Lomperis believes that the authority in question is authority over bodies
and reads in the tale a split between the physical body and metaphysical
questions of virginity and mortality.[172] Derek Pearsall, Jill Mann, and Lee
Patterson focus on the issue of genre, seeing the tale as a saint's life that
has been grafted onto a political story.[173] Anne Middleton argues that the
genre in question is the exemplum and maintains that the tale is a demonstration of the exemplum's inability to consider moral ambiguity.[174] These
disparate readings, some dismissing the *Physician's Tale*, others lauding it,
and still others taking a more neutral stance toward its aesthetic success or
failure, all point to a fundamental sense of disunity that readers experience
in the tale, whether between the politics claimed and those written, between mind and body, between genres, or between our expectations of a
genre and its limits. From different perspectives and for different reasons
all contend with what seems an incommensurability of parts—the long encomium to Virginia's virtue, the long, apparent digression on governesses
and parents, the sudden moment when Virginius beheads his daughter, his
even more sudden and seemingly unmotivated advocacy that Claudius be
pardoned, and the hasty ending that treats none of the issues in the story
itself—and their failure to fit properly together. The disproportion or disunity of the tale that these readings note is not, furthermore, a function of
its basic plot, as we can readily see from the far more harmonious versions
of the story told by Livy, Jean de Meun, John Gower, and Giovanni Boccaccio.[175] The disunity, whether intentional, salutary, or a terrible mistake,
arises from the way Chaucer tells the story, and most particularly from the
additions he makes to it. I believe that Chaucer's additions and changes to
his source material, which create the disunity or disproportion of the tale,
are consistent. All work to turn the tale away from the theme of justice (the
explicit point of the story in the *Roman de la rose*) and toward the idea of
what it is that shapes a person and how she comes to understand and experience the world, even to the point of agreeing that she should die. The
changes move toward exploring what we would today call "ideology,"
whether we use the standard modern definition of a person's imaginary
relationship to her actual conditions of existence, or whether we use
Chaucer's question of why a person might consent to her own death. Al-

though I argue that the tale is, in this sense, broadly political, I arrive at this conclusion through a method that is formal. My argument is not about politics per se but about the ways that all of Chaucer's changes and additions work to set up a framework for calling our attention to how Virginia reaches her decision when she agrees that she should die and why she might make that decision. I therefore examine in turn the changes Chaucer makes to the story before explaining what I take to be their import, because I believe that they achieve this import only when read together.

The changes Chaucer makes can be divided into three main parts: first, the long discursus by and about Nature on the formation of Virginia's particular beauty and virtue; second, the abstract discussion of the responsibility governesses and parents bear for the children in their charge; and third, the scene where after hearing Apius's judgment Virginius comes home to tell Virginia of what transpired and Virginia agrees to her own death. The first two parts of this scheme are completely original with Chaucer; in the third part he moves the action from the public sphere of the open court to the private sphere of Virginius's house, where he has Virginius not only perform the act of beheading but also discuss the action with Virginia beforehand—it is here that Chaucer adds Virginia's voice to the story. Chaucer's modifications, however, start even before this scheme, with the way the tale begins.

In the *Roman de la rose,* the story, after a nod to Livy, begins with Apius.[176] Such a starting point makes sense because Jean de Meun uses it to illustrate the evils of justice gone wrong. Chaucer, after a nod to Livy, begins instead with Virginius, by calling him a knight, which establishes his role in society, and then showing that Virginius has all that a secular knight needs to be good: he is "fulfild of honour" (6.3), a virtue that is both personal and public, "and of worthynesse" (6.3), the catch-all virtue, used also for the knight in the *General Prologue,* which shows not a particular quality but instead that he deserves whatever he has as well as his rank. This general worthiness presumably encompasses the many friends of whom we next learn, magnifying our sense of his public virtue, and "greet richesse" (6.4), a detail that not only confirms his station but also, as the story progresses, shows us that his problems do not stem from an inability to pay an appropriate sort of a bribe and that, unlike Apius, Virginius either would not or could not use his influence through friends and wealth to change the situation in which he will find himself. Virginius's good character and status, rather than the character of the judge, thus frames the story.

Although the discussion then moves to Virginius's daughter, it moves to her not in herself, through a discussion of her general qualities (the way we met Virginius), but through a discussion of her relationship to nature.

Nature has, of course, a constitutive hand in forming every person. Here the narrator's interest lies in showing that Nature could do no more for any person than she did for Virginia:

> For Nature hath with sovereyn diligence
> Yformed hire in so greet excellence,
> As though she wolde seyn, "Lo! I, Nature,
> Thus kan I forme and peynte a creature
> Whan that me list; . . . (6.9–13)

Throughout her hypothetical speech and the contemplation of Virginia's beauty that follows Nature's imagined direct discourse, the emphasis is on Nature's agency: Nature forms and paints, we are told five times in eleven lines; Nature shapes all creatures and decides "what colour that they han or what figures" (6.28); Nature did her best with Virginia. The speech, given by Nature, emphasizes her own self primarily. She presents Virginia as a showpiece of her own craft. The encomium thus implies a causal link between nature and character.

The next paragraph about Virginia begins again with Nature's agency before moving into a discussion of Virginia's manner and virtue. The shape of the paragraph implies the possible guiding hand Nature has in her virtue, even while Virginia's manner and character are presented as possibly her own. The narrator begins the enumeration of Virginia's virtues by giving her his all-encompassing approval ("In hire lekked no condicioun / That is to preyse" [6.41–42]) to let us know that if we happen to think of an unmentioned virtue the omission should be attributed to narratorial negligence rather than a hidden fault. With that disclaimer comes a list, which ends by noting that she finds polite ways to excuse herself from inappropriate situations, neither offending others nor compromising herself.[177] This characteristic stands out as particularly important because it is the one place in the catalog where Virginia clearly determines her own actions, where the agency is entirely her own:

> And of hir owene vertu, unconstreyned,
> She hath ful ofte tyme syk hire feyned,
> For that she wolde fleen the compaignye
> Where likely was to treten of folye. (6.61–64)

By the time we have come to this point we have learned that every beauty and virtue that could be given to Virginia upon her creation has been given to her, and we see here that in instances where she, by her own agency, can avoid situations that might become "ful perilous," as the narrator, a few lines later, calls these gatherings, she removes herself (6.69). We are thus presented with two, potentially complementary, explanations for virtue and virtuous behavior, one emphasizing the role of nature, the second a person's own decisions.

Rather than using these explanations alone as background to the plot, the narrative moves to an abstract account of the importance of governesses. The passage has been read as a comment on Katherine Swynford, Chaucer's sister-in-law, who was governess of John of Gaunt's daughters, his mistress, and finally his wife, and her possible role in the elopement of one of her charges.[178] While contemporaries may have seen the discussion as politically pointed, it also works to provide another account for the creation of virtuous behavior. The narrator addresses governesses directly:

> And ye maistresses, in youre olde lyf,
> That lordes doghtres han in governaunce
>
> . . . .
>
> Thenketh that ye been set in governynges
> Of lordes doghtres oonly for two thynges:
> Outher for ye han kept youre honestee,
> Or elles ye han falle in freletee
> And knowen wel ynogh the olde daunce,
> And han forsaken fully swich meschaunce
> For evermo; . . . (6.72–81)

The narrator begins by using the word "governance," which for Chaucer had primarily political connotations as well as the more general meaning of having a controlling or determining influence over events or people.[179] After planting the seeds of this potential analogy between governesses and rulership, the address moves away to assert two reasons that women might be entrusted with this job: they have either maintained their virtue or, having fallen, have a superior understanding of how to guard against similar falls in others. A person's effectiveness as a governess, therefore, is entirely covered by matters of virtue. We have already seen, of course, that lack of virtue was not Virginia's problem, so whatever befalls her clearly cannot be blamed on her governess, but the narrator takes the opportunity of discussing the already exonerated governess to make clear the stakes in having "governance" over a young woman:

> Looke wel that ye unto no vice assente,
> Lest ye be dampned for youre wikke entente;
> For whoso dooth, a traitour is, certyn
> And taketh kep of that that I shal seyn:

> Of alle tresons sovereyn pestilence
> Is whan a wight bitrayseth innocence. (6.87–92)

The language here turns explicitly political. Although the governess governs, innocence is placed in the role of the sovereign or principle that could be betrayed. Such a betrayal turns one into a traitor, and not just any traitor but the worst possible sort. The passage makes less clear the relationship between "assent" and "wicked intent." If you assent to vice you will be damned for your wicked intent, but whether you are held responsible if your intent was not wicked is left ambiguous. The passage establishes that treason, however, arises from the betrayal of innocence whatever the intent behind that betrayal.

Speaking of those who have governance over innocence, the narrator does not stop at governesses but turns next to parents, who also fill that role:

> Ye fadres and ye moodres eek also,
> Though ye han children, be it oon or mo,
> Youre is the charge of al hir surveiaunce,
> Whil that they been under youre governaunce. (6.93–96)

If governesses have charge only of matters of virtue, parents' responsibilities are not so limited: their purview extends to all aspects of protecting their children. The term "governance" links what the narrator will say about parents to what has been said about governesses, making clear that the subject is not parents versus governesses so much as the role each has in governing children. The narrator goes on to warn parents where they might go wrong: "Beth war, if by ensample of youre lyvynge, / Or by youre necligence in chastisynge / That they ne perisse; . . ." (6.97–99). We thus see that parents teach not only by instruction but also by example and by omission. Unlike governesses, parents cannot rest content with guarding virtue, but must live exemplary lives and chastise children if they go wrong. To omit either of these elements in parenting sets up parents, too, as potential "traitors" to innocence.

Not content with this analogy, the narrator turns to another before moving back to the particular story of Virginia:

> Under a shepherde softe and necligent
> The wolf hath many a sheep and lamb torent.
> Suffiseth oon ensample now as heere,
> For I moot turne agayn to my matere. (6.101–04)

Here the parents are rather conventionally depicted as the shepherds of innocence whose negligence can lead to the destruction of the lambs whatever the "intent" behind the negligence (and here that negligence seems almost entirely removed from the "evil intent" attributed earlier to the betrayal of innocence). The analogy turns briefly from the political to the pastoral in order to emphasize that any harm that may come to children is the responsibility of the parents who should guard them. To say that one example here and now is enough implies that another may follow later, elsewhere, as indeed it does in the story of Virginia. At the same time, we can read the last couplet as an indication that one example, the story of Virginia, must suffice to illustrate the proverbial wisdom about sheep, shepherds, and wolves, because the narrator must now move on to that story.

Many have noted the seeming incongruity of these passages. Brian Lee defends this incongruity against its critics, although he calls the passages a digression, by noting that as "the subject of the tale is the guardianship of a young girl, . . . the digression, though long, is not inappropriate."[180] This defense, logical as it is, does not answer Anne Middleton's charge that the emphasis on governesses and parents in these passages is "theoretically inappropriate. Their stress on the passive malleability of youth contrasts strangely with the moral self-sufficiency we have already heard praised in Virginia; and the peculiar absence of any mention of love as the root of parental discipline runs counter to the whole burden of Nature's speech."[181] While Middleton sees these contradictions as appropriate because they point out the limits of the exemplum form, I would argue that they are important because they demonstrate that what is at work is not a linear argument, in which the elements proceed from conclusions established along the way, but an inclusive list that presents all possible answers regardless of their relationship to one another. Any of these elements could account for behavior; all are possible explanations of virtuous action. In writing about the causes of behavior, Chaucer posits a number of plausible answers. The long introduction to the matter of the tale provides four different accounts of the causes behind virtuous behavior: it may be given by nature; it may arise from an individual's own agency; it may be a result of the "governance" applied by governesses; or it may come from the rule and tending of parents. Virginia is placed very specifically within this theoretical framework: Nature has done everything possible to "forme and peynten" her well (6.21); she exercises her own agency wisely; and she has no governess. Only the influence of parents is left, then, as a locus for behavior that might seem, to us, wrong or ill-considered. As the narrator moves, finally, from this long introduction to the story of Virginia, then, he has brought us back full circle to Virginius, the very place he began.

From here the plot of the story follows the *Roman de la rose* through Apius's refusal to hear Virginius's case for his own paternity, along the way calling Apius's plan "how that his lecherie / Parfourned sholde been" (6.150–51) a "conspiracie" (6.149), employing again the political diction we find throughout the warnings to adults. Where in the *Roman de la rose* Virginius acts immediately in the open court,[182] in the *Physician's Tale* he goes home to sit in his hall,

> And leet anon his deere doghter calle
> And with a face deed as asshen colde
> Upon hir humble face he gan biholde
> With fadres pitee stikynge thurgh his herte
> Al wolde he from his purpos nat converte. (6.208–12)

Although his obstinacy clearly cannot be condoned, it must be contrasted with Apius's lecherous "conspiracie," even if both end in the "betrayal" of Virginia. His face, dead as cold ashes, is a detail akin to a blush in Chaucer—a sign of genuine emotion that cannot be feigned. Furthermore, the narrator presents us with the information about Virginius's interior state and explicitly tells us that he feels struck through the heart— a feeling that either does or does not exist and is not subject to manipulation.[183] By identifying this emotion as "fadres pitee," furthermore, Chaucer explicitly links Virginius's feelings to his role as a parent, the role in which he is supposed to provide guidance for his daughter.

Virginius's love and emotion cannot be in question, then, when he addresses his daughter:

> "Doghter," quod he, "Virginia by thy name,
> Ther been two weyes, outher deeth or shame,
> That thou most suffre; allas, that I was bore!" (6.213–15)

In Jean de Meun's telling of the story, Virginius, seeing that he had no choice but to submit to Apius, exchanged "shame for injury" and beheaded Virginia, neither voicing his reasoning nor consulting her or anyone else.[184] In Chaucer's story, however, Virginius clearly presents his daughter with an either/or decision: either death or shame.[185] These alternatives are problematic because there would presumably be many other ways to deal with the situation: Virginia could run away; she could go into hiding; Virginius could stall for time while he called together all their friends who were pointedly mentioned when we were introduced to Virginius; and on and on. The idea of course is not that Virginia and her father should have followed these options, leading to a happier ending, but that the choice with which Virginius presents his daughter is blatantly false. Its falseness is highlighted not only by the way Virginius was presented at the beginning of the tale, but also by Virginia herself. Virginia has good reason to question an alternative so severe, which she does: "Goode fader, shal I deye? / Is ther no grace, is ther no remedye?" (6. 235–36). She first asks, in other words, for a solution that invokes religious justice and privilege: Is there no grace? Her second question—Is there no remedy?—could be a reiteration of the first, but it also queries whether a more practical solution might be sought—Could not something else be done?—pointing us to the obvious conclusion that indeed many other things could be done.

Virginius's answer, however, is definitive: "No certes, deere doghter myn" (6.237). Virginia asks whether she may complain, swoons twice, rises,

> . . . and to her fader sayde
> "Blissed be God that I shal dye a mayde!
> Yif me my deeth, er that I have a shame;
> Dooth with youre child youre wyl, a Goddes name!" (6.247–50)[186]

In asking for her death Virginia accepts both the dichotomy Virginius proposes (death or shame) and his governance over her (he should do his will with his child).[187] It turns out, audiences of the story other than the Host tend to agree, that this is bad governance, perhaps mirroring Apius's own, though without the "wicked intent"; but Virginius's plea for Claudius's clemency at the end, which Chaucer includes even as he rushes through the story, shows us that Virginius himself cannot be considered "unworthy" even if he does misuse his sovereign powers over his daughter. Furthermore, in placing Virginia's acceptance of her father's interpretation alongside her acceptance of his right to govern her, Chaucer makes clear that the responsibility does not lie entirely with Virginius: Virginia embraces her father's logic as well as his power and, voicing both, consents to her own death.

In the *Physician's Tale*, then, Chaucer tells of a young woman who actively agrees that she must die because she accepts both her father's understanding of her situation and his right to govern her. Chaucer changes the story of Apius and Virginius to make it work through the shaping influences on character and action that might lead to Virginia's decision. There is Nature, which can "forme and peynte" but not teach; there are virtue and good behavior, which Virginia possesses; there is the possible influence of a governess, which does not in this case affect her; and there are parents, who must teach by example and by chastising when appropriate. The *Physician's Tale* shows us the very bad example Virginius's conclusion about his daughter sets for her and its shocking result. Chaucer's original "beginning" for the story, which takes up over a third of its whole, works to set up an experiment with one carefully controlled variable—parental teaching—and the tale shows us how this one variable can overcome all else by creating Virginia's consent to her own death. Given these variables, she recognizes her father's governance and asks to die.

Critics have tended to deemphasize the weight of Virginia's voice. Anne Middleton, expressing a sophisticated form of a common critical stance, writes that since Virginius has already decided that Virginia must die, offering her a chance to speak primarily emphasizes her role as an object. Virginius here, she argues, tries to take the place of Nature.[188] This argument, however, depends on the idea that Nature was "right" and the passage about parents was "wrong." It also minimizes the importance of Virginia's agency—an aspect of her character that Chaucer emphasizes when he explains how she found ways to remove herself gracefully from potentially inappropriate situations. I cannot see any reason for Chaucer to add words that he did not mean, whether in praise of Virginia or in her voice. That Virginius had made up his mind could not have prevented Virginia from disagreeing with him, even if this would not have changed the outcome. These facts, as well as a reading that sees the introductory material as cumulative rather than right and wrong, lead me to take seriously Virginia's words. This moment also, I believe, makes problematic Angus Fletcher's argument that "Virginia's virtuous behavior places her outside of traditional power structures," even as Virginius, by recognizing Apius's governance, "relegitimates the very hierarchies that Virginia's portrait has dispelled."[189] Virginia herself recognizes her father's governance. Although Apius knows that her virtue would make her unwilling to submit to his advances, these advances would not normally be part of his judicial power. By conceiving his plot with Claudius he turns them into a form of judicial authority, and he clearly does expect her to submit to this (now judicial) authority or there would be no point to his plan.

In showing us the way consent can be created, Chaucer does not entirely erase the political themes of his source material, even if he does transpose them. The crucial scene of the story moves, as I have noted, from the public sphere to the private, but rather than understanding this shift as a way of omitting politics from his story, I believe we must see it as a way of positing a broader idea of what constitutes politics than we find in his sources. Chaucer uses explicitly political language in his discussion of governesses and parents and their control over their charges and in describing Apius's plan. This diction is not simply residual. Apius is called a traitor by Jean de Meun; Chaucer, in the material he adds, moves the idea of treachery from the realm of judges to that of governesses and parents.[190] Such political language works in two ways. In the first instance, it poses Innocence, an abstract quality that resides in young people, as sovereign, in order to compare any negligence to treason. The rest of the story points to the idea that leading a young woman to agree to her own death might indeed be considered negligent. This analogy broadens the political sphere, which in turn allows Chaucer to venture upon an analysis of the ways treason and betrayal work. Treason and betrayal are, as we have seen, the words Chaucer uses in connection with his discussion of governance. In this tale, betrayal and treason do not work by giving away secrets or plotting to kill the sovereign. Instead, they work through miseducation and negligence that might lead the sovereign (in this case personified Innocence in the figure of Virginia) into believing that her own destruction is her best option.

At the same time, this political language encourages us to see Virginia as exemplifying not only virginity but also the political subject. Virginia is under the control of her father, who believes he has her best interests in mind even if we believe he does not, and of Apius, who definitely does not mind her interests at all. She agrees with her father and believes she makes the right decision because of the way he presents choices to her ("outher death or shame"). Chaucer thus has good reason to use a young woman, not a man, as the most fitting way to represent people as a whole, and particularly as the most fitting way to represent men. Men, in the political realm, are on the whole not powerful agents, but subject to others, some of whom care about them and many of whom think only of their own needs. The young woman, whom all recognize as having little power over the fate of her own body, is in this case the proper allegorical embodiment of men, who, Chaucer seems to say, do not have as much power as they think they do, especially when they agree with those who hold real power over them.[191] The question for them, as for Virginia, is one of what creates their agreement.

The point, then, in calling the *Physician's Tale* an exploration of ideology is to emphasize that when Chaucer told a political story he did not tell it as a story about the outward administration of judgment and justice, as his sources did. In the *Physician's Tale* politics and governance instead become the process of getting people to agree with you, the process of creating consent. Virginius does this through the choices he presents to his daughter. Governance as it most affects us every day, the *Physician's Tale* demonstrates, is not so much a question of good judges and bad judges (although good judges and bad judges are a part of it) as it is a question of who controls the ways we learn to think and what power we have over the people and systems who have this control. If Virginia continued to refuse her father and Virginius cut off his daughter's head despite her protests, this tale would be an easy story of tyranny. Virginia, however, not only did not refuse the person who had the most direct claim to control her actions, she actively agreed with him and his assessment of her own best interest. The story thus presents two kinds of bad governors: in Apius we see the crudely bad, who ultimately has to flee; in Virginius we see the unknowingly bad, who first persuades his daughter that she should die and then persuades the crowd that they should not kill the "conspirators." The success of Virginius's governance lies not in his ability to make judgments but in his ability to describe reality in such a way that others, most particularly his own daughter, come to agree with him. In the *Physician's Tale* such agreement is created so comprehensively that Virginia not only agrees that her father should kill her, she also reaches the same conclusion as her father that they have no other choice. The tale poses the question of what might make a young woman agree to her own death, and then answers it by stressing the way those who have control over her educate her and teach her to understand reality. In doing so, it depicts the processes that create consent.

Thomas Aquinas on Marriage Formation

Thomas Aquinas considers consent in the formation of marriage in his commentary on Peter Lombard's *Sentences*. He does not, indeed in a commentary form perhaps cannot, ask Chaucer's question of how consent is created, because the form demanded that he address points in Peter Lombard's text rather than raising new questions of his own. Neither is he content, however, with canon law's decision that spoken consent must be understood to signify interior will. In his commentary, Aquinas tries to consider spoken consent not from the point of view of an enforceable contract or the other party, as canon law does, but from a vantage point that emphasizes the sacramental bond at stake in the question. In his writing we see the difference between the way consent is construed from a legal and from a theological perspective. This difference in turn shows us another fissure in the understanding of consent, belying again the assumption in justifications of trade that consent is easily known and universally recognizable.

The disciplines of canon law and theology were closely related: canonists needed to understand and explain laws of God and Church that could be followed; theologians needed to interpret God's laws for individuals in ways that offered them the best hope of salvation. They were not, however, by any means identical. In his writing on the formation of marriage, Aquinas finds the imperatives of law and theology incompatible precisely because of the way each construes consent. For canon law, words signify consent. When they cannot, in cases of excessive force or fear, judges turn to fiction. For Aquinas, however, neither words alone nor fiction are adequate responses, since what needs to be sought is sacramental truth. In this section I turn to Aquinas's writing on the formation of marriage, not because it is typical of the general written view among theologians in the thirteenth century, but because by looking at it I believe we can see a disjunction between the ways that law and theology thought about consent. In Aquinas's hands the division between the disciplines makes it impossible to accept either the analysis of law or the analysis of literature that we have seen. In accepting neither analysis Aquinas casts important light on the forms that contestation of the idea of consent could take.

Thomas Aquinas's writing on the formation of marriage appears in his *Scripta super libros sententiarum,* widely considered his first mature work.[192] As we have seen, the *Sentences* had been recommended by the Fourth Lateran Council in 1215, were used as a teaching text by the Franciscan Alexander of Hales around 1223–27, and had quickly become a required university text in the study of theology.[193] Their centrality to theological learning is made clear in a text of the Dominican constitutions of 1234, which stipulates that provinces ought to provide those friars marked out for theological study with three basic books: the Bible, the *Sentences,* and Peter Mangiador's *Historia scolastica.*[194] Commenting on the *Sentences* was, by the time Aquinas was a student in the middle of the thirteenth century, a necessary part of becoming a master in the faculty of theology. In 1252–53 Aquinas was sent from Cologne, where he had been studying with Albert the Great, to Paris in order to teach the *Sentences* under the guidance of Master Elias Brunet de Bergerac, who had succeeded Albert when Albert left Paris for Cologne in 1248. Commenting on the *Sentences* was thus a stage in Aquinas's training, required by university rules as an integral step in the progression to master of the *Sentences* and admittance to the theological faculty in Paris.[195] Aquinas set upon his task by following his own later dictum "always distinguish." The result is a series of distinctions within the framework laid out by Peter and by the Alexandrine and Innocentian decretals that does not sit comfortably with any of them.[196]

Aquinas agrees with Peter Lombard's statement that consent is the efficient cause of marriage, but Aquinas, unlike Peter, divides marriage into two parts, spiritual and material. These two parts do not constitute a single act, according to Aquinas. Instead, matrimony is two acts simultaneously, "a kind of spiritual joining together, in so far as matrimony is a sacrament, and a certain material joining together, in so far as it is directed to an office of nature and of civil life."[197] Recognizing the dual nature of matrimony, however, is not alone sufficient, because matrimony is not simply two separate acts conducted simultaneously. Rather the material joining creates the spiritual joining, not on its own but by divine power: "the spiritual joining is effected by divine virtue by means of the material joining."[198] In this sense the material joining (the one that we can control) effects the spiritual joining. Because the spiritual joining is the certain result of the material joining, the material joining becomes the outward, worldly sign of the spiritual joining.

Aquinas here posits two separate unions rather than a single union with dual signification. Because he posits this double bond, he explains that the double consent of the parties to marriage does not form the marriage, even though he follows Peter in quoting the idea that "it is not coition but consent that makes a marriage."[199] Matrimony, Aquinas explains, is a union of persons directed to one purpose. Consent effects this union. The union cannot be explained as the consent itself but instead as the consequence of the consent. Consent thus creates a double joining. Neither of the bonds resides in the consent, although both are the effect of it. By this account marriage becomes a sort of chain reaction, initiated by consent, which effects the material union, which in turn effects the spiritual union. All stages of this chain remain, for Aquinas, distinct from each other. In order to keep this distinction intact throughout the various levels of marriage he explains that "consent signifies not the union of Christ with the Church, but His will whereby His union with the Church was brought about."[200] Since consent is not the material union itself, it cannot signify a union. Consent instead constitutes the will to have the union, which in turn brings it about; similarly, it signifies Christ's will rather than the union that resulted from that will.

Although consent brings about the actual union and people can generally agree to something without voicing that agreement, marital consent does require words, according to Aquinas, in order for the various joinings that result from it to take place. He reasons here not with the canonists that others (and most importantly the prospective spouse) must be able to know of the consent. Instead he reasons doubly, as befits his idea of the double result of marriage, by virtue first of the sacramentality of marriage and then of its status as a worldly contract.[201] On one hand, every sacrament requires a "sensible sign," and this sign, in matrimony, is the consent made perceptible to the senses through language.[202] Without this sign we would have no way of knowing that the sacrament had taken place. At the same time that marriage is a sacrament, though, it is also a material joining, or a contract. Since material contracts require words of mutual binding, so too matrimony, as a worldly office, requires these words. The words, then, fill two functions, each separate from the other, but each relating to one part of the two unions that result from marriage. Aquinas does not explain why, if the sacrament of marriage is a result of the material joining of marriage, a separate sign might be necessary. Nor does he explain why these signs need to be verbal (why the old Roman law practices of a cere-mony or a ductio or an exchange of gifts, for example, would not suffice).

The division between the two aspects of matrimony should be reiterated when Aquinas next, following Peter, turns to the question of whether words of present consent make a marriage in the absence of inward con-sent. We have already seen that *Tua nos duxit* and the commentary tradi-tion around it had established a division between the internal forum of the conscience and the external forum of the Church in the case of a person who consents outwardly without meaning it ("John takes you for a wife" solemnly sworn by the man whose name was not John). As we have seen, Innocent III had explained that the man was not married; the canonists insisted that this was true only in the forum of his conscience, where he was also guilty of fornication and deceit, but that he must be treated as mar-ried in the external forum. We might expect that when Aquinas reached this question he would take up the distinction between internal and ex-ternal forums because he uses it elsewhere; because it mirrors his insis-tence on distinguishing between material joining and spiritual joining; and because there is a tradition of making this distinction. But he does not. Instead he writes that "expression of words without inward consent makes no marriage."[203] He does not qualify this judgment, but he does explain it. The explanation he provides follows the sacramental nature of mar-riage. All sacraments, he notes, require correct intention in order to take place. Just as the person who undergoes baptism as a joke or to deceive does not receive the sacrament of baptism, so the person who states his consent without meaning it does not enter into a marital union. Baptism, however, does not work as an appropriate analogy because it has a mater-ial sign but is not also a material contract. But here Aquinas carries through with the insistence that the expression of present consent without inward consent effects no marriage at all, neither spiritual nor material. To the possibility that the liar thus benefits from his lie by using words of consent in order to gain sexual favors, Aquinas responds that the liar does not ben-efit since the Church will judge him married even if he is not and since he has lied, for which he is punished in the tribunal of his conscience. In such a case, though, where Church courts do declare him married and compel him to take the woman he deceived as his wife, Aquinas advises him to suf-fer excommunication or to run away. As we have seen, this is the advice that canonists traditionally reserve for the man whose first marriage can-not be proved if he afterward speaks witnessed words of consent to a sec-ond woman. In this situation, canonists worried, ecclesiastical courts, working within rules of legal evidence that demand two witnesses, would necessarily rule that the man stay with the second wife because evidence existed of the second marriage only. Rather than living in adultery with the second woman and abandoning a spouse, the canonists suggested that such a man run away with the first woman (his true wife). When the canonists offer this advice, in other words, it is because the man, whatever his inward intent, had already spoken words of consent to the first woman, rendering his second marriage invalid despite the courts' inability to find it so. Aquinas instead gives this advice to the man who had mental reservations. Mental reservations, in other words, make the marriage as false for Aquinas as a first living wife makes a second wife for the canonists.

To the canonists' concern for the other party to the contract, which Aquinas recognized when he wrote about the "material contracts," here he replies only that "if mental consent is lacking in one of the parties, on neither side is there a marriage, since marriage consists in a mutual joining together."[204] To the problem that in this case no one will ever know with certainty whether he or she is married, Aquinas replies that since "we must presume good of everyone" there probably is no fraud in most marriages and that parties without express evidence of fraud will be "excused from sin on account of ignorance" if it later turns out that they have been committing fornication with a person to whom they thought they were married.[205] In this discussion Aquinas, unlike the canonists, clearly has no interest in any legal or enforceable standard. Instead he gives married people permission to believe they are married, although he presents the possibility that they are not. "Marriage," here, loses the material aspect he earlier established and becomes understood solely in terms of its sacramentality. Another way of understanding this shift is to say that here Aquinas returns to his earlier idea that words of consent are only signs. If they do not signify as they ought to because the consent to which they refer was never present, the words themselves become empty, and so the relationship they represent, material and spiritual, never comes into being. As a proposition about referentiality this makes sense. As Aquinas stated earlier, however, marriage is also a contract. As a practical proposition his position means that a contract into which you believe you have entered can at any moment be shredded by the other party. Whatever the theological and semiological soundness of this idea, it cannot be good law. In defining marriage here, however, Aquinas's interest lies not in protecting parties but in defining a sacramental truth.

Aquinas's concession to the law comes in his explanation of why the man who speaks words of consent without meaning them should leave his wife even though the Church will declare him married. Although he is not really married, "the Church judges according to outward appearances," according to Aquinas, who goes on to add "nor is she deceived in justice, although she is deceived in the facts of the case."[206] This qualification seems important for two reasons. First, it removes earthly justice from truth. In ordering the man to adhere to his putative wife the Church is wrong in terms of the marriage itself but not in terms of justice, which clearly resides apart from the actual marital union. The second reason the distinction seems important is that if in claiming that the Church is "deceived in the facts of the case" Aquinas means to refer to the fact of the man's absence of inward consent, then the statement makes no sense. If the man has been ordered to return to his wife, he must have left her. If he left her because he never inwardly consented to the marriage, he surely could mention this to the court (as we have already seen, people often mentioned such reservations to the court in marriage suits). So the Church would not, in fact, be deceived as to his reason for leaving the woman. The only way the idea that the Church "is deceived in the facts of the case" can make sense is for "the facts of the case" to indicate how marriages are made, believing them to be the result of words rather than interior consent. Whether Aquinas means to criticize the Church is unclear to me, but his insistence on understanding marriage as a sacrament and the ecclesiastical courts' insistence on enforcing marriage law lead him here to a seemingly untenable position vis-à-vis Church law.

Aquinas continues to dismiss the aspect of marriage that is "an office of nature and of civil life," as he had called the nonsacramental aspect of marriage, when he moves on to consider whether carnal intercourse after verba de futuro makes a marriage.[207] As we have seen, Alexander III held that if a couple had consented to marriage through verba de futuro and then had intercourse they were married. Innocent III had refined the logic of this ruling by explaining that the intercourse did not itself create the marriage but rather signified that consent had already been given. Aquinas, however, rejects this idea entirely. Only the consent of both parties can create a marriage. Carnal intercourse, he explains, follows marriage, it does not make it. Consent to carnal intercourse is consent to carnal intercourse, he points out, not consent to marriage, and so it signifies nothing other than itself—except, as he admits, in the eyes of the law. He here explains explicitly that "we may speak of marriage in two ways": one is the "tribunal of conscience" and the other "external judgment," which he equates with "the judgment of the Church."[208] In the tribunal of the conscience, carnal relations following words of future consent do not make a marriage. This makes particular sense in light of his contention that carnal relations following words of present consent also do not make a marriage in the absence of internal consent, no matter what words are spoken or acts committed. It is only the double internal consent of both parties, expressed in words, that can create a marriage, as he has already explained. In the external tribunal, however, "judgment is given in accordance with external evidence."[209] He concedes that the act of carnal intercourse generally signifies consent, and so the Church rules that consent was present in cases of carnal intercourse following promises of marriage. Aquinas here sets up a second double system (tribunal of the conscience and tribunal of Church law) that does not, in his writing on marriage formation, correspond to the first double system (spiritual joining and material joining) that he posited.

Aquinas posits two kinds of tribunal, but it is clear that the two kinds of judgment are in no way equal. One is true, the other is the best ecclesiastical judges can do. There should be no illusions, however, that the second is particularly adequate: "In truth he who has carnal intercourse consents by deed to the act of sexual union," Aquinas writes, "and does not merely for this reason consent to marriage except according to the interpretation of the law."[210] He here opposes truth, on one hand, to the interpretation of the law, on the other. Church law may have its reason for judging, but its judgment works against what Aquinas conceives of as the truth of the situation.

In the responses to this point Aquinas does acknowledge the problems that arise because marriage and carnal relations always involve two people, rather than one. Since carnal relations are sign enough for the Church that consent has been given, Aquinas admits that a woman who exchanged verba de futuro with a man might think that her betrothed wished to consummate the marriage if he urged sexual relations. If the woman, after such urging, engaged in sexual relations with her betrothed but the man mentally consented only to the carnal relations, not to the marriage, the woman is, according to Aquinas, excused from the sin. She is not, however, married. She is not, furthermore, even excused from the sin if there are signs that the man probably did not intend his actions to consummate the marriage, such as "if they differ considerably in birth or fortune."[211] In such cases the woman should realize that whatever the man's words or actions he does not really intend to marry her. Such a case becomes more problematic for the man, however, if he takes the woman's virginity, since "sin is not forgiven unless restitution is made," as Augustine had explained, and the most appropriate form of restitution would seem to be marriage (which, we should remember, Aquinas assumes has not taken place despite the Church's judgment that it has).[212] If the man promises one woman marriage with verba de futuro, has sexual relations with her but inwardly does not consent to the marriage, and then subsequently marries another woman, he cannot provide restitution to the first by marrying her, Aquinas explains (again in contradiction of Church law, which would find him married to the first woman). In such cases, "it suffices" for the man to provide a dower for the marriage of the first woman, unless he is of higher rank than she, or there is some other such sign that he had not meant his words and actions to the first woman, "because it may be presumed that in all probability she was not deceived but pretended to be."[213]

In thus advocating solutions to actual problems that might arise given his interpretation of marriage, Aquinas treads a fine line between ideas of spiritual and material contract and tribunals of conscience and Church law. After accepting that the external tribunal necessarily works according to external evidence while the tribunal of the conscience does not, Aquinas writes as though people ought to follow the tribunal of the conscience rather than Church law. Once he combines these two systems, internal and external, however, he works according to the internal tribunal on questions of whether a person must stay with his betrothed whom he deceived into having carnal relations (he need not) but according to the external tribunal when deciding how to compensate her (if external evidence points to the idea that she only pretended to be deceived, no compensation is necessary). But once we are willing to take this external evidence, rather than trusting her word, it comes down to a question of whom we allow to operate on a pledge of intention and whom we hold to external evidence. Aquinas here avoids this problem by working within the cultural expectation that women are likely to pretend to be deceived when it might work to their advantage. The fact that the example works along these familiar lines is rhetorically astute but does not obviate the logical problem it presents.

All of these problems point to the conclusion that external and internal forums cannot really be mixed, and Aquinas is not, in fact, advocating that they should be. The real difficulty raised by the hypothetical example of the man who sleeps with the woman he has promised to marry is that even Aquinas, with his insistence on the forum of the conscience, feels the need to come up with a course of action to be taken when problems arise. But courses of action require decisions and judgments based on external facts. The tribunal of the conscience may have a claim to reality that no external tribunal can equal, but it is not and cannot be social or communal. Once Aquinas must advocate action toward another person, based not on one's own internal consent but on someone else's internal disposition, he, too, must resort to external actions as ways of judging internal intentions. In other words, Aquinas replicates the processes of Church law that he seems intent on criticizing. At the same time, he seems to provoke the question by providing, independent of Peter Lombard, a hardest-case scenario. If Aquinas were content to answer only the case in *Tua nos duxit*, he could advocate that the repentant man who had spoken words of consent to a woman without meaning them should repeat the words, this time meaning them because he truly repented of his deception. Such a solution would result in a binding marriage in both the tribunal of the conscience and the tribunal of the law. By positing a marriage to a second woman after a first woman had been deceived, however, Aquinas calls forth a situation that cannot be answered in a wholly satisfactory way with regard to all who thought they had contracts.

The succession of difficulties in Aquinas's arguments about marriage formation come, I believe, from his attempt to recognize the rulings of Church law while explaining the theological workings of marriage as a sacrament. On one hand, he claims the greater truth of the sacrament. Given this greater truth, he advises people to act according to the sacramental, rather than the judicial, nature of marriage when the two conflict. At the same time, this advice leaves no avenue for judging, the situation in which the law finds itself, other than the less acceptable standards the law had already devised. Because the legal and sacramental offices of marriage diverged at a fundamental level, Aquinas defines them as separate offices, but this division was one that he could not maintain because of the material reality of marriage and the other person party to it. The legal and theological systems were, in this case, incompatible in ways that become most clear when we see Aquinas's efforts to resolve them.

Writing about trade, as we have seen, asserts the necessity of consent but then takes the fact of trade (in the absence of clear fraud or physical force) as a sign that consent has occurred. By the thirteenth century, the law held that consent created marriage. To state, therefore, that marriage served as a sign that consent had taken place provided no help in verifying either marriage or consent. In the unhelpfulness of this formulation we see perhaps most clearly the tautology of the prescription as it appears in writing about trade. For cases of marriage law, jurists had to determine how consent, an interior act, could be known externally. First they looked to language. Those who wrote about marriage law thought carefully about what language clearly indicated consent and what language did not. So, as we have seen, they decided that "I will take you as my spouse" did not necessarily signify consent, but that "I will have you as my spouse" or "I take you as my spouse" did. Then they complemented their precise linguistic understanding by trying to evaluate when seeming signs of consent did not really signify consent at all. To this end they employed the standard of the constant man. As we have seen, the constant man, used in discussions of marriage, differs from the good man, used in disputes about pricing, because the good man is an actual person, whereas the constant man is an imaginary standard. This standard demonstrates a willingness to consider when individual signs of consent might not bear their usual meaning. At the same time, it results in the absence of an external standard and the necessity of inscribing acts of imagination and fiction into the law. The widespread understanding of these problems and the solutions the law determined for judging consent show that these ideas about consent and how it was understood were not abstract discussions that interested only a few scholars. Rather, these ideas were as widespread as trade itself, and more widespread than writing about trade.

Chaucer and Aquinas's writings, free from the need to provide actual remedy, complicate further this consideration of ways we can or should determine consent. In the *Physician's Tale,* Chaucer creates a story that diverges both from the jurists' concern that the language of consent does not guarantee its presence and from the dictum in writing on trade that consent guarantees fairness. In imagining Virginia's story, the tale questions not only whether consent always guarantees fairness but also how consent is created. It shows a situation in which a person's consent is both unfair and against her own interest. The question is not the jurists' of whether she does consent, since Chaucer makes her consent clear, but is one of why she would consent. Chaucer thus distinguishes between consent that guarantees fairness and consent that is created externally.

Aquinas's writing on marriage formation draws a different distinction between kinds of consent. It addresses the problem of knowing consent by instituting a double standard for legal knowledge, on one hand, and penitential knowledge, on the other. The external forum may accept words as signs of consent, but the internal forum may not. The double standard Aquinas posits here is not a simple reinscription of the familiar distinction between the lower standards of the law and the higher standards of theology that we saw in writing about the just price, where the law allowed a discrepancy of up to one half of the just price whereas theology allowed no discrepancy at all. Instead, in writing about marriage formation Aquinas contends not that we should uphold a higher standard but that the higher standard is the only true one. It is also, however, one that cannot be judged by other people, whether through language or through imagination. The result is an assertion that however necessary consent may be, it can never be externally known.

4. COMMUNITY

Accounts of trade posit the community as its beneficiary. In John Duns Scotus's formulation, trade is so important to the community that government would even have to pay people to act as merchants if they did not do so voluntarily.[1] In this statement the community appears on a large scale and everyone benefits from trade. Although some writers would seem to posit a smaller community (like the one that is formed in Oresme's tableau of farmer and shepherd), all agree that the hallmark of trade is that the community is better off having traded than not having traded. Were this not the case, the trade would not have taken place, since exchange only occurs when each trader values the object she will acquire more than the one she will relinquish. Otherwise it would be a case of coercion or fraud, not trade. This picture, the one drawn in accounts of trade, raises the immediate question of who exactly is part of the community. Is it only the two people involved in any particular exchange, as it would seem in Oresme's initial tableau? Or is it everyone who uses a particular currency, as it would seem later in his treatise? Or is it everyone who lives within a particular topography or climate, as in Richard of Middleton's formulation that trade allows people in grain-producing lands to drink wine?

This question of who makes up the community is different from those raised in considerations of value and consent. The question left unasked about value in accounts of trade was how value should or could be decided. The question left unasked about consent in accounts of trade was how consent could be determined. Neither of these questions, however, troubles the idea of community. Determinations of both value and consent depend on combining internal and external standards and knowledge. For value in trade, there had to be a personal measure by which one person valued sheep more than grain and another personal measure by which the other person valued grain more than sheep in order to arrive at the external standard by which a certain number of sheep were equal to a certain amount of grain. For consent, the challenge lay in finding an external indication of an internal decision. Community, the supposed beneficiary of trade, is instead a wholly external concern. (We are still a long way off from Benedict Anderson's imagined communities.) The question here is what it means to contend, as accounts of trade do, that the community benefits. This question breaks into the smaller elements of determining who is included in the community and in what way those included could all benefit.

This chapter takes London as a test case of the idea of community. London should be an easy case for identifying a group for whom we could define the notion of community with great certainty. The primary avenue for noncitizens to become citizens of London was through guild membership, and the level of trade specialization developed to an extent that even those who celebrated the Aristotelian polis could hardly have imagined. The term "commonalty" usually referred, at the very least, to the citizens of London and the "common profit" to their collective interests. I begin this chapter with the idealized London community in the middle English alliterative poem *St. Erkenwald*. The poet draws a far more detailed picture of who might make up this community than we find in any account of trade. The poem tells of the miracle of the saint who through a tear baptizes a long-dead virtuous pagan judge from London's past. It explains this miracle in terms of a larger community of Londoners, past and present, who are described with great energy and care. The old Londoner's administration of justice to and for the larger community presents the opportunity for Erkenwald's miracle. The miracle in turn is described in terms of the larger community of which Erkenwald is the head, but also a part. I then turn from the fictional London of *St. Erkenwald* to the historical London of craft guilds. The records of London craft guilds speak almost incessantly of the common good, the commonalty, and the common profit. Examining these records exposes deep contestation over who might be included in such a group. More important, the way the records construct these terms reveals a "common good" that is never common, to the mutual benefit of both parties, as accounts of trade assert. This common good seems rather to come at the cost of some who ostensibly should be part of the community. These records also show that ignorance or fraud, qualities that were supposed to invalidate a trade, were perpetual possibilities in all trades. I turn finally to the fifteenth-century ballad *London Lickpenny*, whose speaker is unable to enter the London community formed by trade. His exclusion highlights a side of that community that writers on trade do not consider. Whether this exclusion is the fault of trade and the communities it creates, or the fault of the speaker who does not know how to trade, however, is one that the ballad does not fully resolve.

The idea of community in the European middle ages is unlike the ideas of value and consent not only in posing an external problem rather than one that combines internal and external standards but also in the amount of attention that it has received. Part of this attention is due to the widespread use of the term and the large number of medieval discourses that employ it. As Antony Black has pointed out, community was an ideal "proclaimed in popular idiom, official ideology and formal philosophy."[2] The ideal itself was not described in consistent vocabulary. M. S. Kempshall lists twenty-seven terms that could easily be used to define some form of the common good, some of which could refer interchangeably to God or the good of a small group of people. He notes that even so rigorous a thinker as Thomas Aquinas was "inconsistent, even indiscriminate, in his use of terminology" and that Aquinas treats the idea itself differently in various works.[3] Where the term was used, it could have a wide range of meanings, from a precisely defined, juridically organized group of people to an inchoate multitude.[4]

Terminological difficulties, however, have not deterred scholars from examining such a widespread idea, which played an important role in metaphysical, political, and legal thought. The idea has received most attention as it relates to a debate about the respective claims of individuals and groups in the middle ages and the justifications for challenging existing hierarchies. The standard picture has held that the rediscovery of Aristotle's *Politics* and *Ethics* played a crucial role in the thirteenth- and fourteenth-century secularization of political power.[5] This narrative has been questioned in a number of ways. Not content to rely so heavily on Aristotle for crucial medieval ideas of community, Pierre Michaud-Quantin has explored the way Roman and medieval legal texts from before 1260 construct notions of community.[6] M. S. Kempshall has questioned the importance of Aristotle for secular political development by analyzing scholastic treatments of the common good, arguing that Aristotle could be deployed on behalf of either royal or papal authority.[7] Susan Reynolds has taken a more on-the-ground approach to the question, offering a synthetic account of a variety of different medieval collective activities.[8] The sheer variety of the forms of collective identity described in her account calls into question the notion of a single community or common good. My interest, however, lies not in metaphysical or political conceptions of community, but in the ways that writing about late medieval London complicates the idea of community presented in justifications of trade.

The Myth of Unified Community in *St. Erkenwald*

Judging by the stories that survive, Erkenwald, a seventh-century bishop of London, spent much of his time on the move.[9] He founded two abbeys, one for his sister Ethelburga at Barking and another for himself at Chertsey. According to one legend, when it became clear during construction at Barking that the carpenters had cut a crucial beam too short, Erkenwald and Ethelburga each took one end of the huge beam with their bare hands and stretched it to the correct length. Another story tells of the two-wheeled litter Erkenwald had built when he grew too weak to travel by other means in order that he might continue making his accustomed preaching journeys. During one trip a wheel fell off the cart. The journey nevertheless continued so smoothly that it was some time before anyone noticed that a wheel was missing. The single remaining wheel stayed on its axle and the ride proceeded as usual until Erkenwald reached his destination. As we might expect for such a well-traveled saint, his death set off an argument over where he should be buried. The nuns at Barking, the monks at Chertsey, and the people of London all claimed him and his remains as their own. This disagreement itself became the occasion of another miracle, by which Erkenwald made clear that he wished his bones to reside in London. A shrine to him was constructed in St. Paul's Cathedral. In the years following his death he became so closely associated with the place that, according to Christopher Brooke, it is something of a wonder that the name of the London church was never changed during the central medieval wave of renaming English churches dedicated to Saints Peter and Paul in favor of local saints and that we should still know the cathedral as St. Paul's rather than St. Erkenwald's.[10]

The middle English alliterative poem *St. Erkenwald,* written in the late fourteenth or early fifteenth century, picks up on Erkenwald's travels, his construction projects, and his association with London.[11] While workmen redig the foundation for a new St. Paul's they come across a miraculously preserved body, dressed like a king. People have no idea who the corpse is, despite their attempts to recover his identity from memory, stories, and written records. At the time of the discovery Erkenwald is off on one of his many journeys. He returns to London and after much prayer commands the body to talk. The body tells the bishop that he was a virtuous judge who controlled London at a time so long ago that "hit is to meche to any mon to make of a nommbre."[12] Erkenwald and the people of London, assembled to view the marvel, hear of the judge's exemplary justice, the high esteem in which he was held, and his current lot outside of heaven. As "a paynym vnpresete" (an ignorant pagan) who never knew of Jesus' plight or mercy or virtue (286–87), he explains, he was left in limbo during the harrowing of hell (291–92). Deeply moved, Erkenwald wishes he could bring the judge back to life for a moment, just long enough for the baptism that would save him, and sheds tears for the judge. One of them, falling on the judge, turns out to hold the power of baptism. His preserved body and clothes remain just long enough to tell us that his soul has reached heaven.

It has long been noted that, in Elizabeth Salter's words, "the whole poem is redolent of the City" and "makes insistent and expert reference to London."[13] This point has not, however, been connected with the miraculous baptism of which the poem tells. In the desire to understand the central miracle of *St. Erkenwald,* its London setting has been largely set aside in favor of comparisons with the medieval legend of Trajan, the righteous heathen emperor whose soul goes from hell to heaven on account of his own virtue and Gregory the Great's intercession.[14] It has also been understood as participating in a number of contemporary controversies, ranging from Pelagian views about baptism, to the relative roles of laity and clergy in preserving history and maintaining civic order, to royal politics of the 1380s and 1390s.[15] I would like to propose that whatever contribution it may have made to political and religious debates of its day, the central miracle of the poem can be joined with Salter's observation about the specificity of the poem's ties to London. Such a joining provides a way of understanding the poem in its communal context that is not dependent on specific political polemics the poet may have intended. At the same time, I will argue that the poem works not to divide Londoners, presenting activities in which the laity should not engage, but to unite them behind the voice of Erkenwald embracing the pagan judge.[16]

Insisting that the poem can, on one hand, be understood as a statement about the community of London, while, on the other hand, trying to divorce it from the specific political London of its time may require a word of explanation. The centrality of London to a poem written in a Cheshire dialect has long raised curiosity.[17] Salter suggested that "perhaps the poem was written for westerners living and working in London, by a poet who himself was an immigrant."[18] Ruth Nissé and Frank Grady have both located the poem more specifically in the London of the late fourteenth century, suggesting that it makes a statement about royal policies. Nissé sees the poem as a challenge to royal policy of the 1380s and 1390s, while Grady views it as a royalist response to the events of 1388. I believe that it is somewhat problematic to understand the poem as a reaction to specific political events when we do not know the date of the poem and therefore must in part postulate this based on how we perceive its reaction to specific events or policies. This problem is made particularly acute by the fact that the two outstanding scholars who have studied it with reference to contemporary political events disagree completely about the political comment it makes and the events on which it is commenting. Although it is possible that the poem could respond to the parliament of 1388 or Richard II's policies toward London in the 1390s at a remove of several years, or even decades, this possibility further complicates the way we understand *St. Erkenwald* as a political poem. The fundamental disagreement between Nissé and Grady necessarily complicates any view of the efficacy the poem may have had as a political statement. Whatever the poem's stance on particular political events, the miracle of *St. Erkenwald* restores a member of London's community to his rightful place in heaven, where all other virtuous members of the city expect to find themselves. Whether or not it presents a London choosing sides between royal and parliamentary power, the poem most certainly draws a picture of London surprised and moved to tears when it finds one of its most prominent members denied a place in heaven. By placing the just ruler of London past in a Christian heaven the poem closes a potential division between righteous members of the London community past and present. In doing so it offers a vision of a unified community.

The poem begins by placing us geographically, "At London in Englonde" (1). The poet emphasizes the close connections between the person of Erkenwald, the city of London, Christian history, and the story that we will hear, reiterating twice more in the first five lines that "[t]her was a byschop *in þat burghe*" (3) and that "[i]n his tyme *in þat toun*" (5) the church's rebuilding, of which we will hear, takes place. The historical record that often prefaces alliterative poems is of the rededication of English heathen temples to Christianity performed by Augustine of Canterbury (rather than the more common political history of Britain).[19] The poem's prefatory matter brings the connection between the general conversion of England and the story at hand back to London once more by explaining that London, "þe metropol and þe mayster-toun" (26), links Augustine to Erkenwald through time because "of þis Augustynes art is Erkenwolde bischop / At loue London toun" (33–34). London thus unites the story's past and present.

With the connection between Augustine and Erkenwald established, the poem turns to the people who make up the community over which the bishop presides. The next seventy lines of the poem tell of the finding of the tomb and Londoners' inability to guess whose body lies within it. This narrative clearly does not require seventy lines on its own. Instead, the lines are filled with the bustle and labor of London life. Masons were made to work in the rebuilding of the cathedral, the poet tells us, and their work is described in appreciative, if not especially knowledgeable, detail: how they use various tools to hew the hard stones, how it took "many" of them to perform the work, how they needed to dig down to the foundation so that they could insert the correct structural supports, and how deep they delved before they found the tomb. We see, in other words, not only a body found but the ongoing labor that produced the finding and which the finding interrupted.

Once the tomb thus uncovered has been described, we are presented with a parade of London life. "All," the poet tells us, pondered out loud what the tomb could mean. The "all" who speak are at least partially enumerated in the lines that follow: they include many hundred courtly men, burgesses, beadles, masters' men, leaping lads, the mayor and his retinue, the sexton, and workmen, all explicitly mentioned (55–70). "Þer commen þider of alle kynnes so kenely mony / Þat as alle þe worlde were þider walon wytin a honde-quile" (There came thither many of all kinds so quickly that it was as though all the world were found gathered there within an instant) (64–65). No one class of people, as the list shows, came, but all people. At the same time, the poet presents the people of London as "all the world." The information that news was "token to þe toun," not the world, and the time span make a hyperbolic reading of "all the world" inevitable (it is particularly unlikely that all the world could arrive so quickly), although the shortsighted view of "all the world" allies the speaker with the denizens of many urban centers both before and since the poem's composition (one thinks particularly of the *New Yorker*'s map of the United States from the perspective of a New Yorker, which shows an outsized Manhattan dwarfing the rest of the country).

These people, clerical and lay, from all stations of London life, do not stand quietly in a line like an allegorical representation of all the people. They make noise, speculating out loud, forming a "route wyt ryngande noyce" (a crowd with ringing noise) (62), above or through which the sexton makes his order to unlock the tomb known. The poet again emphasizes physical work, this time that of opening the tomb. He narrates the process of wedging in levers and using iron crowbars, stressing the skill of the "wy3t werke-men" (strong workmen) (69) who finished the job quickly despite the tomb's large size. The description of the miraculously preserved and richly dressed body within the tomb similarly highlights the labor that must have created his garments. Gordon Whatley finds a cognate of *St. Erkenwald*'s comment that the corpse's clothes were "als bry3t of hor blee in blysnande hewes / As þai hade 3epely in þat 3orde bene 3isturday shapen" (as bright of their color in gleaming hues as if they had been made in that yard yesterday) (87–88) in the Trajan story in Jacopo della Lana's commentary on Dante's *Commedia,* which remarks that the emperor's tongue was as well preserved as if it had been buried that hour.[20] However close the narrative point in the two works, the difference between their descriptions is instructive. Della Lana comments on "freshness" that could not be preserved through time naturally and thus posits the body's seemingly recent burial as the indication of the miracle. The *Erkenwald* poet instead stresses the work that goes into making clothes that naturally decay over time. This natural decay should eventually erase not only the dead person's body but also the visible record of the cloth-makers' labor.

The fine clothes appeared in such pristine condition that if the creation of the cloth, the embodied labor of the people who made it, did not occur recently, their labor was miraculously preserved along with the preternaturally fresh body.

The appearance of the body not only fosters the belief that the corpse must have been buried recently, it also creates more talk as "each person" asks whether anyone remembers the corpse, since "he has ben kynge of þis kithe as couthely hit semes" (it plainly seems that he has been king of this church) (98). The people do not wonder silently or ponder rhetorically. Instead they voice their questions, seeking answers from others in their midst. Seeing that the body has been buried beneath the church and that he is dressed as a king, "each person" immediately takes him for a leader of the church, the community of which they are a part. There follows a list of the ways they expect they should be able to identify such a person: by title, token, tale in church record or in a book, or memory. As John Scattergood points out, the list shows the uselessness of lay methods of storing knowledge about the past.[21] It also points to the uselessness of normal clerical methods of storing such knowledge in this case, since no record can be found in church documents either. The dean of the cathedral later sums up the situation by telling the bishop that no one can remember the man and that a weeklong search through the cathedral library has proved futile. The problem stems from the fact that the laity and clergy alike assume that the body was a member of their community. They are correct to the extent that the judge was an important person in London, their geographical community, but incorrect in assuming that he was a member of the Christian community. As someone who was not a member of the Christian community, the community has no record of him.

Erkenwald, too, later repeats this mistake of thinking the body is part of his own Christian community, even after knowing the judge was a pagan, by assuming that the justice of the judge's actions in and for London assured his soul a place in heaven. This assumption leads Erkenwald to commit something of a faux-pas by asking the soul confined to limbo to tell him "of þi soule in sele quere ho wonnes / And of þe riche restorment þat raȝt hyr oure Lorde" (of where thy soul in bliss resides and of the rich restitution that our Lord gave her) (279–80). The bishop and the people alike recognize the judge as one of their own but misapprehend the community that ties them together. And bishop and people alike are shocked and saddened to hear that the judge's soul languishes, as he says, in dark death (294).

This expectation that the judge's soul should reside in heaven has been tied to the belief, expressed in Pelagian theology and *Piers Plowman,* that a truly just person needs no sacraments to attain heaven.[22] There is a reason

this particular bishop and these particular people might be so quick to believe that this judge's soul resides in heaven. The body declares that it was
"never king nor caesar nor knight" (199), but a man of the law, a "master-
man" who controlled the city (201–2). By the rank of his birth, then, the
people were mistaken in identifying him as king or bishop. Rather he was
a common man, not low, but of lesser rank than many of the "gay grete
lorde[s]" listening to him and perhaps even the kind of master the "masters' men" in the audience knew well. At the same time, however, he was
deputy and principal judge whose jurisdiction, he carefully notes, is the
same geographical location as that of Augustine and Erkenwald: London,
or the New Troy.[23] "I was of heire and oyer in þe New Troie," he says, and
"in my power þis place was putte al to-geder"; "I iustifiet þis ioly toun"; and
"alle Troye" lamented his death (211, 228, 229, 246). The city, which at
the beginning of the poem linked Erkenwald to Augustine, now links both
to the judge. In the forty years he presided over the area, not only did he
practice exemplary justice but the wider community, although resistant at
times, recognized his virtues. "Alle Troye" not only noisily mourned him,
they dressed him as befit a king to honor his "honesté of heghest enprise,"
the crown signifying his rank as "kynge of kene iustices / Per euer wos
tronyd in Troye" (king of learned justices that were ever enthroned in
Troy) (254–55). The poet stresses the people's agency in this process, as
the judge explains that "[a]lle menyd my dethe, þe more and the lasse /
And þus to bounty my body þai buriet in golde" (247–48). It is "[a]ll the
people, greater and lesser" who perform the long list of actions to honor
him: they "cladden," "gurden," "furrid," and "coronyd" him (clad, girded,
furred, and crowned) (249, 251, 252, 254). Heavenly recognition mirrors
the communal recognition, showing itself in the miraculous preservation
of his clothes and face. His careful and just rule led to the reward of "un-
spoiled" skin and clothes without the benefit of embalming or other
earthly science.

Although the judge speaks directly in response to Erkenwald's questions, by asking the questions Erkenwald is again brought together with the
larger Christian community of London over which he presides. He bids the
body to speak not in his own name but in God's name, querying the judge
"on God's behalf" (181) and only after the Holy Ghost, during Erkenwald's long night of prayer, had shown him the proper way to proceed. He
asks these questions, however, not in private examination but in public conversation. He does so at the front of a local hierarchy of which he clearly
comes first. Before he went to the tomb "elegant great lords" had listened
to him say mass, as they often did, and yielded to him as he passed them
in the nave (134–35, 138). The scene demonstrates that lords and bishop
formed part of the same community and that the lords recognized the

bishop's place over them. When Erkenwald arrived at the tomb he was followed by a "great throng" and came to examine it beside "the mayor," "mighty men," "macers," and "the dean of the dear place" (141, 143–44). The civic and ecclesiastical hierarchy of London, in other words, come together before the tomb, all acknowledging the bishop at their head. Nor does this larger community disappear while the judge tells Erkenwald his story. In the middle of their conversation, after the judge has described his actions on earth but before he has addressed the status of his soul, the poet reinserts the larger community, telling us:

> Quil he in spelunke þus spake þer sprange in þe pepulle
> In al þis worlde no worde, ne wakenyd no noice
> Bot al as stille as þe ston stoden and listonde
> Wyt much wonder forwrast, and wepid ful mony. (217–20)

[While he thus spoke in the tomb there sprung in the people in all this world no word, nor arose no noise, but all stood as still as the stone and listened unsettled with much wonder, and very many wept.]

The silence during the judge's speech contrasts with the noise before and after the exchange between Erkenwald and the judge. In addition to creating a sense of drama, as T. McAlindon points out, calling our attention to the crowd's silence serves to keep our focus on the whole audience of the tale, rather than just the bishop.[24] That only the bishop speaks does not indicate that the others have left or are unimportant or have reactions that are in any way inappropriate. In fact, the tears of "very many" anticipate Erkenwald's own tears a few lines later.

We have seen so far two kinds of recognition: the London community of Erkenwald's time and heaven have recognized the judge's virtue; and Erkenwald and his own London community recognize or misrecognize in the corpse a person who they believe should belong to their community. To these we can add a third: the judge himself, dead though he is, recognizes Erkenwald and the Christian community from which he says he is excluded. The corpse's first word, after Erkenwald bids it to speak, is "Bisshop" (193). The corpse thus not only knows who has been speaking to him, he recognizes Erkenwald's place in a Christian church that did not exist during his own lifetime. He further recognizes the Christian community by declaring the power of Jesus over "[a]l heauen and helle . . . and erthe bitwene" (196) and by proclaiming God's greatness even as he bemoans his own fate of having lived before Jesus. Along the way he also displays a fair knowledge of the sacrament of baptism and the rewards it makes possible. The judge was a key part of the London community of his own time, recognized by the community itself and by heaven. Although he could not be Christian, he recognizes the Christian community of the future.

The Christian community returns this recognition, after hearing the judge's story of his life and afterlife, by weeping over his exclusion from heaven: "[A]lle wepyd for woo þe wordes þat herden" (all who heard the words wept for woe) (310). This "all" includes not only the great crowd of people but also the bishop himself, who gives voice to the reason for his tears when he wishes that the judge might come to life just long enough to be baptized. Erkenwald's own tear effects this baptism and the judge remains just long enough to tell the crowd what has happened. The poem ends, however, not with this seeming resolution, but by focusing on the larger community:

> Þen wos louynge oure Lorde wyt loves vp-halden,
> Meche mournynge and myrthe was mellyd to-geder;
> Þai passyd for the in processioun and alle þe pepulle folowid
> And alle þe belles in þe burghe beryd at ones. (349–52)

[Then there was praising of our Lord with hands upheld, much mourning and mirth were spoken aloud together, they passed forth in procession and all the people followed and all the bells in the city rang at once.]

The picture with which the poem ends is that of London, the place the poem began. It ends, however, by showing that the Christianization the poem initially narrated as London's past has now been made complete. Not only have the churches been rededicated, and not only has the foundation of St. Paul's been redug, but the virtuous head of the older London community has been reincorporated into the new Christian community. The London in the poem's closing lines is not a place of buildings, it is a place of people and noise, mourning and joy voiced together aloud through the city's ringing bells. London remains a place of hierarchies, the bishop rightly taking his place above the mayor and both rightly taking their places at the head of the procession. It is also a place, however, where they are joined and followed by "all the people."

Saint Erkenwald tells of the miracle by which the virtuous Londoner of old is reincorporated into the present London community. It tells of the process by which two separately defined communities, one "virtuous Londoners," another "Christians," are brought together into a single community with no division. *St. Erkenwald* makes the problem of the "virtuous pagan" particularly acute because the pagan is not just any pagan, he is the pagan who ruled London virtuously and who was recognized as a wise and just magistrate by the Londoners of his own day. The poem thus creates not only a series of transformations, as others have noted, but also a series of parallels: the Londoners of the past, who recognized a good magistrate and the Londoners of Erkenwald's day, who similarly recognize the virtue of their bishop; the judge, whom the people think must have been "king of this church" and Erkenwald, who is the head of the London church; and the city itself, as it was and as it is in Erkenwald's time.[25] The miracle of the poem rejoins these elements, as the Londoners of Erkenwald's time recognize the virtue of the judge, allying themselves with the Londoners of the past, and the soul of the virtuous judge, through the intercession of his later counterpart, the holy bishop, moves to heaven. The soul of that most exemplary Londoner thus takes its place where it belongs, and the community itself forms the last tableau of the poem, celebrating its wholeness.

London Craft Guilds and the Common Profit

Baptism, not justice, is the miracle at the heart of *St. Erkenwald*. Yet the poem explains the miracle in terms of a greater London community. The virtuous judge brought justice to all the Londoners of his day, and the poem highlights the Londoners who were Erkenwald's contemporaries, describing them sometimes by occupation and rank (burgesses, beadles, masters' men, builders, the bishop) and sometimes as the unified whole they create (the "alle þe pepulle" of the poem's end). Although it takes a saint to perform a miracle, it is a miracle that the whole community celebrates.

This idea of a whole community, however, mentioned as the beneficiary of exchange in accounts of trade and depicted so fulsomely in *St. Erkenwald*, gets called into question when we turn to records of the London craft guilds. London craft guild charters and ordinances of the fourteenth and fifteenth centuries continuously mention the common good, the common profit, and the commonalty as both their justification (the regulations should be enacted for the common profit) and their final end (the enacted regulations do work for the common profit). These documents, however, unlike *St. Erkenwald*, construct the common good or commonalty in ways that exclude people whom we might, from the poem or from accounts of trade, expect to be members of it. By examining the charters, ordinances, and complaints, we see both the language of community that seems to celebrate a whole and the ways that the "common good" seems always to come at the cost of some of its members.

In this section I examine the way London craft guilds are described in their regulations, approved by the city and sometimes granted by the crown, and in actions pertaining to them in city records. Paying attention to the language of these records suggests that the notion of what the common good or common profit might mean is in fact far more fraught than we tend to allow. In these documents we see at least three ways that the "commonalty" splits against itself, making the notion of a "common" profit contradictory. In the first instance, some guilds implicitly exclude members of other guilds and crafts from their definition of the "common people"; in the second instance, the community is split between buyers and sellers, each with very different interests and senses of the common profit; and in the third instance the community of the craft guild itself fractures, as some members turn against others. In all cases the unified community, so beautifully drawn in *St. Erkenwald* and evoked in accounts of trade as well as in the guild charters and ordinances, turns out to have interests that are irreconcilable rather than common.

Craft guilds played a crucial role in London civic life of the fourteenth and fifteenth centuries. By 1319 the only avenue to citizenship for someone not born in London was through the craft guilds: six members had to present the applicant to the mayor and alderman, vouching for his skills and character.[26] Craft guilds elected wardens who helped in the governance of city life; by the later fourteenth century they are seen as instruments of city government in some instances.[27] The political factions of London split along the lines of the professional guilds, in smaller matters and during two major periods of civic unrest.[28] In 1351–52 and 1376–84 members of the Common Council, a body that played a vital role in the government of London and eventually controlled all of the city's finances, were elected by crafts rather than by wards.[29] The political organization of the city along craft lines mirrored its economic organization. The economy of London was based on trade (both internal and overseas), manufacturing, and the service industry.[30] Trading and manufacturing were, in turn, organized and regulated along guild lines.[31] Craft guilds were also part of the justice system of the city since craft guild members charged before the city with an offense relating to their crafts were judged by fellow guild members.[32] The importance of craft to identity can be seen in the city records, which invariably identify the people they name by trade, regardless of whether the record has anything to do with the profession.[33]

The beginning of the fourteenth century saw a marked increase in the number of documents that bear on the regulation of guilds.[34] Some craft guilds were granted royal charters, usually in language copied verbatim from the guilds' petition for them. More commonly we find ordinances pertaining to crafts in the *London Letter-Books,* which tend to record the executive and administrative activities of London. Sometimes these ordinances take the form of official approval for regulations the craft had already created, sometimes they note rules that the mayor and aldermen found necessary for the regulation of city life. Records pertaining to the crafts also appear frequently in the *Plea and Memoranda Rolls,* which do not necessarily note anything different than the *Letter-Books* but tend, over time, to concern themselves with the enforcement of rules and regulations.

In 1327 Edward III granted a charter to the London goldsmiths that explains the need for a chartered guild by sketching the current state of affairs. "Recently," it asserts,

> merchants, both native and alien, have been bringing into this country from foreign lands counterfeit sterling . . . , and of this money none can have knowledge save by melting down. Moreover there are many practicing the goldsmiths' craft who keep their shops in dark lanes and obscure streets, and buy vessels of gold and silver secretly, making no inquiry as to whether the vessel was stolen or lawfully bought, and melt it down at once and turn it into plate and sell it . . . ; and also they make counterfeit articles of gold and silver such as coronals, brooches, rings, and other jewels . . . selling their wares to mercers and other people who have no knowledge of such things. And the cutlers in the cutlers' quarter cover tin with silver so thinly that the silver can never be separated from the tin, and then sell this tin covered with silver as fine silver to the great damage and deception of us and all our people.[35]

The solution to this conglomeration of problems, seemingly more appropriate to a film noir than fourteenth-century London, turns out to be the goldsmiths' charter, granted "for the common profit of us and of our people."[36] The guild will regulate the craft and search out and amend any misdeeds, dispensing "due punishment to wrong-doers."[37] If necessary, it calls upon the mayor and sheriffs to help it carry out its regulations. Given the dark lanes, the secret dealings, and the silver that can never be separated from the tin, it might seem that the goldsmiths had an almost overwhelming task on their hands. If their ability to carry out this mandate could be questioned, however, certainly it would seem that the reasoning could not: surely no one, after all, would argue that stolen goods, counterfeit gold, cheated Londoners, and silver that could never be separated from tin work in any way but "to the great damage and deception of us and all our people." Surely no one would argue that stopping these abuses could work in any way but "for the common profit of us and our people."

The goldsmiths' charter, although unusual in its eloquence and the frankness with which it worries about those who can purchase "vessels of gold and silver" and "coronals, brooches, rings, and other jewels," is typical of the charters granted to London craft guilds in presenting the regulation of the craft as a measure that will work for "the common profit." It is also typical in making palpable the need for regulation that it asserts by enumerating the ways that the status quo works against the common profit.

Motifs of darkness and secrecy that stand for duplicity and deceit also become regular features in fourteenth- and fifteenth-century craft regulations.[38] In the same year that Edward III granted a charter to the goldsmiths, he also granted a charter to the London girdlers (makers of horses' girdles) "for the common profit of our people."[39] Like the goldsmiths' charter, its claim to benefit the common profit was made on the basis of the ills regulation would curtail. In this case the charter mentions persons who "garnish [girdles] with false work, such as lead, pewter, and tin, and other false things; whereby the people of the said city [London] and of the realm are deceived, to the great loss of themselves, and the scandal of the good folks of the trade" as the evildoers the guild would prevent.[40] Other London craft guild charters follow the same rhetoric. The skinners' charter, for example, also granted in 1327, was to serve "for the common advantage of the commonalty of our realm to the same city [London]," "seeing that the premises are for the advantage of the people of our realm," and the drapers' charter was granted in 1364 for "the common profit of the people," remedying the "great damage and loss" that "have of late accrued to us and all the people of our realm."[41]

Trade ordinances that the city approved follow the same formula. The city granted the hostlers and haymongers' regulations in 1327 "for themselves and for all the commonalty" to prevent "the great damage of the folks and of all the people";[42] in 1331 the butchers' ordinances were amended "to the profit of the commonalty";[43] poultry-sellers' regulations were approved in 1345 "for the common advantage of all the citizens";[44] in the same year spurriers' articles were granted "for the common profit";[45] and in 1347 the glovers' ordinances were granted "to the great profit of all the common people."[46] From 1316 to 1416 this language becomes standard in the craft ordinances the city approves. Over forty documents approving craft regulations justify themselves explicitly in terms of the common profit, common good, good of the commonalty, or common advantage that they will promote.[47] Even more make reference to the damage to and deceit of the common people that the ordinances and articles will prevent.[48]

Guilds Excluding Other Guilds

Despite this agreement on the importance of working toward the common advantage and the need to eradicate any habitual damage and deceit of the common people, the group constituted by "common" was subject to vigorous competition. The first and most obvious kind of competition for the idea of whom the commonalty includes is when the guilds exclude each other from the idea of the common good. This competition arises in a number of different ways. In some cases it seems a matter of factionalism. We have seen this already in political divisions and civic unrest that run according to guild affiliation. It appears also in street violence, as when, in 1267, a disagreement between tailors, on one side, and goldsmiths, on the other, led some of those professions to "go armed throughout the streets of the City, creating most severe conflicts among themselves" for three nights in a row.[49] The gathering drew in other crafts, as well: dealers in broadcloth, for example, supported the tailors. The melee was said, by the end of the third night, to have attracted together "more than five hundred of these mischievous persons," none willing to put an end to the fighting because "every one was waiting by force of arms to take vengeance on his adversary."[50] Disputes between the fishmongers and skinners led to violence on more than one occasion, as when in 1340 "an affray" took place "owing to an old quarrel": the fishmongers who tried to help their colleague were set upon by skinners, and some skinners who then tried to stop the fight were "wounded in the head" with knives by other fishmongers.[51] Dissension still appears to have been going strong three years later when "men of the misteries [guilds or crafts] of Fishmongers and Skinners" were called to "take steps for putting down disturbances that had arisen between men of each mistery and for better preserving the peace."[52] The fishmongers and goldsmiths engaged in open violence against each other in 1339.[53] In 1327 the fight seems instead to have been between the saddlers and almost everyone else. "[T]he men of the trade of the saddlers of the City of London, of the one part, and the men of the trades of the joiners, painters, and lorimers [makers of bits and metal work for reins]" came together, "on either side strongly provided with an armed force," and "exchanged blows and manfully began to fight."[54] The result was that several people were "wickedly, and against the peace . . . killed, and others mortally wounded," while "the greater part of the City was in alarm, to the great disgrace and scandal of the whole city."[55] These examples of violent factionalism can be understood as de facto challenges to the idea of the common good: the groups on either side of these conflicts did not think the other was acting for the common benefit and tried to take matters into their own hands, which led, according to the record, to a breach in the reputation and dignity of the city as a whole.[56]

The dissension between communities of crafts also took forms that were less violent but seem more intent on excluding other crafts from the "commonalty." We see this clearly in the charters and ordinances themselves, as when the goldsmiths' charter accuses cutlers of covering "tin with silver so thinly that the silver can never be separated from the tin." The charter proposes that the cutlers' own profit opposes the common profit and thus draws a line between the cutlers and the commonalty.

The allegation against the cutlers, it turns out, is among the milder aspersions cast upon other crafts. The drapers' charter, using language taken from the drapers' own petition, complains at great length of dyers, fullers, weavers, and others who "have neither been apprenticed to, nor sufficiently instructed in, the mysteries of the dealing in Drapery." "And," the charter continues,

> on account of their ignorance, and because of the great engrossment which they make unwisely in all manner of cloth, the dearness of cloth has become so great that it cannot be easily reduced, and also various frauds have been practiced in the making and sale of cloth, such as by false drapers and shearmen, and cloth of demy grain sold for scarlet; and the Dyers, Weavers, and Fullers . . . also perpetrate many frauds in their work which cannot be well detected except by Drapers who have full knowledge of such work, and what is worse, the Dyers often change the wool and the Weavers the yarn and the Fullers the whole cloth, buy other cloths by way of forestalling and then sell them to Drapers, and thus the cloth is twice bought before it comes to open sale. . . . The which things amongst others are the chief cause of the excessive dearness of the merchandise of cloth, and also because of the like frauds and defaults great damage and loss have of late accrued to us and all the people of our realm, and greater will befall us, which God forbid, if a remedy be not speedily applied.[57]

The drapers thus position themselves against other crafts but with the community, which, they assert, is now paying too much for cloth. The crafts that compete with the drapers do not, in this charter, constitute part of the "us and people of our realm" who have suffered damage and loss. The drapers provide a taxonomy of reasons that the practices of other crafts (at least when they try to engage in the drapers' work) form a threat to the whole. The malpractice runs from simple incompetence (the "ignorance" of others) to outright deceit (the "frauds that have been practiced"). It harms not only the individuals who are thus taken in (no one, after all, wants to be the victim of professional ignorance or fraud) but also the entire cloth-buying community, since one result of these practices is the general "excessive dearness of the merchandise of cloth." Though the drapers might therefore assert that they act for the good of the community, this community clearly does not include dyers, weavers, or fullers.

Nor do crafts confine the ways they place other crafts in opposition to the community to petitions for their own charters. Complaints about how other crafts work against the common good could take a range of forms. Each voices the idea that another group, in pursuing its own interests, has been harming the interests of the group making the complaint and the larger community they try to serve. In 1335, for example, weavers charged that burellers (middlemen in the cloth trade) were having their servants weave, while the burellers countercomplained that the weavers "sought to monopolize the craft of weaving cloth in the City."[58] Disputes between the two groups had a long history. In 1300–1301, for example, the burellers had complained that the weavers refused to complete work that the burellers could not, by city regulation, give to anyone else.[59] Complaints and countercomplaints were also common in other trades that were forced to work together. In 1395 a disagreement between cordwainers (workers of cordovan leather, often made into shoes) and cobblers over who could work on what kind of shoes led finally to the agreement "that no person who meddles with old shoes, shall meddle with new shoes to sell; and that every manner of work that may be made of new leather belongs to the new workers, without their meddling with any old work."[60] The leathersellers worried in 1372 not about who might practice what craft, but that the dyers, on whom they depended, were charging artificially high prices "by covine among themselves" for dying leather, a complaint similar to the one voiced in 1349 by cordwainers who charged that curriers were charging too much for the leather they sold.[61] The saddlers and fusters (who made the wooden frames of saddle trees) lodged frequent complaints against each other, often including charges of price fixing.[62]

All of these cases mount a double challenge to the easy idea that the community benefits from exchange that we saw in accounts of trade. In the first place, the interests of the group charging too much clearly stood at odds with the interests of the groups being charged. In this sense trade did not benefit the whole community; it benefited one part of the community or the other. In the second place, when one step in producing a commodity becomes too expensive or poorly executed, then the community of all who use that commodity suffers. All suffer, that is, except the group charging too much. Their profit comes at the expense of the community and thus excludes them from the community that suffers.

In 1408 the cutlers voiced another sort of complaint that resulted from the fixed division of different kinds of crafts. The cutlers sold "knives fully prepared and decorated," but due to the regulations surrounding trades the knives were actually constructed by members of three different crafts: bladesmiths forged the blade, cutlers crafted the handle, and sheathers created the sheath. The sheaths, cutlers charged, were "being not properly made," which resulted in harm to the cutlers, who were held responsible for any defects in the knives, including the sheaths, since they sold the entire knives to "all buyers."[63] This complaint against the sheathers, intent on demarcating a line between crafts that buyers did not draw, can be seen as a case of community working too well. The perceived common responsibility for the craft of the knife, the cutlers declared, was not common at all. They were eager to distinguish themselves more completely from the sheathers, who, they believed, were causing "blame and scandal" to be "charged upon the said trade of the Cutlers."[64]

In all of these cases, those making the complaints carefully aligned themselves with the commonalty against the malefactors who would not work, or who would not work at a reasonable rate, or who did work without having been properly trained. We also see professions allying themselves with the common people against unauthorized persons practicing various parts of crafts, as when it is explained that cappers sell people caps that turn their heads colors by dint of working with unauthorized dyers or caps that stink because they have not been properly fulled, "in deceit of the commonalty."[65] Professions also express concerns about the health of the community (of which they are a part) in worries about unregulated and unscrupulous merchants smuggling goods in and out of London, as when the cappers explain that shoddy caps are not made by them, but smuggled into the city by foreign merchants, "to the no small deception of the whole people of the realm and the manifest hurt of the aforesaid cappers."[66] The few unscrupulous, then, be they noncitizens or entire professions, were accused of harming the community, which was made up of the guild itself united with all honest people. The alleged unscrupulous thus become excluded from the community that has been harmed by dint of having harmed it.

This stance of the guild and larger community together, united in their "common" interests against the ignorant and fraudulent, is one that appealed to guilds but made jurists suspicious. Jurists on the whole were not necessarily adverse to the idea of craft guilds. Following Gratian's advice to turn to Roman law when canon law did not provide explicit guidance, they tended to consider medieval craft guilds as variations on the *collegium*, the Roman law designation for a formal group of associates.[67]

According to Justinian's *Digest,* craft workers (with a very few exceptions) could only form such a group by permission of the senate or emperor.[68] Medieval jurists got around this problem by following the lead of Bassianus, who in the late twelfth century wrote that every association is permissible that has as its purpose the protection of the justice of each of its members.[69] In the thirteenth century Hugolinus (d. post 1233), professor of Roman law at Bologna, and Accursius (d. 1263), in the *Glossa ordinaria* to Roman law, reiterated this view, as did Pope Innocent IV (1243–54), a student of both Roman and canon law and a law professor at Bologna before his ecclesiastical career.[70] Innocent was even more specific on the permissibility of craft guilds. Craftsmen, he wrote, may "set up a college, providing they do so for some just cause, for example to defend their own and others' *justitia,* to prevent fraud in their profession and for similar reasons."[71] A lot hinges on the way we translate *justitia*. We can understand it as "rights" (craftsmen may set up a college to defend their own rights), in which case London guild ordinances repeat the reasons the lawyers give for sanctioning guilds, providing explicit cases in which members believe that their rights, both individual and corporate, had been violated because they were not properly formed in an assembly, while at the same time self-reflexively granting themselves the rights that the behavior to which they object violates. We could also, however, understand *justitia* as "justice" (craftsmen may set up a college to defend their own justice), which would return us to the problem of community raised by the writing about the "common good," because justice is, for medieval writers, a relational virtue.[72] To translate *justitia* as justice therefore begs the question of justice between whom.

Sellers versus Buyers

The matter becomes more complicated, however, because not all lawyers agreed with Bassianus and Innocent IV. The most significant dissenting opinion was that of Bartolus (1313–57), the most famous late medieval commentator on Roman law. Bartolus argued that craft guilds did not have the right to restrict the number of people who could practice any given trade: the guilds may not, he wrote, make "a law by which another is prejudiced, as for instance if they made a law that only certain persons and not others can exercise that craft."[73] The important point here is not that London guilds were, by virtue of their selective apprenticeship system, in continual violation of this position (true though this may be), but that it clearly recognizes that the interest of guild members was often in direct competition with the interest of nonmembers. Furthermore, it is a competition that the larger community does not always stand to win. The point is illustrated by the case of the weavers at the beginning of the fourteenth century. In 1300 and again in 1321 the weavers were accused of trying to stimulate demand for English cloth artificially by restricting membership and impounding looms of some members found guilty of theft. Although most guilds restricted membership, the weavers' actions were unusual in their scope and effects. The number of looms in operation apparently fell from around three hundred in 1290 to around eighty in 1300. By destroying looms, however, the weavers aroused great indignation and stimulated new foreign competition. The city juries that heard charges against the London weavers condemned many of their practices as outside the limits of acceptable craft regulation, calling them "of new made and not of old used."[74]

In restricting new membership and impounding looms the weavers exhibited a solidarity as understandable as it was futile, trying to protect themselves against changes they could not stop. Their actions showed clearly the way communities compete by putting the guild members' own interests ahead of their buyers and therefore creating (or trying to maintain) bonds among craftsmen rather than between an individual weaver and his or her trading partner. The city's findings against the weavers' claims of their right to these practices demonstrates an awareness of the harm that might come to the larger economic community if the smaller community of weavers had its way in protecting itself.

The ways in which communities of craftsmen could work together against, rather than as part of, a community that included buyers also took far more mundane forms that come to light in various accusations of endemic cheating. Bakers were particularly prone to such charges, perhaps an unsurprising fact given the common nature of the product they sold (most people ate bread, even if they did without vessels of silver and gold) and the potentially disastrous effects of a bad product (having dye run down your head in the rain from a bad cap might have been a nuisance, but it was as nothing compared to being poisoned).[75] In some cases the bakers seem not to have had great concern for the condition of the bread they sold, being charged, for example, with offering "putrid" bread that would have been "poisonous" to eat.[76] Most often, however, they were accused of intentionally selling bread deficient in weight.[77] Such accusations appear repeatedly, sometimes taking even more devious turns, as in the case of Robert Porter who, knowing that the bread was underweight, inserted a piece of iron into the loaf.[78] Although there is no indication that bakers on the whole were in the habit of adding iron to bread, a more frequent tactic seems to have been making loaves of deficient weight and then hiding until the bread was cold and therefore could not be properly weighed. A charge from 1331 declares that "the bakers of this city do withdraw themselves from the same, and hide in the mills and elsewhere in the foreign, to escape the punishment which they ought to have for their false loaves . . . to the great damage and in deceit of all the people."[79] Five years later the mayor and aldermen, "for the common advantage of those dwelling within the city," took it upon themselves to regulate what they saw as an unacceptable state of affairs:

> In these days the bakers of the city . . . were following their calling stealthily, like foxes, that so they might not be found by the officers of the said City, in case it should so happen that default in their loaves were found. Wherefore, . . . for promoting the common advantage . . . when the bread of any baker in the city . . . should be taken by the officers of the City, and found hot, the

baker aforesaid being *non inventus* or lying in concealment, such bread should be carried unto the Chamber of the Guildhall, and there ... be weighed.

The weight was then to be recorded, so that the penalty that would have been assessed had the baker been found would be assessed whenever he turned up, "no regard being had to the intervening lapse of time or the fact of the said bread having become dry in the interval."[80] The rules are remarkable in a number of ways. First, there is the image of bakers moving about "stealthily like foxes," not because their bread is necessarily deficient in weight, but on the chance that it might be, as though sneaking around the city and lying in concealment were easier than weighing bread as it was made. Next there is the assertion of how universal this practice had become: this is not a charge against one or two people (like the accusation of adding iron to loaves), but claims to describe the way "the bakers of the city" practice their trade "in these days." Finally, there is the solution, which knows all too well the way these bakers wiggle out of charges by waiting until the bread is dry and then explaining that it naturally weighs less than it did when it retained moisture. The mayor and aldermen, here, seem determined to close this loophole that had clearly been used before.

The community also fractured into the opposing interests of buyers and sellers in more standard ways than hiding from one another stealthily like foxes. In 1339 a group of carpenters was found to have kept wages artificially high by "intimidat[ing] men from taking work for less than 6*d.* a day and an after-dinner drink."[81] In 1344 the pouch-maker Robert de Storteford got into trouble when he found that he was unable to sell his goods at a price as high as that he had sworn to uphold. The other pouch-makers charged him with perjury, which led him to complain before the city, which in turn resulted in the pouch-makers being charged with illegally fixing prices.[82] Although not typically so drawn out, similar charges of price fixing were not unusual.[83] There were also standard accusations of simple cheating, as when Thomas Lanleye and others, "contriving how to deceive the common people," sold inferior goods as silver, or when a tapestry was found to have been made "of linen and thread beneath, but covered with wool above, in deceit of the people."[84] Sometimes the cheating was not simple at all, but quite elaborate, as when a large number of bakers were found to have had tables, called "moldingbordes," specially made so that they had secret holes that opened and closed "after the manner of a mouse-trap." When people brought their bread to be baked, the dough was put upon the table, while someone from the baker's household was "sitting in secret beneath such table; which servant, so seated beneath the hole, and carefully opening it, piecemeal and bit by bit craftily withdrew some of the dough aforesaid, frequently collecting great quantities from such dough, falsely, wickedly, and maliciously."[85] The accusation of malice clearly delineates two groups and their opposing interests: the bakers, although "false" to the people from whom they ingenuously stole dough, showed malice only to those who brought their dough to be baked, not to other members of their own household and not to other bakers who had their own ovens.

In all of these cases, the trade does not work to the advantage of the community, as accounts of trade predict. The challenge these cases pose to accounts of trade, however, is not that a person who is cheated does not benefit from trade. Not only is this unsurprising, it is expected, and expected to such an extent that, as we have seen, fraud invalidates trade. The challenge that these cases pose to trade instead lies in the ubiquity of the charges. If a single baker puts iron in his loaves, that person can be punished by the city. Buyers of bread may also decline to trade with him again. But if all bakers underweigh their bread and then hide "stealthily like foxes," or have tables designed to steal dough, then either fraud becomes a normal part of trade or trading for bread cannot be considered trade at all. The widespread nature of these charges challenges the picture that accounts of trade draw about how any trade takes place.

Although the bakers may have acted "wickedly," it did not take any particular malice or mendacity for the idea of a larger community to fracture as allegiance to the smaller community of the craft took precedence over allegiance to the larger commonalty, as the case of the weavers who impounded looms shows. In part, such allegiance was written into guild ordinances. The carpenters' ordinances, for example, stress that members must assist sick fellow members and their widows and that members should help any fellow members fallen upon hard times. They also highlight the importance of good works like charitable donations.[86] The whittawyers' (dressers of white leather) ordinances make similar provisions.[87] The particular interest in helping other guild members was not, however, always without consequences for the larger community. A shoemaker, for example, who admitted to "beating a stranger who asked too much for the price of a cup" as well as to abusing the alderman who requested that he desist was released with no penalty when others of his craft intervened.[88]

The practice of calling on members of a craft to judge the work of a fellow member when it was deemed substandard also made room for members to support one another against the larger community, as when a cook was charged with selling veal "which, when it came to the table, was found to be hashed up, stinking, and abominable to the human race." The five cooks to whom the case was submitted nevertheless claimed "on oath that the meat was good."[89] Although there may well have been nothing wrong with the meat, the prospect of submitting "stinking and abominable" food to other cooks for judgment raises the possibility of fraternal support taking precedence over public health. The image of Chaucer's cook, with his gangrenous ulcer that is revealed to us in uncomfortable narratorial proximity to his excellent blanchmange, here provides no comfort.[90]

Guild Members versus Fellow Members

The communities of fellow practitioners of a single craft are not the ones accounts of trade primarily envisage as the beneficiaries of exchange. Yet even these did not remain whole and did not have necessarily compatible interests. If the practice of guilds policing their members seems sometimes to pit guilds against the larger community, it also could create pressure within the guild community itself. In some cases guilds passed laws that gave members a vested interest in condemning fellow members. Fishmongers, for example, declared in their statutes that any member who finds another "going beyond the boundaries" "shall himself" take half the fish, while the other half is confiscated.[91] The fishmongers thus had a real economic incentive for telling on each other. A similar incentive was given for nets that were found to be too small (if holes were too small fish that should have been left in the water were instead caught). There does not seem to have been a mechanism for spot-checking nets; the system relied on the fishermen themselves. One case shows the challenge taken up with great enthusiasm when some eight fishmongers were accused at once of using illegal nets.[92] In the end four nets were found legal and returned to the fishermen with their catch, while four were found illegal and burned. The ratio (half right, not bad), makes it seem plausible that at least some accusers were guessing or settling old scores.

Even without an economic interest in acting against fellow members, the system by which guild members appealed to other members as judges when their work was called into question also divided members of the same guild. Allowing craft guild members jurisdiction over questions having to do with the craft was justified by custom and by Roman law, which said that craftsmen were subject to special judges in public as well as private suits.[93] In practice this meant that "reputable" members of the guild were asked to judge fellow members against whom complaint had been brought, as when "Henry de Passelewe, cook, was attached to make answer to the Commonalty of the City of London, and to Henry Pecche," who charged that he had "bought of the aforesaid Henry de Passelewe, cook . . . for himself and his two companions, two capons baked in a pastie, that one of the two capons was putrid and stinking." Passelewe denied the charges, and "said that at the time when he sold the same the said capons were good, and he requested that examination might be made thereof by men of his trade.

Precept was given to the sergeant to summon eight or six good and trusty men of the trade aforesaid." Eight reputable cooks were brought in and sworn, with their names and provenances recorded. The cook, we can only assume, hoped that his fellow members would help him out of the accusation. If this was indeed his hope, he was disappointed, since the eight "said upon their oath that the said capon at the time of sale thereof was stinking and rotten and baneful to the health of man."[94] It is difficult to know whether these strong words come from the eight cooks or the secretary, but Henry de Passelewe was sentenced to the pillory, with the stinking capon carried before him on his way. The case shows that although Henry de Passelewe might have had an idea, or maybe just a hope, of the community that could arise among common members of a craft, the eight reputable cooks had a very different notion. They chose to protect the larger community, or perhaps more of their fellow cooks, by trying to maintain their common reputation. The same choice was made over and over again, by cordwainers, by skinners, by pouch-makers, by goldsmiths, and others.[95] In 1369 a group of fullers even complained that examining cloths kept them so busy that they could not both keep up with the examinations and "attend to their trade as they ought to do."[96] To whatever extent the members who judged believed it was incumbent upon them to uphold the standards of their craft, they saw that their responsibility was to the abstract standards of the profession rather than to the support of every individual member. Individual members were thus fined and shamed (usually made to stand on the pillory with the offending item before them), singled out from the guild to which they belonged.

All of these examples show communities whose members are at odds with one another: members who judge other members must decide between supporting members of their community or supporting the buyers with whom they trade. These cases also reveal the instability of what "community" might mean: what goals it has and who its members are. We see this instability in the guild ordinances' delineation and attempted conciliation of the various interests of craftsmen, consumers, and the kingdom; in the potential incompatibility of the interests of members of a craft and the people with whom they trade, articulated by some jurists and by hundreds of city regulations; and in the competing interests of members of the same craft. The notions of community they describe were not only different but incompatible.

The Closed Community: *London Lickpenny*

If a glance into the London city records about craft guilds shows their inability to agree on any notion of community that does not exclude at least some buyers or some sellers, it also presents a picture of the intricacy of London trade: three different and differently regulated groups, for example, worked on every knife a Londoner might buy. The detail and ubiquity of London trade that emerges from the records appears again in the fifteenth-century ballad *London Lickpenny,* which tells of a provincial's experience seeking legal redress in London. The speaker travels to the city, first to make a complaint before a man of law. He then goes to a judge, a variety of clerks, and Westminster before recording the other items and services on offer in London. Cooks will provide good bread, ale and wine, as well as "rybbes of befe, bothe fat and fine."[97] Others offer strawberry and cherry pies, and all kinds of spices (pepper, saffron, cloves). Still others sell cloths of every variety: lawn, Paris thread, and umple; drapers offer still more cloths, there is more food for sale, as well as pewter pots, not one or two but so many that they "clatteryd on a heape" (91). Musicians ply their trade, some playing and some singing, taverners offer more drink, bargemen offer transportation across the water, and even the speaker's own hood, stolen in the second stanza, appears for sale.

In the ballad, then, London appears in some ways just as those who wrote about the benefits of trade might hope a city would appear. It is a place where anything can be bought. The Londoner who is part of this community is not confined to English cloths, but can purchase cloths from anywhere that might suit his needs, all of which appear in the London markets. The speaker is not part of this community: "[F]or lacke of money I myght not spede," he says over and over again, in refrain to the descriptions of the services and goods on offer. Nevertheless the ballad presents a picture of the specialization and community created and enabled by trade. Although the speaker might be barred from legal advice due to his lack of money, it would be available to all of the people the speaker encounters. Any of the Londoners in the ballad could exchange his or her food or drink or cloths or pots or even musical skills for the legal help from which the speaker is excluded. In fact, just to make clear the point that the economy works by trading all of these things for other things, the first person who wants to sell goods to the speaker asks "[W]hat will ye copen or by" (53), offering to trade for as well as to sell outright his "fine felt hatts" (54) and other items. From the perspective of those who write about the benefits of trade, therefore, we might well conclude that this city is a successful community created and allowed to prosper by exchange.

From the perspective of the speaker, however, who delights in all of these goods but has access to none of them, continually reminding us that "for lake of money I might not spede," the conclusion is not so clear. From his perspective we see a side of trade that Oresme and others who write about it do not mention. It is the perspective of the person who wants to trade but is excluded from the community that trade creates. Such communities demand that you have something to exchange for what you want. If the shepherd wants grain he must give up some sheep. *London Lickpenny* portrays the plight of the person who has no sheep (or oil, or wine) to exchange. It shows a community that the person without goods to trade cannot enter.

There is another way, however, of looking at the community, based so clearly on trade, that *London Lickpenny* presents. We might say that the speaker's problem is not so much that he has no money as that he misunderstands the fact that money is merely an intermediate form through which people convert what they have into what they want; that it works as the Aristotelian place-marker once you have traded what you have but before you have cashed in for what you need or desire. Although the speaker continually bemoans his lack of money, he goes to London wearing a hood. In the first stanza he complains that he cannot give silver to the man of law because his "purs is faynt" (7). It is not until the second stanza, however, after he has made this complaint, that his hood is stolen. The hood, it turns out eleven stanzas later, not only could have been sold but in fact is being sold. The speaker, however, cannot buy it back: "for lacke of money I might not spede." Another person, in this case a thief, will turn the hood into money, whereas the speaker, when in possession of the hood, seems not to have been aware of that potential conversion. Although it is possible, therefore, to see London as a community closed to those without money, it is also possible to see it as a community closed to those who do not know how to trade. If the speaker had simply sold his hood, turning it into money when he first arrived in the city, he would have had silver for the law.

There is another way, too, of understanding this speaker and his exclusion from the community, which is that he wants to partake in its goods without offering anything in return. He asks for the man of law's help but offers nothing for this help, neither silver nor services. He similarly asks bargemen for transportation without cost. And although he regrets his inability to buy any of the goods or services on offer, he seems to have no awareness that lack of money could in any way be amended through trading his own goods or labor, despite the offer to barter as well as to sell. What he wants, in other words, is not trade at all, since what he wants partakes in none of the proportionate reciprocity that is the hallmark of exchange. His exclusion from the community, in this sense, is quite correct since he refuses to engage in the acts on which the community is based.

In drawing out these possibilities I do not mean to defend the legal system or the sale of justice. The ballad certainly does demonstrate "the simple litigant's bewilderment and sense of alienation in the face of professional indifference," as Richard Firth Green has claimed.[98] It does not, however, portray this experience with much bitterness. Instead, as Christine Chism has noted, it "paints a vivid picture of exuberant legal barter."[99] And we might remember that those who wrote about trade did not shirk the fact that lawyers had to be paid for their work: Gerald Odonis even explained that they needed to be paid quite a lot, since they were much more expensive workers than farmers, who, for a lawyer's brief, might trade grain that required a hundred times as much labor as the brief itself. *London Lickpenny* describes the exchange from the perspective of the person who will not or cannot enter into it and therefore cannot become part of its community. These two possibilities, the unwillingness to trade or the lack of goods to trade, are ones those who justified trade do not imagine. They close off the community that trade creates, although the question of just who is at fault is one that *London Lickpenny* leaves humorously open to debate.

The community posited in accounts of trade as the beneficiary of exchange seems indeed to benefit from it in *London Lickpenny*. Or at least it benefits so long as we do not identify with the excluded speaker. Accounts of trade tend not to portray such a figure. But it is not only the unworldly non-Londoner unable to trade who complicates the community so frequently mentioned in accounts of exchange. In those accounts, the community was not so much delineated as invoked. *St. Erkenwald* imagines a way first to detail who constitutes the community and then to include all of its members in the miracle story. The saint performs the miracle, one that the community he leads wishes to see performed for a person who had served the community in the past. The larger community, in their work and wondering and noise, also serves something of the role of a viewer in a painting, drawing the poem's audience into the action and directing our attention. We become, at one remove, part of the crowd about which the poet writes. The miracle story thus creates ever wider circles of inclusion.

Whereas the community becomes ever larger in *St. Erkenwald,* records of the London craft guilds present an idea of community and common good that becomes ever more narrow. The challenge to the idea of community that we find in these records is not that guilds compete with one another. Numerous buyers or sellers of similar objects are built into pictures of trade, particularly in the ways that they envision fluctuations of supply and demand. The difficulty craft guild charters and rules pose for the notion of community is that they construct the common good and the commonalty in such a way that they always exclude people whom we might, from accounts of trade or from *St. Erkenwald,* think should be part of it. The idea of the common good, invoked so frequently in craft guild documents, always comes at a price that others who should be members of the community have to pay. Sometimes the cost is borne by members of a particular trade, as when members of one craft lodge complaints and accusations against another. Sometimes it is borne by the people who trade with crafts-men, as when members of a craft set their prices artificially high. Some-times the community of fellow guild members is broken, as when fishmongers tell on each other for having nets with holes too small, or when cooks uphold charges against a fellow cook. All of these cases reveal ways in which the common good is not common, not because people who trade compete, but because their interests are fundamentally incompatible.

All of these cases reveal too a potential for fraud or ignorance contained in every trade that complicates the insistence we find in writing on trade that fraud or ignorance invalidates exchange. The city may try its best to cut down on such cases: bakers with their moldingboards are punished, and goldsmiths are supposed to police cutlers, and cappers try to keep their eyes on dyers so that people's heads will not turn colors from caps they wear in the rain. But in the difficulty of remedy and the prevalence of asserted or potential deception, we see a picture in which many—maybe even most—exchanges in a community built on commerce may not be trade at all, if we disallow deception and ignorance. Acts of trade that are supposed to bind and aid the community often work in these documents to divide it, or to create relationships through trade that are more parasit-ical than symbiotic.

London Lickpenny shows that even this unhelpfulness toward fellow traders, whether those of the same craft or those who trade for the goods a craftsman makes, may be a sign of belonging to a community that not all can enter. The speaker is excluded from the community because he has nothing to trade. Although we may, as I suggested, view this as the speaker's own fault or limitation in not realizing how trade works or in being un-willing to enter into trade, the first person voice of the ballad invites us to see the situation from the speaker's point of view. Where Aristotle saw ex-change as a form of justice, *London Lickpenny* posits a topsy-turvy version of that relationship in which justice can be gained only through exchange. Justice thus becomes subordinated to the act that was supposed to be gov-erned by it. The ballad's critique, however, is more gentle than a descrip-tion of it might suggest. In part, the indulgence toward this world of trade comes from the poem's good humor. In part it comes also from the possi-bility that the problem lies with the speaker rather than with the commu-nity. He declines an offer to trade and does not think to sell the hood that is later stolen from him and sold by someone else. The problem in this sense is not that the speaker has nothing to trade but that he does not un-derstand how trade works and so is unable to enter a community based upon it. On one hand, we see in the London of *London Lickpenny* the world feared by readers of the *Shipman's Tale,* a world in which everything becomes an equally proper object of exchange, justice no more or less than copper pots. On the other hand, we also see in the poem a profound misunderstanding, on the part of the speaker, of the way money should work. He thinks that he needs money for the various objects and services he desires rather than realizing, as accounts of trade would have him understand, that money stands as a marker in the process of trade, holding the place of his work or goods or time before converting them into that which he wants or needs. All of these writings complicate the idea of community by trying to specify it. Although the fiction of *St. Erkenwald* stands alongside accounts of trade in wanting to celebrate the possibility of a common good, the London craft guild records and *London Lickpenny* suggest that the common good is itself a fiction.

CONCLUSION

If we return to Ambrogio Lorenzetti's fresco of the effects of good government, we might notice that although I, like Bernardino of Siena, described it in isolation, it does not stand alone. Covering the east wall of the Sala dei Nove, it is one of three frescoes that decorate the chamber the Nine used for their meetings. The north wall is covered by an allegory of good government, while the west wall is covered by an allegory of bad government and its effects. The south wall has windows. On the left third of the allegory of good government, we see Justice, below Wisdom and above Concord, presiding over Distributive Justice and Commutative Justice, while the right two-thirds of the wall show Common Good presiding over Peace, Fortitude, Prudence, Magnanimity, Temperance, and Justice. Faith, Charity, and Hope hover above Common Good's head.[1] Below the fresco is an inscription that reads, in part, "Wherever the holy virtue [of justice] rules . . . this gives rise to every useful, necessary and delightful civil effect."[2] Although there has been some debate over whether these virtues are Aristotelian and scholastic or Roman, all agree that the inscription describes what the fresco on the effects of good government depicts, illustrating what these virtues might look like in action.[3]

The fresco of the effects of good government, so dominated by trade, does not, then, stand only as an image of what thriving civic life might be. It also illustrates what the virtues portrayed in the allegory of good government might look like in action. Trade plays a double role in bringing these personifications to life. On one level, it is the material effect of the virtues' presence: if the common good, concord, justice, and all the rest thrive, trade will inevitably result. This trade then gives rise to further prosperity and ties the various kinds of prosperity together, linking shepherd, grocer, tailor, and builder. On a second level, trade stands as a sign, telling us about the kind of place this is: a place where proportionate reciprocity flourishes, a place of prosperous people who get married in style, who harvest goods, who travel back and forth between city and country freely to exchange their surpluses for what they need. In these ways trade stands as a sign that the virtues personified on the adjoining wall are present in the city and countryside.

Considering this double role that trade plays, it is fitting that the town wall with the open gate between the city and countryside should be the central point of the picture of the effects of good government. The open gate allows trade and all of the forms of prosperity that it creates and for which it stands. On the facing wall of the Sala dei Nove, this point is made clear by what is left of the damaged fresco of the effects of bad government. Rather than depicting an open gate, the fresco shows the gate between city and countryside standing pointedly closed. Rather than depicting people who trade, the fresco shows people being robbed. The tailor, goldsmith, grocer, and teacher are all gone. Instead, the only open shop sells weapons. The hunger, destruction, and lawlessness everywhere present are thus shown in the goods for which people cannot trade and in their inability to trade. If the allegory of good government, then, suggests that peace is necessary for the common good to thrive, in both the fresco of the effects of good government and the fresco showing the effects of bad government trade stands as the illustration of the virtues peace allows.

In the preceding chapters, I have suggested that if we isolate writing about trade from other writing and other subjects, we sever the tie that trade represents in Lorenzetti's frescoes. Accounts of trade always portrayed exchange as composed of three constituent parts: value, consent, and community. Without value, the parties would never know how much of one good to trade for another. Without consent, the trade would not take place. The fact of the first two led to the kind of communal benefits we see in Lorenzetti's fresco. On an individual basis, trade allows each person to exchange what he or she values less for what he or she values more. On a larger scale, it allows those in regions of scarcity to gain what they lack. In all cases, it creates a community between buyer and seller based on the mutual benefit that accrues to both. Accounts of trade suggest that the presence of these elements defines trade: if the parties cannot value independently, or do not agree, or do not benefit, then somehow what happened was a result of coercion, or fraud, or force, any of which invalidated an exchange. These elements are therefore not only straightforward in descriptions of trade, they must be straightforward if they are not to cast doubt on the activity as a whole.

Placing the elements of trade back into their larger context and away from our notion of "economics," showing their ties to other areas of medieval life, as Lorenzetti's fresco does and as I have sought to do, reveals a picture of trade that does not emerge from accounts of exchange. For medieval Christian writers, the kind of valuation that occurred in trade depended on a division between true or natural value, on one hand, and economic value, on the other. Economic value, as Augustine explained, was the way people did value rather than the way they should value. One consequence of this distinction was the inability to establish a way to determine economic value. In writing on value and the just price we see authors create a multitude of ways to justify economic valuation after it has occurred. But we can find no suggestions for the way that economic valuation should occur, no guidance for how any person might determine the value of what she wants to trade. For Augustine, another consequence of the distinction between natural and economic value was the similarity between need and desire: the decisions to value food more than a mouse and a jewel more than a servant were equally decisions made on grounds of economic rather than natural value since they equally placed the inanimate above the animate and thus equally reversed the natural scale of valuation. Later accounts of trade, however, tend to concentrate on need while ignoring desire. This concentration is not a further refinement of Augustine's categories; rather, it is an implicit refusal of them, since Augustine's point is the gulf between the way we value and the way God values. The way in which desire largely disappears from later accounts of trade represents not only a way of understanding that these accounts were not descriptive but also a way of understanding why trade might continue to prove theoretically upsetting for people, even as it became a necessary part of life.

Chaucer's *Shipman's Tale* and Henryson's "The Cock and the Jasp" both suggest the connection between need and desire that drops out of most contemporaneous accounts of trade. Chaucer's tale teases us by suggesting a world in which not just any need but also any desire might be converted into and satisfied by money. Henryson's fable concludes by reprimanding the rooster who so carefully distinguished between need and desire because he did not realize that both alike stood in opposition to nonphysical wisdom. The imaginative literature has other ways, too, of thinking through difficulties with the kind of valuation we see in accounts of trade. The *Shipman's Tale* suggests that the line we try to draw between "natural" and "economic" human relations is illusory; the *Franklin's Tale* suggests that natural or absolute values are fragile and can fall easily in the face of far more stable economic values; and "The Cock and the Jasp" posits our own inability to distinguish between the two forms of value. None answers the question left unanswered by theological and legal writing on price and value of how we ought to determine economic value. Each, however, freed from the task authors on price and value set themselves of explaining economic value, questions the kinds of reasoned explanations those authors provide and the assumptions on which their writing is based.

Searching out considerations of consent takes us away from writing about trade, although it still leaves us comfortably within Lorenzetti's depiction of the common good in action. Writing about trade asserts that lack of consent invalidates trade and then somewhat tautologically assumes that trade itself stands as a sign of consent in the absence of clear indications to the contrary. Those interested in defining marriage, however, could not content themselves with the same conclusion. Once they came to define marriage as the consent of the two parties, they needed a more precise way to determine consent than clear force or fraud. They turned first to language. Although their considerations of consent sometimes seem abstruse ("I take you as my spouse" and "I will have you as my spouse" created a marriage but "I will take you as my spouse" did not), we have seen that their conclusions were widely known, understood, and used in fourteenth- and fifteenth-century England. In the commonplace act of marriage, people considered the status of consent in far more detail than scholastic authors did in their accounts of trade. Legal writers on marriage formation also worried about those instances in which the language of consent did not stand as a sign of the interior consent it was supposed to indicate. In these cases they turned to the fiction of the constant man. This fiction provided not a rule but a way of allowing for the failure of the usual rules.

Chaucer's *Physician's Tale* further complicates the way we understand consent by positing a case in which consent does not represent the best interest of the person who consented. In this way Chaucer's story of Virginia challenges the assumption we find in accounts of trade that people will not consent unless they will benefit. It also creates a situation about which jurists cannot ask judges to ponder in marriage cases: the person who agrees but should not have because it will cause her harm (or, in Virginia's case, death). Thomas Aquinas's writing on marriage formation poses a further challenge to both the straightforward requirement of consent we find in accounts of trade and the more detailed attempts to determine consent that we find in legal writing on marriage. For Aquinas, the division between inward consent and outward signs of that consent can never be certainly judged by any person other than the one who gives those signs and God. The jurists needed to determine consent in order to administer the law. For Aquinas, however, any determination of another person's consent was always potentially wrong. The darkness of Aquinas's suggestion that no one can ever know truly whether or not he or she is married is tempered for him by the dual knowledge first that we can all know whether or not our own outward signs of consent are true, and second that God knows the truth of our signs of consent, even if we cannot know the truth about each other.

Accounts of trade posit a general good to the community, but the miracle story of *St. Erkenwald* imagines far more specifically what it might mean for the entire community to benefit. It first details the members of the community and then shows how the saint's miracle brings joy to all and harm to none while widening the community itself to allow the inclusion of the virtuous pagan judge who dispensed justice to a past generation of Londoners. If a miracle allows the entire community to benefit, however, looking into the records of the London craft guilds shows the unlikelihood that the same result can be achieved through trade. Not only do these records show competition among sellers and between buyers and sellers, they show that the "common" good comes always at the price of some members of the community. Sometimes this takes the form of members of one trade, like the drapers, asserting that the "common" good lies with them and the "community" but not with the dyers, who will be harmed by the drapers' proposal. At other times it takes the form of sellers who care about their own benefit to the exclusion of those to whom they sell. At other times it takes the form of members of a guild choosing to support a buyer to the harm of the fellow member who sold to him or her. In each case it suggests that the idea of common benefit so often asserted in accounts of trade may be a fantasy. At the same time, in the series of cases of fraud and the seemingly useless series of punishments, the records suggest that fraud, which was supposed to invalidate a trade, was actually a part of many trades, and potentially a part of all. This possibility in itself, by making the valuation of one party unimportant and making her consent untrue, should have been enough to counter the communal benefits that accounts of trade championed. The ballad *London Lickpenny* presents a further challenge to the idea of community by depicting the ways in which anyone who does not possess goods to trade is excluded from a community built upon it.

If returning value, consent, and community from the isolation of accounts of trade back into larger conversations about them allows us to see that these accounts were argumentative and selective rather than descriptive, it also has another benefit. In understanding that these accounts were not realistic descriptions of life in the market, it places them back into the great tradition of medieval analysis of which they are a part. Medieval analysis often worked by isolating problems and thinking them through separately from their "real life" context in order better to understand them and eventually better to understand the context from which they are taken. We might think here of scholastic methodology, which drew ever finer distinctions so that it could examine one issue at a time. Or we might think of Elizabeth Fowler's recent elucidation of the way medieval authors used the "social person," or abstract and conventional representation of a person (monk or wife or merchant, for example), not to depict individuals but to understand topoi many individuals inhabit, even as they inhabit other topoi as well.[4] Or we might think of allegory itself and the way it shuns mimesis, valuing instead analysis and clarity.

Some have admired Lorenzetti's fresco of the effects of good government for the perspective and foreshortening with which it shows the wall that divides city and country, and many have noted its skillful details and realistic touches (the city architecture is recognizably Sienese, there is a label naming the water at the far right "Talamone," a Sienese port, and the striped bell tower of the cathedral at the far left is distinctively Siena's).[5] No one, however, would argue that the picture itself is a realistic picture of Siena, or indeed any town or countryside. Instead, as we have seen, the fresco presents a vision of what the personified virtues on the adjoining wall might look like in action. It is also allegorical in itself. The countryside produces both summer and winter crops; people perform agricultural tasks appropriate to both spring and fall; and the dancers, as I have noted, are not only disproportionate in scale to the rest of the fresco, they appear at a time when dancing was not allowed in the streets of Siena. We recognize, however, that Lorenzetti's failure to portray Siena as it really was, as he saw it on the streets outside of the Sala dei Nove every day, is not a failure at all. Rather, it is a success in illustrating the forms those personified virtues might take in a Sienese setting.

This too, I believe, is the way we must understand accounts of trade. Rather than lauding them for a mimesis they can never achieve, we must understand them as part of a larger tradition of medieval representation and analysis. This tradition does not seek to rival Dickens or Balzac, let alone the photograph or documentary. Neither positive nor negative depictions of trade show the world as it was, although both contain elements of reality: some merchants doubtlessly were greedy, as those who condemned trade charged, just as trade doubtlessly did help many individuals and communities, as those who supported it asserted. Those who wrote accounts of trade did not look around them, realize how the market actually worked, and then run to jot it down. Instead, like Lorenzetti, they thought about how trade should work and what, at its best, it might look like.

ABBREVIATIONS

CCSL   *Corpus Christianorum series Latina.* Turnhout: Brepols, 1953–.

Dig.   *The Digest of Justinian.* Latin text ed. Theodor Mommsen with the aid of Paul Krueger. English trans. Alan Watson. 4 vols. Philadelphia: University of Pennsylvania Press, 1985.

Inst.   *Justinian's Institutes.* Ed. Paul Krueger. Trans. Peter Birks and Grant McLeod. Ithaca: Cornell University Press, 1987.

PL   *Patrologiae Latinae cursus completus.* Ed. Jacques-Paul Migne. 221 vols. Paris, 1844–55.

X   *Decretales Gregorii IX (Liber extra).* In *Corpus iuris canonici.* Ed. Emil Friedberg. 2 vols. Leipzig: Tauchnitz, 1879–81. Repr. Union, N.J.: Lawbook Exchange, 2000. 2:cols. 1–928.

NOTES

Introduction

1. Those who have performed such work include De Roover, "Concept of the Just Price," 418–34; Baldwin, *Medieval Theories;* De Roover, *Two Great Economic Thinkers;* Baldwin, *Masters, Princes, and Merchants,* 1:261–311; Gordon, *Economic Analysis,* 122–235; Langholm, *Price and Value;* Langholm, *Economics;* Langholm, *Legacy of Scholasticism;* and Wood, *Medieval Economic Thought.*

2. The problem of understanding the writings of Thomas Aquinas as representative of medieval thought has been quite correctly pointed out. This particular explanation, however, is quite typical, as will become apparent.

3. Thomas Aquinas, *Commentaria in X libros ethicorum* 5.9, to Aristotle 5.5 (*Opera omnia* [Parma ed.], 21:172). Translation from Thomas Aquinas, *Commentary on Aristotle's* Nicomachean Ethics, 310.

4. Biller, *Measure of Multitude,* 296–382.

5. Newman, *God and the Goddesses,* 291–327; Freedman, *Images of the Medieval Peasant,* 133–73.

6. Sombart, "Capitalism," 195–208; Nussbaum, *Economic Institutions of Modern Europe,* 17–57. This view has persisted among nonmedievalist specialists. See, for example, Rima, *Development of Economic Analysis,* 27; Roth, *Origin of Economic Ideas,* 29–30 (part of a chapter called "The Preposterous Origins"). This sense of the lack of medieval economic thought has also resulted in many accounts of the history of economic thought that go back only as far as mercantilism (or sometimes only to Adam Smith). See, for example, Hunt, *History of Economic Thought;* Blaug, *History of Economic Thought;* and Oser and Bruce, *Evolution of Economic Thought.*

7. Langholm, *Legacy of Scholasticism,* 1–11, 139–200; Langholm, *Economics,* 3–8, 85, 333–37, 360–61; De Roover, *Two Great Economic Thinkers,* 40–42.

8. On usury, the standard studies remain Noonan, *Scholastic Analysis of Usury,* and Nelson, *Idea of Usury.* Medieval writers sometimes discuss legitimate trade in descriptions of usury in order to distinguish one from the other, explaining why they are different. See, for example, Giles of Lessines, *De usuris,* 413–36, and Alexander of Alessandria, *Traité de morale économique.* On the just price, Baldwin, *Medieval Theories,* has not been superseded.

9. On the sophistication of actual monetary policies, for example, see Mate, "Monetary Policies in England," 37, 44–46, 53–59; Spufford, *Money and Its Use,* 109–263; Mayhew, "Modeling Medieval Monetisation," 55–77; and Spufford, *Power and Profit,* 12–59.

10. Kaye, *Economy and Nature*, 11. See also Kaye, *Economy and Nature*, 2, 5–8, 11–12, 14, 29–30, 36, 40, 50, 57, 94; Wood, *Medieval Economic Thought*, 206–9.

11. Kaye, *Economy and Nature*, 11; Wood, *Medieval Economic Thought*, 206–9.

12. See, for example, Gilchrist, *Church and Economic Activity*, 23–47; Little, *Religious Poverty and the Profit Economy*, 3–41; Bolton, *Medieval English Economy*, 331–33; Le Goff, *Time, Work, and Culture*, 107–21; Wood, *Medieval Economic Thought*, 2–6.

13. I think particularly of poems such as the *Libelle of Englyshe Polycye*, which talks about the national balance of trade; *Winner and Waster*, which puts forward arguments for both saving and spending; Thomas Hoccleve's work, which mentions money and counterfeit a number of times; Geoffrey Chaucer's *Complaint of Chaucer to His Purse*, which regrets how empty it is; and *Sir Launfal*, a romance about a knight with a cash-flow problem. For discussions of the "economic" components of these texts see Scattergood, *"Libelle of Englyshe Polycye"*; Trigg, "Rhetoric of Excess in *Winner and Waster*"; Roney, *"Winner and Waster*'s 'Wyse Wordes,'"; Scattergood, *"Winner and Waster* and the Mid-Fourteenth-Century Economy"; Meyer-Lee, "Hoccleve and the Apprehension of Money"; Strohm, *England's Empty Throne*, 128–52; Strohm, *Hochon's Arrow*, 75–94; Smith, *Arts of Possession*, 72–107, 154–87.

14. Barron, "London 1300–1540," 400.

15. On the fresco in general, see Frugoni, *Pietro and Ambrogio Lorenzetti*, 73–78; Starn, *Ambrogio Lorenzetti*, 7–23, 68–87; Norman, *Painting in Late Medieval and Renaissance Siena*, 100–103. On the fresco's "pictorial peculiarities," see Baxandall, "Art, Society, and the Bouguer Principle." In the foreground of the city there is a somewhat incongruous group of dancers. Because they are disproportionately large and because dancing was not allowed on the streets of Siena when Lorenzetti painted the mural, they have been understood as allegorical. Most argue that they are an allegory of harmony. Quentin Skinner contends instead that they represent "the joy we naturally feel at the rule of justice and the resulting attainment of peace." See Skinner, "Ambrogio Lorenzetti's *Buon Governo* Frescoes," 26, and more generally Skinner, *Visions of Politics*, 2:103–17.

16. Debby, "Ambrogio Lorenzetti's Frescoes in Saint Bernardino's Siena Sermons," 275; trans.: 276 n. 7.

1. The Story of Trade

1. Oresme, *De moneta*, ed. and trans. Johnson, 4. All references are to this edition.

2. See, for example, Kaye, *Economy and Nature*, 37–55; Langholm, *Price and Value;* and Langholm, *Wealth and Money.*

3. Tertullian, *De idololatria* (*CCSL*, 2:1110); quoted in Baldwin, *Medieval Theories*, 14. See also Gilchrist, *Church and Economic Activity*, 51.

4. Ambrose, *De officiis ministrorum*, 3.9 (*CCSL*, 15:174).

5. Acts 5:1–10.

6. Ambrose, *De officiis ministrorum*, 3.6 (*CCSL*, 15:168–69); Baldwin, *Medieval Theories*, 14–15.

7. Augustine, *Enarrationes in Psalmos*, 33.14 (*CCSL*, 38:291). See also Gilchrist, *Church and Economic Activity*, 51.

8. Cassiodorus, *Expositio psalmorum*, 70.15 (*CCSL*, 97:635); translation from Baldwin, *Medieval Theories*, 14.

9. For the collections preceding the *Decretum*, see Baldwin, *Medieval Theories*, 34, and Little, *Religious Poverty and the Profit Economy*, 38; Gratian, *Decretum*, D. 5 c. 2 (*Corpus iuris canonici*, 1:col. 1240).

10. Matthew 21:12. All quotations are from the *Douay Rheims Holy Bible*. For this episode see also Mark 11:15, Luke 19:45, and John 2:14–16. Cassiodorus's questions

are in Gratian, *Decretum*, D. 88 c. 13 (*Corpus iuris canonici*, 1:col. 310). On the dates when these texts were incorporated into the *Decretum*, see Baldwin, *Medieval Theories*, 14, and Winroth, *Making of Gratian's Decretum*, 198.

11. Gratian, *Decretum*, D. 88 c. 11 (*Corpus iuris canonici*, 1:col. 308). Here and throughout I am the translator of Latin texts when no translator is specified. On this passage see also Little, *Religious Poverty and the Profit Economy*, 38; Baldwin, *Medieval Theories*, 38; Langholm, *Economics*, 102–3; Gilchrist, *Church and Economic Activity*, 50–51.

12. Peter Lombard, *Sententiae*, 4.16.2 (*PL*, 192:col. 878).

13. See, for example, Pirenne, *Histoire économique de l'Occident médiéval*, 169; Gilchrist, *Church and Economic Activity*, 49–58; Little, *Religious Poverty and the Profit Economy*, 38–41; *Fasciculus Morum*, 155, 165, 343–47, 373, 437, 459, 557, 697; *An Alphabet of Tales*, 328–30, 372–73; Owst, *Literature and Pulpit in Medieval England*, 95–96, 171–72, 293, 352–61.

14. Gratian, *Decretum*, D. 88 c. 12 (*Corpus iuris canonici*, 1:cols. 309–10).

15. John Baldwin makes this argument: *Medieval Theories*, 38–39.

16. See, for example, Gilchrist, *Church and Economic Activity*, 23–47; Little, *Religious Poverty and the Profit Economy*, 3–41; Bolton, *Medieval English Economy*, 331–33; Le Goff, *Time, Work, and Culture*, 107–21; Wood, *Medieval Economic Thought*, 2–6.

17. Thomas of Chobham, *Summa confessorum*, 301.

18. Roland of Cremona, *Summae*, question 251 (705).

19. Raymond of Peñafort, *Summa*, 244–47.

20. On Conrad of Höxter, the *Summa fratris Conradi*, and its influence on Raymond's *Summa*, see Langholm, *Economics*, 108–11.

21. William of Rennes, *Glossa*, to *recto fine*, in Raymond of Peñafort, *Summa*, 248. In the edition, this gloss is erroneously ascribed to John of Freiburg.

22. Langholm, *Economics*, 114–15, notes that all follow William's gloss almost verbatim.

23. Alexander of Hales, *Summa theologica*, 4:723–24.

24. Alexander of Hales, *Summa theologica*, 4:722.

25. Alexander of Hales, *Summa theologica*, 4:722.

26. Aristotle, *Politics*, 1256a–b. Citations will be to the version printed in the *Aristoteles Latinus*, 29.1. Here, see *Aristoteles Latinus*, 29.1:12–15.

27. Aristotle, *Politics*, 1256b (*Aristoteles Latinus*, 29.1:14). English translation from Aristotle, *The Politics*, trans. Lord, 45–46.

28. Aristotle, *Politics*, 1257a (*Aristoteles Latinus*, 29.1:15; Lord trans., 46).

29. Aristotle, *Politics*, 1252b (*Aristoteles Latinus*, 29.1:5; Lord trans., 37).

30. I signify the English terms as "commerce" and "business" because this is how Lord translates them. The terms in Greek, like the English ones Lord uses, are roughly synonymous. The important point, clearly made in the medieval Latin translations, is that a distinction be made between "good" and "bad" trade. There were two Latin translations of the *Politics* current in the later middle ages. The incomplete version comprising the first three books is provisionally attributed to William of Moerbeke and is the version printed in the *Aristoteles Latinus*. In this version the Greek words are simply transliterated as "crimatisticam" and "kapelica." There is also a complete Latin translation (reprinted in the Leonine edition of Thomas Aquinas's works) that is positively attributed to William of Moerbeke in three manuscripts. The complete version translates *kapêlikê*, or trade by acquisition, as "campsoria," which Latin readers would have understood as money-changing, already suspect. This translation suggested great tolerance for commercial activity, with a caveat against love of money, which makes men confuse economic means with economic ends. The point in either version remains that natural exchange gives rise to money, which can be used either well or ill. See Aristotle, *Politics*, 1257a (*Aristoteles Latinus* 29.1:15; *Politics*, trans. Lord, 46; Thomas Aquinas,

Opera omnia [Leonine ed.], 48:44, 102–3). On the medieval Latin translations of these terms, see Langholm, *Economics*, 178.

31. Aristotle, *Politics*, 1257a (*Aristoteles Latinus*, 29.1:15; Lord trans., 46).

32. Aristotle, *Politics*, 1257a (*Aristoteles Latinus*, 29.1:16; Lord trans., 47).

33. This explanation of the function of money was common by the late thirteenth century: see Kaye, *Economy and Nature*, 137–46, 170–99.

34. Aristotle, *Politics*, 1257b (*Aristoteles Latinus*, 29.1:16; Lord trans., 47).

35. Aristotle, *Politics*, 1256b (*Aristoteles Latinus*, 29.1:14; Lord trans., 46).

36. Aristotle, *Politics*, 1257a (*Aristoteles Latinus*, 29.1:15–16; Lord trans., 47).

37. Aristotle, *Politics*, 1257b (*Aristoteles Latinus*, 29.1:16; Lord trans., 47).

38. Aristotle, *Politics*, 1257a (*Aristoteles Latinus*, 29.1:16; Lord trans., 47).

39. William of Auxerre, *Summa aurea*, 3.48.3 (3:910).

40. Aristotle, *Nicomachean Ethics*, 5.2, 1130b. Citations will be to the revised version of Robert Grosseteste's translation, which is printed in *Aristoteles Latinus* 26.1–3, fasc. 4. Here, see *Aristoteles Latinus*, 26.1–3:457. For the English translation, see *Nicomachean Ethics*, trans. and ed. Ross, 111.

41. Aristotle, *Nicomachean Ethics*, 5.3, 1131a (*Aristoteles Latinus*, 26.1–3:458; Ross trans., 112).

42. Aristotle, *Nicomachean Ethics*, 5.3, 1131a (*Aristoteles Latinus*, 26.1–3:458; Ross trans., 113).

43. Aristotle, *Nicomachean Ethics*, 5.4, 1132a (*Aristoteles Latinus*, 26.1–3:460; Ross trans., 114–15).

44. Aristotle, *Nicomachean Ethics*, 5.5, 1132b (*Aristoteles Latinus*, 26.1–3:462; Ross trans., 117–18).

45. Aristotle, *Nicomachean Ethics*, 5.5, 1132b (*Aristoteles Latinus*, 26.1–3:462; Ross trans., 118).

46. Aristotle, *Nicomachean Ethics*, 5.5, 1133a (*Aristoteles Latinus*, 26.1–3:463; Ross trans., 118–19).

47. Aristotle, *Nicomachean Ethics*, 5.5, 1133a (*Aristoteles Latinus*, 26.1–3:463; Ross trans., 119).

48. Peter of Tarentaise, *In quattuor libros sententiarum commentaria*, 309.

49. Aristotle, *Nicomachean Ethics*, 5.5, 1133a (*Aristoteles Latinus*, 26.1–3:463; Ross trans., 119).

50. Aristotle, *Nicomachean Ethics*, 5.5, 1133a (*Aristoteles Latinus*, 26.1–3:463; Ross trans., 119).

51. Aristotle, *Nicomachean Ethics*, 5.5, 1133b (*Aristoteles Latinus*, 26.1–3:464; Ross trans., 120).

52. Aristotle, *Nicomachean Ethics*, 5.5, 1133b (*Aristoteles Latinus*, 26.1–3:464; Ross trans., 121).

53. Albert the Great, *Ethica* (Second Commentary), 5.9 (*Opera omnia* [Paris ed.], 7:355).

54. Albert the Great, *Commentarii in IV sententarium*, to 4.B.46 (*Opera omnia* [Paris ed.], 29:636).

55. Henry of Ghent, *Quodlibet*, 1.40 (*Opera omnia*, 5:221).

56. Henry of Ghent, *Quodlibet*, 3, quoted in Langholm, *Economics*, 261–62.

57. Giles of Lessines, *De usuris*, 416.

58. Richard of Middleton, *Super libros sententiarum*, 33.3.4 (3:389–90). The translation here is from Langholm, *Economics*, 332–33.

59. Richard of Middleton, *Quodlibet*, 2.23.1 (*Super libros sententiarum*, 4:65); Langholm, *Economics*, 333–34.

60. Richard of Middleton, *Quodlibet*, 2.23.1 (*Super libros sententiarum*, 4:65–66); Langholm, *Economics*, 333.

61. Richard of Middleton, *Quodlibet*, 2.23.1 (*Super libros sententiarum*, 4:65–66); Langholm, *Economics*, 333–34.

62. Richard of Middleton, *Quodlibet*, 2.23.1 (*Super libros sententiarum*, 4:66); Langholm, *Economics*, 334.

63. Richard of Middleton, *Quodlibet*, 2.23.1 (*Super libros sententiarum*, 4:66); Langholm, *Economics*, 334.

64. Bonaventure, *De perfectione evangelica*, 2.3 (*Opera omnia*, 5:161).

65. Giles of Lessines, *De usuris*, 421; Peter Olivi, *Tractatus*, 266. For Walter of Bruges, see Langholm, *Economics*, 322.

66. Giles of Rome, *De ecclesiastica potestate*, 2.1 (38); translation from Giles of Rome, *On Ecclesiastical Power*, trans. Dyson, 33.

67. John Duns Scotus, *Political and Economic Philosophy*, ed. and trans. Wolter, 58 (this is a preliminary edition of question 15 of Scotus's commentary on the fourth book of Peter Lombard's *Sentences*, published in anticipation of the definitive Vatican edition of Scotus's *Opera omnia* still in progress).

68. John of Bassolis, *In quartum sententiarum opus*, 4.15 (f. 85r); Alexander of Alessandria, *Un traité de morale économique*, 126, 128; Remigio of Florence, *Contra falsos ecclesie professores*, 187; Durandus of Saint-Pourçain, *Commentariorum libri IIII*, 4.16.5 (f. 337v–338r).

69. Peter Olivi, *Tractatus*, 263, 253, 257.

70. Francis of Meyronnes, *In libros sententiarum*, 4.16 (f. 203r).

71. John of Bassolis, *In quartum sententiarum opus*, 4.15 (f. 86r); John Duns Scotus, *Political and Economic Philosophy*, 44.

72. For Gerald Odonis, see Langholm, *Economics*, 516–17.

73. Although see Guido Terreni, a Carmelite who similarly argued that an original division of property and goods was for the best, since man was a necessarily social animal and this division facilitated exchange according to mutual needs: Guido Terreni, *Ethics* commentary, 5.11 (Vat.Borgh.328, f.19r).

74. Oresme, *De moneta*, x.

75. Oresme, *De moneta*, 4–5.

76. Oresme, *De moneta*, 4.

77. Oresme, *De moneta*, 16, 35, 11, 37.

78. It is worth noting that when they wrote of money all of these authors were thinking of coined money, rather than a purely abstract measure. Gerald of Abbeville, *Quodlibet* 4, quoted in Cornet, "Les éléments historiques des IVe et VIe 'quodlibets' de Gerard d'Abbeville," 193–96; Giles of Rome, *De regimine principum*, 2.3.9 (370); for Guido Terreni, see Langholm, *Economics*, 503; for other medieval arguments about the properties money should have, see Langholm, *Wealth and Money*, 79–88.

79. Oresme, *De moneta*, 18.

80. Oresme, *De moneta*, 26.

81. Oresme, *De moneta*, 22.

82. Oresme, *De moneta*, 19.

83. This distinction raises the interesting question of whether the prince himself can commit treason. The question revolves largely around whether the guarantee is seen as a personal guarantee or as a guarantee that the prince makes because of his structural position within the state. Although Oresme's arguments would seem to indicate that it is a personal agreement (if the prince violates his word then he is a liar), he later asserts that the reason the name of the prince is put upon the coin is that the prince is structurally in the best position to guarantee it. In this case, the person of the prince could be accused of violating the word of the figure of the prince, in which case the prince could commit treason. Oresme does not, however, explicitly argue anything so extreme.

84. Oresme, *De moneta*, 24. Debasement increased royal revenue because it acted as

a tax on all existing money. The ruler would usually reduce the metal content of new coins, which meant that he could make more coins from each pound of precious metal. He could then pay a higher mint price per pound for precious metal brought to the mint to be recoined, which made it appear profitable for his subjects to bring in their old coin. He could thus phase out the old coin, which made it necessary for even those subjects unwilling to have their money reminted to do so. See Spufford, *Money and Its Use,* 289.

85. Oresme, *De moneta,* 12.

86. Oresme, *De moneta,* 42.

87. Oresme, *De moneta,* 10.

88. Oresme, *De moneta,* 30–31.

89. Oresme, *De moneta,* 16, 40.

90. Oresme, *De moneta,* 40.

91. Oresme, *De moneta,* 40.

92. Wives could leave husbands only in very specific circumstances, the most common being when there had been abuse or both had agreed to live separately. Even in such cases the parties involved could not remarry.

2. Value

1. On a generalized notion of price, see, for example, Wood, *Medieval Economic Thought,* 132–44; Bolton, *Medieval English Economy,* 331–38; for these groupings see, for example, Baldwin, *Medieval Theories,* which is still unsurpassed as an examination of the just price; for analyses on an author by author basis, see, for example, Langholm, *Economics;* Kaye, *Economy and Nature,* 56–78, 101–15.

2. Augustine, *De civitate dei,* 11.16 (*CCSL,* 49:336). For the translation, see Augustine, *City of God,* trans. Bettenson, 448.

3. Augustine, *De civitate dei,* 11.16 (*CCSL,* 49:336); *City of God,* 448.

4. The distinctions in the natural scale are all Augustine's, from *De civitate dei,* 11.16.

5. See Baldwin, *Medieval Theories;* and De Roover, "Concept of the Just Price," 418–34.

6. For the parable of the worker worthy of his hire in medieval writing see Epstein, "Theory and Practice of the Just Wage," 54–57.

7. See for example Soudek, "Aristotle's Theory of Exchange," 34–40; and Meikle, "Aristotle and Exchange Value," 197, 200–201, 210.

8. Albert the Great, *Super Ethica* (First Commentary), 5.7 (*Opera omnia* [Münster ed.], 14:346). The translation of "opus" can be problematic because Albert uses it to mean *work* and occasionally also to mean *need:* see Kaye, *Economy and Nature,* 68. It seems to me that, given the context, here we must understand it as work.

9. Albert the Great, *Ethica* (Second Commentary), 5.10 (*Opera omnia* [Paris ed.], 7:359).

10. Quoted in *MIT Dictionary of Modern Economics,* s.v. "value" (440).

11. Albert the Great, *Super Ethica* (First Commentary), 5.7 (*Opera omnia* [Münster ed.], 14:341).

12. Albert the Great, *Ethica* (Second Commentary), 5.7 (*Opera omnia* [Paris ed.], 7:353).

13. Wieland, "Reception and Interpretation of Aristotle's *Ethics,*" 660.

14. Gratian, *Decretum,* D. 10 d.p.c. 6 and C. 15 q. 3 d.p.c. 4 (*Corpus iuris canonici,* 1:col. 20, col. 752).

15. X 5.32.1 (*Corpus iuris canonici,* 2:cols. 843–84). The *Glossa ordinaria* refers readers of Gratian's comments noted above to this decretal.

16. "Res tantum valet quantum vendi potest." Dig. 9.2.33; 13.1.14; 35.2.63; 36.1.16; 47.2.52.

17. Inst. 3.23. See also Evans-Jones and MacCormack, "Obligations," 150–59.

18. It is thought that the first use of the term *laesio enormis* is by the post-glossator Cinus (1270–1333). See Baldwin, *Medieval Theories,* 18 n. 68.

19. Dig. 35.2.63. See also Dig. 13.4.3.

20. Baldwin, *Medieval Theories,* 20.

21. Dig. 35.2.63.

22. Robert of Courson, *Summa,* 10.18 (Ms. Paris, BN lat. 14524, ff. 51v–52r).

23. Thomas of Chobham, *Summa confessorum,* 301–2.

24. Thomas of Chobham, *Summa confessorum,* 302.

25. Thomas of Chobham, *Summa confessorum,* 301.

26. Albert the Great, *Ethica* (Second Commentary), 5.7 (*Opera omnia* [Paris ed.], 7:353).

27. Rufinus, *Summa decretorum,* to 14.3 (341–42); Alexander of Hales, *Summa,* 4: 725; Thomas Aquinas, *Summa,* 2-2.77.4 (*Opera omnia* [Leonine ed.], 9:154); Hostiensis, *Summa aurea,* col. 1859. For Huguccio and Guy of l'Aumône, see Baldwin, *Medieval Theories,* 41, 64–65.

28. Thomas of Chobham, *Summa confessorum,* 301; Peter Olivi, *Tractatus,* 266.

29. Guido Terreni, *Ethics* commentary, 5.9 (Vat.Borgh.328, f. 42r).

30. Rufinus, *Summa decretorum,* to 14.3 (341); Stephen of Tournai, *Summa,* to 14.3 (220, copying Rufinus); Peter Olivi, *Tractatus,* 266; Henry of Ghent, *Quodlibet,* 1.40 (*Opera omnia,* 5:227); Bernardino of Siena, *Quadragesimale de Evangelio aeterno,* sermon 33 (*Opera omnia,* 4:143). On Bernardino of Siena, who followed Olivi's analysis very closely, see also De Roover, *Two Great Economic Thinkers,* 11, which should be read in conjunction with the remarks of Langholm, *Economics,* 345.

31. Richard of Middleton, *Quodlibet,* 2.23.1 (*Super libros sententiarum,* 4:65–66).

32. Peter Olivi, *Tractatus,* 255.

33. Azo, *Summa,* to C.4.44 (col. 417); Placentinus, *Summa codicis,* to C.4.44 (176); Accursius, *Glossa ordinaria,* to Dig. 13.4.3 (1:cols. 1396–97); Peter the Chanter, *Summa de sacramentis et animae consiliis,* III (2a):416; Robert of Courson, *Summa,* 10.18 (Paris, BN lat. 14524, ff. 51v–52r); Henry of Ghent, *Quodlibet,* 1.40 (*Opera omnia,* 5:222); Giles of Lessines, *De usuris,* 421; John of Bassolis, *In quartum sententiarum opus,* 4.15 (f. 86r); Francis of Meyronnes, *In libros sententiarum,* 4.16 (f. 204r); Guido Terreni, *Ethics* commentary, 5.11 (Vat.Borgh.328, f. 42r).

34. X 5.19.6.

35. Alexander of Hales, *Summa,* 4:724; Thomas Aquinas, *Summa,* 2-2.77.4 (*Opera omnia* [Leonine ed.], 9:154); Giles of Lessines, *De usuris,* 428; Peter Olivi, *Tractatus,* 266; Guido Terreni, *Ethics* commentary, 5.11 (Vat.Borgh.328, f. 42r); Bernardino of Siena, *Quadragesimale de Evangelio aeterno,* sermon 33 (*Opera omnia,* 4:143).

36. Cited in Langholm, *Economics,* 256. Paul Freedman makes the sensible point that this is not actually true: some commodities are undesirable despite their rarity and therefore do not command a high price. I am grateful to Professor Freedman for allowing me to read a copy of his unpublished paper, "Spices and Medieval Ideas of Scarcity and Value," in which this observation appears.

37. Giles of Lessines, *De usuris,* 419; Richard of Middleton, *Quodlibet,* 2.23.1 (*Super libros sententiarum,* 4:65–66); Henry of Ghent, *Quodlibet,* 1.40 (*Opera omnia,* 5:228); Peter Olivi, *Tractatus,* 255; Guido Terreni, *Ethics* commentary, 5.10 (Vat.Borgh.328, f. 42r).

38. Henry of Ghent, *Quodlibet,* 1.40 (*Opera omnia,* 5:230).

39. Langholm, *Economics,* 518.

40. Guido Terreni, *Ethics* commentary, 5.10 (Vat.Borgh.328, f. 42r); Richard of Middleton, *Quodlibet,* 2.23.1 (*Super libros sententiarum,* 4:65–66).

41. Henry of Ghent, *Quodlibet*, 1.40 (*Opera omnia*, 5:229).
42. Peter Olivi, *Tractatus*, 259; Guido Terreni, *Ethics* commentary, 5.11 (Vat. Borgh.328, f. 42r).
43. Thomas Aquinas, *Commentaria in X libros ethicorum*, 5.9, to Aristotle 5.5 (*Opera omnia* [Parma ed.], 21:172); Henry of Friemar, *Ethics* commentary, to Aristotle 5.5. Latin passage quoted in Langholm, *Price and Value*, 113; Walter Burley, *Ethics* commentary, to Aristotle 5.5, my translation. Latin passage quoted in Langholm, *Price and Value*, 93; for Odonis I follow the translation in Langholm, *Economics*, 519.
44. Albert the Great, *Ethica* (Second Commentary), 5.10 (*Opera omnia* [Paris ed.], 7:358–59); Richard of Middleton, *Quodlibet*, 2.23.1 (*Super libros sententiarum*, 4:66); Peter Olivi, *Tractatus*, 255; Durandus of Saint-Pourçain, *Commentariorum libri IIII*, 4.5.2 (f. 303v); Guido Terreni, *Ethics* commentary, 5.10 (Vat.Borgh.328, f. 42r); Antonino of Florence, *Summa*, 2.1.16 (2:col. 255). For Antonino of Florence, see also De Roover, *Two Great Economic Thinkers*, 22–23.
45. Accursius, *Glossa ordinaria*, to Dig. 35.2.63 (2:col. 1597); Henry of Ghent, *Quodlibet*, 1.40 (*Opera omnia*, 5:221); Godfrey of Fontaines, *Quodlibet*, 5.14 (*Les Quodlibet*, 3:67); Peter Olivi, *Tractatus*, 261; John of Bassolis, *In quartum sententiarum opus*, 4.15 (f. 86r); John Buridan, *Questiones super libros ethicorum*, to Aristotle 5.16 (f. 106).
46. Henry of Friemar quoted in Langholm, *Economics*, 545; John Buridan, *Questiones super libros ethicorum*, to Aristotle 5.16 (f. 106).
47. Richard of Middleton, *Quodlibet*, 2.23.7 (*Super libros sententiarum*, 4:70).
48. Albert the Great, *Ethica* (Second Commentary), 5.10 (*Opera omnia* [Paris ed.], 7:359).
49. Giles of Lessines, *De usuris*, 424; John of Bassolis, *In quartum sententiarum opus*, 4.15 (f. 86r).
50. Peter Olivi, *Tractatus*, 259; Richard of Middleton, *Quodlibet*, 2.23.1 (*Super libros sententiarum*, 4:65–66). For Henry of Friemar and Gerald Odonis, see Langholm, *Economics*, 544, 519.
51. Quoted in Langholm, *Economics*, 519.
52. Peter Olivi, *Tractatus*, 255.
53. Thomas Aquinas, *Summa*, 2-2.77.2 (*Opera omnia* [Leonine ed.], 9:151); Bernardino of Siena, *Quadragesimale de Evangelio aeterno*, sermon 35 (*Opera omnia*, 4:191).
54. Robert of Courson, *Summa*, 10.18 (BN lat. 14524, ff. 51v–52r); Thomas of Chobham, *Summa confessorum*, 301.
55. Alexander of Hales, *Summa*, 4:724–5; Thomas Aquinas, *Summa*, 2-2.77.4 (*Opera omnia* [Leonine ed.], 9:154); Giles of Lessines, *De usuris*, 428; Peter Olivi, *Tractatus*, 266; John Duns Scotus, *Political and Economic Philosophy*, 56–59; Hostiensis, *Summa aurea*, col. 1859. For Huguccio, see Baldwin, *Medieval Theories*, 41.
56. Quoted in Kaye, *Economy and Nature*, 152 n. 158.
57. Peter Olivi, *Tractatus*, 259.
58. Durandus of Saint-Pourçain, *Commentariorum libri IIII*, 4.25.3 (f. 365).
59. Thomas of Chobham, *Summa confessorum*, 301; Henry of Ghent, *Quodlibet*, 1.40 (*Opera omnia*, 5:228); Thomas Aquinas, *Summa*, 2-2.77.4 (*Opera omnia* [Leonine ed.], 9:153–54); Peter Olivi, *Tractatus*, 266; Guido Terreni, *Ethics* commentary, 5.11 (Vat.Borgh.328, f. 42v).
60. John Duns Scotus, *Political and Economic Philosophy*, 58, my translation.
61. Baldwin, *Medieval Theories*, 48–49.
62. Giles of Lessines, *De usuris*, 420.
63. Giles of Lessines, *De usuris*, 423.
64. John Duns Scotus, *Political and Economic Philosophy*, 58, my translation.
65. Alexander of Hales, *Summa*, 4:724; Thomas Aquinas, *Summa*, 2-2.77.4 (*Opera omnia* [Leonine ed.], 9:154); Peter Olivi, *Tractatus*, 259–60.
66. Langholm, *Economics*, 285.

67. Langholm, *Economics*, 474.

68. Guido Terreni, *Ethics* commentary, 5.9 (Vat.Borgh.328, f. 41v).

69. Thomas Aquinas, *Commentaria in libros ethicorum*, 5.9, to Aristotle 5.5 (*Opera omnia* [Parma ed.], 21:172).

70. Peter Olivi, *Tractatus*, 254–55.

71. Langholm, *Economics*, 473.

72. John Duns Scotus, *Political and Economic Philosophy*, 44, my translation.

73. Francis of Meyronnes, *In libros sententiarum*, 3.37 (f. 176r).

74. Giles of Lessines, *De usuris*, 428, 430.

75. Langholm, *Economics*, 285.

76. Guido Terreni, *Ethics* commentary, 5.9 (Vat.Borgh.328, ff. 41v–42r).

77. Azo, *Lectura super codicem*, to C. 4.44 (342); Accursius, *Glossa ordinaria*, to Dig. 35.2.63 (2:col. 1597); Odofredus, *Lectura codicis*, to C. 4.44.2 (f. 246v); Alexander of Hales, *Summa*, 4:723; Albert the Great, *Commentarii in IV sententiarum*, to 16.B.46 (*Opera omnia* [Paris ed.], 29:638); Giles of Lessines, *De usuris*, 422; Henry of Ghent, *Quodlibet*, 1.40 (*Opera omnia*, 5:222); Richard of Middleton, *Quodlibet*, 2.23.3 (*Super libros sententiarum*, 4:67); Antonino of Florence, *Summa*, 2.1.8 (cols. 127–28). For Alexander of Tartagni, see Langholm, *Economics*, 260 n. 38.

78. Langholm, *Economics*, 260 n. 38.

79. Accursius, *Glossa ordinaria*, to Dig. 35.2.63 (2:col. 1597); Odofredus, *Lectura codicis*, to C. 4.44.2 (f. 246v).

80. John of Bassolis, *In quartum sententiarum opus*, 4.15 (f. 86r).

81. John Duns Scotus, *Political and Economic Philosophy*, 44.

82. Peter Olivi, *Tractatus*, 254.

83. Langholm, *Economics*, 473.

84. Langholm, *Economics*, 515–16.

85. Baldwin, *Medieval Theories*, 55 n. 108.

86. My attention was first called to this illustration by Baldwin, *Medieval Theories*, 55.

87. Hostiensis, *Summa aurea*, col. 943.

88. *Liber sextus*, regula 27 (*Corpus iuris canonici*, 2:col. 1122).

89. John Duns Scotus, *Political and Economic Philosophy*, 42.

90. Langholm, *Economics*, 262.

91. John of Erfurt, *Summa confessorum*, 1.6.7 (2:457); Hostiensis, *Summa aurea*, col. 943; Innocent IV, *Commentaria super libros decretalium*, 5.19.5 (f. 517r).

92. See Baldwin, *Medieval Theories*, 24–27, 46.

93. Langholm, *Economics*, 448. Kaye argues that the common distinction between the allowances of human and divine law followed different models of equalization, one arithmetical and the other geometrical. The point of drawing the distinction also may have been to posit not only different models of equalization but also different systems of judgment. Human law, which allowed more latitude than divine law, judged by external scales (what others paid for the same goods in the same place at the same time). Divine law did not so much equalize differently as judge according to intention, since divine law did not determine prices, as we have already seen. See Kaye, *Economy and Nature*, 94.

94. William of Auxerre, *Summa aurea*, 3.48.3 (3:932).

95. Baldwin, *Medieval Theories*, 69.

96. Raymond of Peñafort, *Summa*, 244; William of Rennes, *Glossa*, to *peccant*, in Raymond of Peñafort, *Summa*, 235–36. In the edition, this gloss is erroneously ascribed to John of Freiburg. For Huguccio, see Baldwin, *Medieval Theories*, 41.

97. Raymond of Peñafort, *Summa*, 244; Godfrey of Trani, *Summa super titulis decretalium*, 5.19 (f. 222r). For Laurentius Hispanus, see Baldwin, *Medieval Theories*, 48.

98. X 5.19.6.

99. X 5.19.19.

100. Peter Olivi, *Tractatus*, 257.

101. Quoted in Langholm, *Economics*, 285.

102. Godfrey of Fontaines, *Quodlibet*, 5.14 (*Les Quodlibet*, 3:67); Giles of Lessines, *De usuris*, 423–24; John Duns Scotus, *Political and Economic Philosophy*, 46, 48; Francis of Meyronnes, *In libros sententiarum*, 3.37 (f. 176r).

103. Francis of Meyronnes, *In libros sententiarum*, 4.16 (f. 203r).

104. Baldwin, *Medieval Theories*, 53.

105. Baldwin, *Medieval Theories*, 76–77; De Roover, *La pensée économique des scolastiques*, 56–58.

106. Kaye, *Economy and Nature*, 98.

107. Robert of Courson, *Summa*, 10.18 (BN lat. 14524, ff. 51v–52r).

108. Thomas Aquinas, *Summa*, 2–2.77.2 (*Opera omnia* [Leonine ed.], 9:151). The translation is based on that by the fathers of the English Dominican Province: Thomas Aquinas, *Summa theologica*, 3:1509.

109. This whole discussion presupposes that alchemists do not make pure gold: "If true gold *were* to be made by alchemy, it would not be unlawful to sell it for true, for nothing prevents art from employing certain natural causes for the production of natural and true effects." See Thomas Aquinas, *Summa*, 2–2.77.2 (*Opera omnia* [Leonine ed.], 9:151). The translation is based on that by the fathers of the English Dominican Province: *Summa theologica*, 3:1509.

110. Many have noted this point. See, for example, Cooper, *Oxford Guides to Chaucer*, 279.

111. Silverman, "Sex and Money in Chaucer's *Shipman's Tale*," 329–36.

112. Donaldson, ed., *Chaucer's Poetry*, 931, 932; Strohm, *Social Chaucer*, 100, 102; Patterson, *Chaucer and the Subject of History*, 356.

113. All quotations from the *Shipman's Tale* are from *The Riverside Chaucer*, ed. Benson. References are to line numbers in this edition.

114. This asserted causality is another way of describing the equivalences established throughout the tale that John Ganim links to double entry bookkeeping. See Ganim, "Double Entry in Chaucer's *Shipman's Tale*," 294–305.

115. Robert Adams, among others, argues that the merchant's miserliness is both sexual and monetary, based on his wife's complaint that he fails to pay his marriage debt. See Adams, "Concept of Debt in *The Shipman's Tale*," 85–102, who argues overall for the implication of sin as religious debt to God in the various debts of the *Shipman's Tale*. There is no particular reason, however, to believe that the merchant does not fulfill his marriage debt, both from the construction of the wife's complaint and from his behavior once he returns from his business trip.

116. For another account of the importance of the architecture in the tale, see Hahn, "Money, Sexuality, Wordplay, and Context," 236.

117. Hahn points out that according to the *Middle English Dictionary* these words "occur only in the *Shipman's Tale*, with close parallels . . . in gild records." See Hahn, "Money, Sexuality, Wordplay, and Context," 236.

118. Derek Pearsall has drawn attention to the merchant's insistence on keeping his friendship with the monk apart from business, notwithstanding the loan of a hundred francs. Pearsall sees the merchant as a character who needs to present to himself an image of himself that he will find satisfactory. See Pearsall, *The Canterbury Tales*, 209–17.

119. Hahn, "Money, Sexuality, Wordplay, and Context," 243.

120. In this connection we might note that Jill Mann, discussing gender roles in Chaucer's writing, lists "the marital relationship of the *Shipman's Tale*" as an example of the fact that "the Canterbury Tales is not entirely lacking in examples of traditional gender roles." Mann, *Geoffrey Chaucer*, 186.

121. For Robertson see *A Preface to Chaucer*, 376.

122. Patterson, *Chaucer and the Subject of History*, 351.

123. Thomas Aquinas, *Summa*, 2–2.77.1 (*Opera omnia* [Leonine ed.], 9:147).

124. Strohm, *Social Chaucer,* 101.

125. Many have noted this point. See, for example, Pearsall, *The Canterbury Tales,* 144.

126. All quotations from the *Franklin's Tale* are from *The Riverside Chaucer.* References are to line numbers in this edition.

127. Baker, "Dorigen's Complaint," 56–64.

128. See Hoy and Stevens, *Chaucer's Major Tales,* 87; Brewer, "Towards a Chaucerian Poetic," 242.

129. "Trouthe" in fact had a more complex meaning than the simple translation "truth." See especially Green, *A Crisis of Truth,* 1–40.

130. All quotations from "The Cock and the Jasp" are from Robert Henryson, *Poems of Henryson,* ed. Fox. References are to line numbers in this edition. Although the order of the *Fables* has been the subject of much argument, the Prologue ends by pointing the reader to the tale of the Cock and the Jasp ("And to begin, first of ane cok he wrate, / Seikand his meit quhilk fand ane jolie stone, / Of quhome the fabill ye sall heir anone"), and Fox carefully refutes the idea that the Prologue was meant to stand in the middle of the *Fables* (see *Poems of Henryson,* lxxv–lxxxi). On this probable order, see also Gray, *Robert Henryson,* 32–33.

131. John Lydgate, *Minor Poems,* ed. MacCracken. All references are by line number to this edition.

132. Pearsall, *John Lydgate,* 196. Lois Ebin reaches a more understated version of the same conclusion. See Ebin, *John Lydgate,* 106–8.

133. This connection is also noted by Fox: *Poems of Henryson,* 195. It is made more plausible by Henryson's probable training in canon law. Marianne Powell notes that in the Vulgate *scientia* corresponds to what we would translate as "understanding" or "wisdom." See Powell, *Studies in Henryson's Morall Fabillis,* 106.

134. Burke, *Rhetoric of Religion,* 14–15.

135. Walter's collection of fables may or may not have been the only version of this story that Henryson knew. Fables were widely used as pedagogic tools, particularly in teaching schoolboys Latin. Walter's version was popular but, as Fox points out, it would be difficult to prove that Henryson had not read a different version. It is almost certain, however, that Henryson based his fable on Walter's. See *Poems of Henryson,* xlix, as well as xliv–l for a complete discussion of sources.

136. In Phaedrus's telling, and in all subsequent tellings until Walter's, the jewel is a pearl rather than a jasper. Walter's reasons for the change are uncertain. Fox, after studying medieval lapidaries, concludes that there is no discernible substantive reason for the change and that it must therefore have had to do with meter. See *Poems of Henryson,* 194–95.

137. *Babrius and Phaedrus,* 279.

138. Joseph Jacobs, quoted in *Babrius and Phaedrus,* lxxxiii.

139. This is true of all four medieval versions of Romulus's *Fables* transcribed in Hervieux, *Les fabulistes latins,* vol. 2.

140. *Caxton's Aesop,* ed. Lenaghan, 74.

141. Richard of Middleton, *Super libros sententiarum,* 33.3.4 (3:389).

142. *Poems of Henryson,* 195–96; and Fox, "Henryson's *Fables,*" 341–48. For a very different (and notably Phaedrean) reading of this fable, see Benson, "O Moral Henryson," 215–17.

3. Consent

1. Peter Olivi, *Tractatus,* 253, 257, 263; Francis of Meyronnes, *In libros sententiarum,* 4.16 (f. 203r); John of Bassolis, *In quartum sententiarum opus,* 4.15 (f. 86r).

2. John Duns Scotus, *Political and Economic Philosophy,* 44.

3. For Gerald Odonis, see Langholm, *Economics*, 516–17.

4. Aristotle, *Nicomachean Ethics*, 5.11, 1138a (*Aristoteles Latinus*, 26.1–3:475; Ross trans. 134); Langholm, *Legacy of Scholasticism*, 33.

5. Langholm, *Legacy of Scholasticism*, 39–40.

6. Aristotle, *Nicomachean Ethics*, 3.1, 1110a (*Aristoteles Latinus*, 26.1–3:410; Ross trans. 48–49).

7. Thomas of Chobham, *Summa confessorum*, 508.

8. William of Auxerre, *Summa aurea*, 3.48.1 (3:913–14); Peter of Tarentaise, *In libros sententiarum commentaria*, 309; Alexander of Hales, *Summa*, 4:914–15; Thomas Aquinas, *Summa*, 2–2.78.1 (*Opera omnia* [Leonine ed.], 9:156). For more examples, see Langholm, *Legacy of Scholasticism*, 61–65.

9. Langholm, *Legacy of Scholasticism*, 65.

10. William of Auxerre, *Summa aurea*, 3.48.2 (3:920).

11. A point stressed by Langholm, *Legacy of Scholasticism*, 67.

12. Albert the Great, *Super III sententiarum*, 3.37.15 (*Opera omnia* [Paris ed.], 28:711).

13. Thomas Aquinas, *In libros sententiarum*, to 3.37.1.6 (*Opera omnia* [Busa ed.], 1:409).

14. Durandus of Saint-Pourçain, *Commentariorum libri IIII*, 3.37.4 (f. 281v).

15. Antonino of Florence, *Summa*, 2.1.9.14 (2:col. 153); Langholm, *Legacy of Scholasticism*, 68.

16. *Besete v. Peper* (1382), York Dean and Chapter Court book, 1357–1471, which I cite from the appendix to Helmholz, *Marriage Litigation*, 223–24. Translations are my own unless otherwise noted.

17. On the general competition between common law and canon law in England at this time see Helmholz, *Canon Law and English Common Law*, and Van Caenegem, *Birth of English Common Law*. On common law being content to leave marriage cases to ecclesiastical courts, see Helmholz, *Marriage Litigation*, 1–5; and Sheehan, "Formation and Stability," 229–30, 232–33. For a discussion of the interdependence of canon and common law, including an exploration of the extent to which canon law was part of the *ius commune*, see Kuttner, "Some Considerations," 349–63. Christopher Brooke points out that legislating monogamy was in the interest of both church and lay authorities. See Brooke, *Medieval Idea of Marriage*, 126–28.

18. The strongest testimony to this fact is the number of cases of clandestine marriages (that is, marriages that went against Church law by taking place away from any church) that survive. See especially Helmholz, *Marriage Litigation*, 28; Sheehan, "Formation and Stability," 249–50; and Sheehan, "Marriage and Family," 213–14. For a statement of the general problem see Helmholz, *Marriage Litigation*, 4–5. For cases where at least some of the parties seem to be trying to regulate their own affairs see, for example, *Brown alias Lymyngton v. Brown alias Lymyngton* (1471), transcribed in McSheffrey, *Love and Marriage*, 76–78, and the thirty-four cases described by Helmholz in *Marriage Litigation*, 60–61 and 135–37.

19. Anders Winroth has argued for two recensions of the *Decretum:* a first, shorter, and more consistent recension, which he dates 1139–40, and a second, longer, and less coherent recension, which he dates no later than 1158. The cases and dicta I discuss come primarily from Winroth's list of those included in the first recension; where they come from what he believes is the later recension I note so explicitly because I am interested in establishing a rough chronology. On the dating of the recensions, see Winroth, *Gratian's* Decretum, 136–45. On those parts of the generally accepted *Decretum* included in what he calls the first recension, see the appendix to Winroth, *Gratian's* Decretum, 197–227.

20. See, for example, Winroth, *Gratian's* Decretum, 1–33; Brundage, *Medieval*

Canon Law, 47–49, 154, 190–94; Brundage, *Law, Sex, and Christian Society,* 229–34; and Smith, *Medieval Law Teachers,* 19–20.

21. Gratian, *Decretum,* D. 1 c. 7 (*Corpus iuris canonici,* 1:col. 2). English from *Gratian: The Treatise on Laws,* trans. Thompson and Gordley, 6.

22. Gratian, *Decretum,* C. 27 q. 2 d.p.c. 34 (*Corpus iuris canonici,* 1:col. 1073).

23. This, for example, is how Brundage understands Gratian's position. Brundage points out that Gratian "cited with approval a number of venerable authorities who had expounded the coital theory of marriage" and that after the promise of marriage but before consummation both parties could agree to enter religious orders. While these points are certainly true, it seems less clear to me that they place Gratian significantly in the coital school of marriage since he also quotes, with approval, venerable authorities who emphasize that consent is necessary for marriage, and since if husband and wife both agreed to enter religion they could do so even after a completed marriage. See Brundage, *Law, Sex, and Christian Society,* 236–38, and Gratian, *Decretum,* C. 27 q. 2 c. 16–18 (*Corpus iuris canonici,* 1:cols. 1066–67). *Causa* 27 q. 2 c. 18 is part of the second recension, although d.p.c. 18, like the whole of canons 16 and 17, is part of the first.

24. Gratian, *Decretum,* C. 34 q. 2 c. 5 (*Corpus iuris canonici,* 1:col. 1259; part of second recension).

25. Gratian, *Decretum,* C. 27 q. 2 c. 30–32 (*Corpus iuris canonici,* 1:col. 1072).

26. Gratian, *Decretum,* C. 31 q. 2 d.p.c. 4 (*Corpus iuris canonici,* 1:col. 1114). For an extensive discussion of this conclusion, see Sheehan, "Choice of Marriage Partner," 1–33.

27. Eph 5:32. For a brief overview of the place of marriage among sacraments in the middle ages see Pelikan, *Christian Tradition,* 3:211–12.

28. The discussion that follows is drawn from Le Bras, "Mariage," cols. 2123–2317.

29. On the problem of Joseph and Mary's relationship see especially Resnick, "Marriage in Medieval Culture," 350–71.

30. Peter Abelard, *In annuntiatione Mariae,* sermon 1 (*PL,* 178:381); Hugh of St. Victor, *Quaestiones in epistolas Pauli,* 61 (*PL,* 175:524). Peter Lombard's discussion of marriage is found in Peter Lombard, *Sententiae,* 4.26–30 (*PL,* 192:909–18).

31. Peter directly echoes Hugh's language. Where Hugh wrote "Causa efficiens est consensus materialis per verba de praesenti expressus," Peter explains "Efficiens autem causa matrimonii est consensus." Hugh of St. Victor, *Quaestiones in epistolas Pauli,* 61 (*PL,* 175:524); Peter Lombard, *Sententiae,* 4.27.3 (*PL,* 192:910).

32. Brundage, *Law, Sex, and Christian Society,* 264 n. 36.

33. On the place of the *Decretum* in the schools see Rashdall, *Universities of Europe,* 1:128–32; Brundage, *Law, Sex, and Christian Society,* 232; Smith, *Medieval Law Teachers,* 19–22; and Baldwin, *Scholastic Culture,* 72. On the place of the *Sentences* in the schools see Rashdall, *Universities of Europe,* 1:474–76; Sheehan, "Choice of Marriage Partner," 14, and Baldwin, *Scholastic Culture,* 83.

34. Just as the canonists are those who studied canon law. Although each would have known a good deal of the other law and the groups may, in practice, even have overlapped occasionally, the doctors of each formed their own *collegia.* See Kuttner, "Some Considerations"; Rashdall, *Universities of Europe,* 1:147; and Smith, *Medieval Law Teachers,* 21–22.

35. Donahue, "Case of the Man," 8.

36. Dig. 35.1.15. For a consideration of this maxim in the middle ages, see Donahue, "Policy of Alexander the Third," 253–54.

37. Donahue, "Case of the Man," 9–11.

38. Donahue, "Case of the Man," 11–28.

39. X 4.1.15 (*Corpus iuris canonici,* 2:cols. 666–67). The phrase is "cui potius adhaerere deberet."

40. It is standard to refer to these traditions as, respectively, the Bolognese or Italian school (indicating those who followed Gratian) and the Parisian or French school (indicating those who favored Peter Lombard's theories). I have avoided this common terminology because I believe it is confusing. The two greatest proponents of the "French school" were Pope Alexander III, who taught at Bologna as Rolandus Bandinelli before he became a cardinal, and Huguccio, one of the most important Bolognese decretists of the middle ages. Furthermore, by the time Huguccio wrote, it is not clear, as I note below, that he followed the "Parisian" Peter Lombard so much as the Bolognese pope. The short time between Peter Lombard's *Sentences* (1155–58) and Alexander III's marriage decretals (1159–81) does not allow us to know of any clear tradition in Paris of following Peter rather than Alexander III on this question.

41. For the argument that this provision is part of the "French tradition" of Peter Lombard, see Brundage, *Law, Sex, and Christian Society*, 264. I feel less certain, having been unable to find it in the writings of Peter Lombard or Hugh of St. Victor.

42. Alexander did rule that a marriage could later be declared null if it were demonstrated that it could not be consummated: X 4.2.9 (*Corpus iuris canonici*, 2:col. 676). Some emphasize that this provision went a long way toward restoring the centrality of consummation to marriage (see, for example, Brundage, *Law, Sex, and Christian Society*, 334–35). I find the provision less significant because it leaves intact the idea that marriage is complete before consummation. It also seems to have been exceptionally difficult to win a ruling dissolving a marriage based on this claim. In one case, for example, the claim was made and after waiting three years the couple resorted to another claim; in another, the marriage was declared void, but when the husband subsequently married and produced offspring he was ordered to go back to his first wife and the second marriage was declared the invalid one: see Sheehan, "Formation and Stability," 261.

43. X 4.9.1 (*Corpus iuris canonici*, 2:cols. 691–92). See also Donahue, "Policy of Alexander the Third," 256–57.

44. X 4.1.6 (*Corpus iuris canonici*, 2:cols. 662–63).

45. X 4.1.14 (*Corpus iuris canonici*, 2:col. 666).

46. X 4.1.15 (*Corpus iuris canonici*, 2:cols. 666–67).

47. X 4.3.2 (*Corpus iuris canonici*, 2:col. 679).

48. See, for example, Donahue, "Policy of Alexander the Third," 267, and Sheehan, "Choice of Marriage Partner," 14–15, 30–33. Shannon McSheffrey points out that there is not a necessary contradiction between the choice of the offspring and that of the parent. See McSheffrey, "Consent and the Making of Marriage," 155–69.

49. Paucapalea, *Summa*, to C. 27 q. 1 pr. and C. 27 q. 2 (112–14). For discussions of the positions discussed in this paragraph see also Le Bras, "Mariage," cols. 2155–57, and Brundage, *Law, Sex, and Christian Society*, 256–64.

50. Rolandus, *Summa*, to C. 27 pr. and q. 2 c. 5, 16–17, 33–34 (114, 127, 129, 131–33). It is now accepted that the canonist Rolandus who wrote this summa is not the same as Rolandus Bandinelli, who later became Pope Alexander III. See Noonan, "Who Was Rolandus?" 21–48.

51. See transcription of *In primis hominibus* from British Library MS Royal 11.B.XIII, ff. 86vb–87ra, in Brundage, *Law, Sex, and Christian Society*, 264 n. 34.

52. Rufinus, *Summa decretorum*, to C. 27 pr. (430–32).

53. Donahue, "Policy of Alexander the Third," 254 n. 14; Donahue, "Case of the Man," 23–26, 32–33.

54. Quotation and translation from Donahue, "Case of the Man," 13.

55. Quoted in Donahue, "Case of the Man," 15.

56. Although it is not clear that Martinus regards a ductio as absolutely necessary, since he believes a man should be able to be married even if he does not have a house of his own. See Donahue, "Case of the Man," 15–17.

57. See Donahue, "Case of the Man," 18–23; Brundage, *Law, Sex, and Christian Society*, 266–67.

58. Brundage, *Law, Sex, and Christian Society*, 265.

59. Brundage, *Law, Sex, and Christian Society*, 265–66; Smith, *Medieval Law Teachers*, 27–29.

60. Huguccio, *Summa*, to C. 27 q. 2 (746).

61. Brundage, *Law, Sex, and Christian Society*, 233.

62. The changes to marriage law the council advocated were not officially adopted until its twenty-fourth session in November 1563.

63. X 4.1.22 (*Corpus iuris canonici*, 2:col. 669).

64. X 4.4.5 (*Corpus iuris canonici*, 2:cols. 681–82).

65. *Decrees of the Ecumenical Councils*, canon 51 (1:258).

66. The court cases studied by Michael Sheehan and Richard Helmholz seem to bear out this concern. Of the marriage cases heard between 1374 and 1382 in Ely, for example, over 70 percent (89 of 122) were performed away from the parish church and therefore considered clandestine, while of the cases that involved marriage formed by words of present consent in the Canterbury deposition book of 1411–20, over 90 percent (38 of 41) took place away from the church. It may be, of course, that marriages that took place as the canons prescribed were less likely to be contested, but the numbers are still remarkably high. On these numbers and the high incidence of clandestine marriage see Sheehan, "Formation and Stability," 249–51; Helmholz, *Marriage Litigation*, 28; and Donahue, "Policy of Alexander the Third," 267–68.

67. *Decrees of the Ecumenical Councils*, canon 50 (1:257).

68. Sheehan, "Marriage and Family," 17–18; Sheehan, "Marriage Theory and Practice," 412–25, 437–38, 440–42.

69. Homans, *English Villagers*, 169; Helmholz, *Marriage Litigation*, 27–30; and Sheehan, "Formation and Stability," 236–39.

70. Le Bras, "Mariage," cols. 2158–61; Brundage, *Law, Sex, and Christian Society*, 269.

71. Sheehan, "Marriage Theory and Practice," 409–51, 458–60, and Sheehan, "Choice of Marriage Partner," 17–18.

72. On the general form and aims of the summa for confessors see Boyle, "Summa for Confessors," 126–30.

73. Tentler, "Summa for Confessors as an Instrument of Social Control," 103–26, and "Response and *Retractatio*," 131–37.

74. Sheehan, "Choice of Marriage Partner," 21–22.

75. Thomas of Chobham, *Summa confessorum*, 145. For his whole discussion of marriage, see 144–93.

76. Thomas of Chobham, *Summa confessorum*, 145–46.

77. Thomas of Chobham, *Summa confessorum*, 146.

78. Thomas of Chobham, *Summa confessorum*, 69–75.

79. Quoted in Sheehan, "Choice of Marriage Partner," 23 n. 51.

80. Quoted in Murray, "Individualism and Consensual Marriage," 135 n. 40.

81. Quoted in Murray, "Individualism and Consensual Marriage," 138 n. 47.

82. Johannes Andreae, *Sponsalibus et matrimoniis*, f. 3v.

83. For the legists' options and conclusions see Donahue, "Case of the Man," 28–41.

84. Sheehan, "Choice of Marriage Partner," 28–29.

85. Sheehan, "Choice of Marriage Partner," 30.

86. Thomas of Chobham, *Summa confessorum*, 177–78. In this insistence Thomas may have gone against common practice, but he was following canon law: it is made clear in X 4.9.1, which had been published in the *Compilatio prima* (compiled by Bernard of Pavia, probably completed in 1191).

87. Murray, "Individualism and Consensual Marriage," 136.

88. Clark, "Decision to Marry," 497–511.

89. Leonard Boyle takes this position. See Boyle, "The *Oculus Sacerdotis,*" 86.

90. John Mirk, *Instructions for Parish Priests,* 68. For the dating, see *Instructions for Parish Priests,* 9.

91. John Mirk, *Instructions for Parish Priests,* 182.

92. *Lay Folks' Catechism,* xvii.

93. *Lay Folks' Catechism,* xv, xvii.

94. In the cases that follow, and particularly in the conclusions drawn about the way marriage law was practiced, it is important to note that all the evidence I discuss comes from England and that conclusions must therefore be limited to marriage law in England. There is evidence that marriage law in France was practiced and applied somewhat differently: marriages created by verba de futuro followed by sexual relations, for example, seem to have been much more common in France than in England. See especially Donahue, "Canon Law," 144–58. For more general discussions of the extent to which canon law on marriage was followed in practice in English ecclesiastical courts see Donahue, "Policy of Alexander the Third," 260–61, 271–79, and Helmholz, *Marriage Litigation,* 187–89.

95. Pollock and Maitland, *History of English Law,* 2:368–69.

96. In addition to the evidence discussed below, it is notable that a number of the cases Poos cites (stretching from the early fourteenth to the early sixteenth centuries, from Kent to Lancashire) use the verb *adhaerere,* which was not a translation of colloquial English (Poos even uses quotation marks when he translates it) and which I believe echoes X 4.1.15. See Poos, "Heavy-Handed Marriage Counsellor," 296 n. 22, 296 n. 23, 296 n. 24, 302 n. 55, 303 n. 57.

97. Brundage, *Law, Sex, and Christian Society,* 237–38.

98. Sheehan, "Formation and Stability," 234–35; Helmholz, *Marriage Litigation,* 28–31.

99. Helmholz, *Marriage Litigation,* 83–84; Donahue, "Policy of Alexander the Third," 267.

100. See Poos, "Heavy-Handed Marriage Counsellor," 294–301.

101. Cases in which parties seem to act on this principle include, for example, those of Anegold, Slory, Pateshull, Cakebred, Saffrey, and Pertefeu, all described by Sheehan, "Formation and Stability," 240–43. *Smalwode v. Twytynge and Hilton* is another similar example. See *Smalwode v. Twytynge and Hilton* (1471), in McSheffrey, *Love and Marriage,* 72–76.

102. Most of the cases that Sheehan classifies as "bigamous" fall into this category because the usual defense is that the person accused has only one spouse—the one he or she prefers. Sometimes this claim is deemed accurate, sometimes not. See Sheehan, "Formation and Stability," 251–53.

103. Sheehan, "Formation and Stability," 249 n. 83.

104. Sheehan, "Formation and Stability," 245.

105. *Lynch v. Holyngbourne* (1374), Canterbury Act book, 1372–75, transcribed in appendix to Helmholz, *Marriage Litigation,* 198–99.

106. Helmholz, *Marriage Litigation,* 61, 61 n. 123.

107. *Grene v. Knyff* (1470), in McSheffrey, *Love and Marriage,* 67–71.

108. Helmholz, *Marriage Litigation,* 107.

109. Sheehan, "Formation and Stability," 235.

110. Sheehan, "Formation and Stability," 242.

111. Sheehan, "Formation and Stability," 241.

112. Sheehan, "Formation and Stability," 238–39, 257.

113. Sheehan, "Formation and Stability," 258.

114. Sheehan, "Formation and Stability," 259.

115. Sheehan, "Formation and Stability," 259.

116. Helmholz, *Marriage Litigation,* 64–65.

117. See, for example, Resnick, "Marriage in Medieval Culture," 360–62; Sheehan, "Marriage and Family," 213; Sheehan, "Formation and Stability," 252–53; and Donahue, "Policy of Alexander the Third," 259.

118. Helmholz, *Marriage Litigation,* 156–57.

119. For declarations on oath of bribery, see Helmholz, *Marriage Litigation,* 158; for collusion in claiming a previous marriage, see Sheehan, "Formation and Stability," 252, and Helmholz, *Marriage Litigation,* 65.

120. Sheehan discusses such conclusions in "Formation and Stability," 252–53.

121. The maxim was "vox unius, vox nullius." This rule seems to have been adhered to closely in marriage cases. See, for example, *Wylson v. Fox* (1402), York Cause papers, fifteenth century, and *Chapelayn v. Cragg* (1303), York Cause papers, fourteenth century, transcribed in appendix to Helmholz, *Marriage Litigation,* 228–30, 230–32. See also Donahue, "Policy of Alexander the Third," 259.

122. *Paston Letters,* no. 721. I have modernized the spelling.

123. Helmholz, *Marriage Litigation,* 163. The translations are his.

124. Helmholz, *Marriage Litigation,* 101, 127.

125. Helmholz, *Marriage Litigation,* 126. Helmholz provides other examples of mutually contradictory defenses, 126–27.

126. X 4.4.5 (*Corpus iuris canonici,* 2:cols. 681–82).

127. Helmholz, *Marriage Litigation,* 63.

128. See, for example, *Cursted v. Tournour* (1421), Canterbury Act book, 1419–25, in appendix to Helmholz, *Marriage Litigation,* 198.

129. For many examples of marriages conditional on parental consent, see McSheffrey, "Consent and the Making of Marriage," 155–69. The condition of a dower of five marks is in *Whitingdon v. Ely* (1487), in McSheffrey, *Love and Marriage,* 56–59.

130. This understanding was made explicit by Innocent III in X 4.5.6 (*Corpus iuris canonici,* 2:cols. 683–84, promulgated in 1203).

131. For a detailed analysis of conditional contracts see Helmholz, *Marriage Litigation,* 47–57. I take my example of a dishonest condition against the substance of marriage from his chart, 50. For other discussions of conditions that are and are not against the substance of marriage see Raymond of Peñafort, *Summa,* 525–29, and Thomas of Chobham, *Summa confessorum,* 147–48.

132. *Hokerrige v. Lucas* (1417), Canterbury Deposition book, 1410–21 and Canterbury Act book, 1416–23, transcribed in appendix to Helmholz, *Marriage Litigation,* 204–07.

133. Helmholz, *Marriage Litigation,* 49–50. The friends' awareness of the rules of present consent creating a valid and lasting bond also presents striking evidence of how popularly this doctrine was accepted, even if the judge believed Joan had acted on time.

134. On error of person see, for example, Peter Lombard, *Sententiae,* 4.30.1 (*PL,* 192:916–17); Raymond of Peñafort, *Summa,* 524–25; Thomas of Chobham, *Summa confessorum,* 174–76; and William of Rennes, *Glossa,* to *si per errorem* and *vel virgo,* in Raymond of Peñafort, *Summa,* 524, 525. In the edition, this gloss is erroneously ascribed to John of Freiburg.

135. X 4.1.26 (*Corpus iuris canonici,* 2:cols. 670–71).

136. X 4.1.26 (*Corpus iuris canonici,* 2:cols. 670–71).

137. X 4.1.26 (*Corpus iuris canonici,* 2:col. 671).

138. See, for example, Innocent IV, *Commentaria super libros decretalium,* to X 4.1.26 (f. 466r); Raymond of Peñafort, *Summa,* 512–13; Antonius de Butrio, *In sextum decretalium volumen commentaria,* to X 4.1.26 (no. 7).

139. X 4.1. d.a.c. 26 (*Corpus iuris canonici,* 2:col. 670). For a consideration of Ray-

mond's work in reforming and restating canons from the *Compilationes antiques* in the *Liber extra* see Kuttner, "Raymond of Peñafort as Editor," 65–80.

140. For a full description of court procedure in marriage cases see Helmholz, *Marriage Litigation*, 112–40. In one case in York in 1373 a defendant even went so far as to challenge the way the examiner had translated his statement because he believed the not entirely accurate translation would lead the judge to the wrong conclusion. The case is described in Helmholz, *Marriage Litigation*, 181–82.

141. William of Rennes, *Glossa,* to *volo te habere,* in Raymond of Peñafort, *Summa,* 511.

142. For a more complete consideration of the problem and the distinctions canonists made in discussing it see Helmholz, *Marriage Litigation*, 36–40.

143. *Bedeman v. Nicholas* (1470), in McSheffrey, *Love and Marriage,* 41. The entire deposition is at 40–42. For other depositions that report similarly ambiguous statements, see *Brocher v. Cardif* (149?) and *Whitingdon v. Ely* (1487), in McSheffrey, *Love and Marriage,* 37, 57–59; and *Lovechild,* described in Sheehan, "Formation and Stability," 245.

144. *Lynch v. Holyngbourne* (1374), Canterbury Act book 1372–75, transcribed in appendix to Helmholz, *Marriage Litigation*, 198–99.

145. For a much more detailed discussion of this problem see Helmholz, *Marriage Litigation*, 40–45. The second example is drawn from his example on 42.

146. See, for example, *Colton v. Whithand* (1398), York Cause papers, fourteenth century; and *Cursted v. Tournour* (1421), Canterbury Act book, 1419–25, transcribed in appendix to Helmholz, *Marriage Litigation*, 196–98.

147. *Paston Letters,* no. 721.

148. See, for example, *Brocher v. Cardif alias Peryn* (149?), *Bedeman v. Nicholas* (1470), *Smalwode v. Twytynge and Hilton* (1471), and *Brown alias Lymyngton v. Brown alias Lymyngton and Bishop* (1471), in McSheffrey, *Love and Marriage,* 37–40, 40–42, 72–76, 76–78.

149. Thomas of Chobham, *Summa confessorum,* 148.

150. Johannes Andreae, *Sponsalibus et matrimoniis,* ff. 3v–4r.

151. Peter of Poitiers, *Sententiarum libri quinque,* 15 (*PL,* 211:1259).

152. John Mirk, *Instructions for Parish Priests,* 78.

153. Raymond of Peñafort, *Summa,* 511.

154. X 4.1.15 (*Corpus iuris canonici,* 2:cols. 666–67).

155. For the constant man in Roman law, see Dig. 4.2.6.

156. Brundage, *Law, Sex, and Christian Society,* 345.

157. Case from 1477, York Cause papers, described in Helmholz, *Marriage Litigation,* 91–92.

158. Case from 1393, Lichfield, Register of Bishop Le Scrope, described in Helmholz, *Marriage Litigation,* 91–92.

159. *Penysthorp v. Waldergrave* (1334), York Cause papers, fourteenth century, transcribed in appendix to Helmholz, *Marriage Litigation,* 221–23.

160. Case from 1442, York Cause papers, described in Helmholz, *Marriage Litigation,* 92–93.

161. *Besete v. Peper* (1382), York Dean and Chapter Court book, 1357–1471, transcribed in appendix to Helmholz, *Marriage Litigation,* 223–24.

162. Case from 1429–32, York Cause papers, described in Helmholz, *Marriage Litigation,* 92.

163. Case from 1362–63, York Cause papers, described in Helmholz, *Marriage Litigation,* 92.

164. *Pulter,* described in Sheehan, "Formation and Stability," 259 n. 126. The case mirrors one ruled on by Pope Clementine III (1187–91), who judged valid the marriage of a woman who said that she had consented to a marriage out of fear and yet had lived peaceably with the man she married for eighteen months. X 4.1.21 (*Corpus iuris canonici,* 2:cols. 668–69).

a non-Christian can attain heaven, although they come to different conclusions. See Whatley, "Heathens and Saints," 330–53; and Grady, *"Piers Plowman, St. Erkenwald,* and the Rule of Exceptional Salvations," 79–86. See also, *St. Erkenwald,* ed. Morse, 20–31.

23. On the way in which London came to be identified as "New Troy" see Clark, "Tri-novantum—the Evolution of a Legend."

24. McAlindon, "Hagiography into Art," 484.

25. On the series of transformations, see especially Petronella, *"St. Erkenwald."*

26. Barron, "London 1300–1540," 400. This practice was repeated regularly in city documents. For example, in the *Liber albus:* "Every person admitted to the freedom of the City shall be of a certain mystery or craft, upon the security of six reputable men of the same mystery or craft." *Liber albus,* in *Munimenta Gildhallae Londoniensis,* 1:157 (*Liber albus,* comp. Carpenter and Whitington, trans. Riley, 140). References to the *Liber albus* throughout are to the *Munimenta Gildhallae Londoniensis* edition, translations are from Riley's translation. Where I have used the translation I include its page number in parentheses. See also *Liber albus,* 1:142; *Calendar of Letter-Book E,* 12–13. There is an indication that becoming a citizen was so valuable that this safeguard did not always work— the city sometimes found it necessary to stipulate that any person or mistery receiving payment for presenting someone to the city would be fined double. See *Calendar of Letter-Book H,* 162.

27. The *Liber albus,* for example, records that these wardens held "full power from the Mayor" to ascertain that "no knavery, false workmanship, or deceit, shall be found in any manner in the said mysteries, and for the common profit of the people": *Liber albus,* 1:494 (424). These representatives regularly took oaths to oversee "well and law-fully" the mystery of which they were master, and to present to the city "all the defaults that you shall find, . . . sparing no one for favor and aggrieving no one for hate." The particular language here is from *Liber albus,* 1:528 (451). See also *Calendar of Letter-Book D,* 3; Barron, "London 1300–1540," 404; Thrupp, *Merchant Class,* 62–63.

28. The most fractious took place between 1376 and 1392 and saw a power struggle between John of Northampton and the drapers (usually known as "the non-victuallers") and Nicholas Brembre and the grocers (usually known as "the victuallers"). Contesta-tions for power along craft lines also became serious in the 1430s. See Nightingale, *Gro-cers' Company,* 228–317; Nightingale, "Capitalists, Crafts and Constitutional Change," 3– 25; Barron, *Revolt in London,* 12–20; Barron, "Ralph Holland and the London Radicals"; Thrupp, *Merchant Class,* 77–80. For the role of craft guilds in London political life more generally, see Williams, *Medieval London,* 157–69, 190–95.

29. Barron, "London 1300–1540," 403–4; Thrupp, *Merchant Class,* 68, 73.

30. Barron, "London 1300–1540," 412–28.

31. Barron, "London 1300–1540," 428–33.

32. There have been recent suggestions that the traditional distinction between craft and professional guilds, on one hand, and religious guilds and fraternities, on the other, is an artificial division that does not take sufficient account of the similar and complex roles both organizations played in late medieval life. See Reynolds, *Kingdoms and Com-munities,* 69–74, and Wallace, *Chaucerian Polity,* 75–76. Davies, "Tailors of London," emphasizes the fraternal and religious aspects of the guild. Not all, however, agree that the division between crafts and religious fraternities should be erased. Caroline M. Bar-ron, for example, in "London Middle English Guild Certificates," emphasizes that the 1389 enquiry into guilds in England concerned itself primarily with informal religious fraternities rather than with professional guilds, and Miller and Hatcher, *Medieval En-gland: Towns, Commerce and Crafts,* 361–79, find it useful to distinguish craft associations from other fraternities, even if the two had some attributes in common. But the ease with which an organization formed for one purpose could be changed to serve another has been emphasized (Reynolds, *Kingdoms and Communities,* 69–70), as have the prob-

lems in assuming that all associations of traders existed for primarily economic motives (Reynolds, *Kingdoms and Communities*, 71–74; Wallace, *Chaucerian Polity*, 76). See also Black, *Guilds and Civil Society*, 14–15, who does not find the division problematic but does point out the wide variety of names for what we call a craft guild. And we could take these arguments further. Both religious and craft associations had important communal functions. Both had religious stipulations. Both tended to be organized by geography; members of the same trade tended to live near one another. The religious guilds therefore also often included many members of the same profession. And both could be included in theories of associational forms and rights organizations. J. L. Bolton, on the other end of the spectrum, does not mention the affinities between religious and professional associations but breaks down the professional associations into two smaller groups: those who created a product (like tanners or weavers) and those who sold products they did not create (like fishmongers and grocers). See Bolton, *Medieval English Economy*, 263–65. In this section I am concerned with London craft organizations alone and altogether. I define the term simply as any association of people that defined itself in terms of its profession. Although the actual functions these organizations performed may in some instances have been similar to those of other associations this definition excludes, my interest here is in the language such groups used to describe themselves through their ordinances and articles. The distinction between craft guilds and religious fraternities is particularly important in London because of the important role craft guilds played in civic government and economic life.

33. For a discussion of the importance of profession to civic identity see also Thrupp, *Merchant Class*, 2–14. For a study that examines the various ways individual identity was negotiated through craft organizations, see Rosser, "Crafts, Guilds and the Negotiation of Work," 3–31.

34. Although this does not necessarily mean that craft guilds were inactive or nonexistent before this flowering of documentary evidence. On the idea that that guilds were organized and acted in a unified and corporate manner well before this time, see Nightingale, *Grocers' Company*, 6–107; Sutton, "Silent Years of London Guild History"; Veale, "Mistery and Fraternity in Thirteenth-Century London." For the increase of markets in thirteenth-century England, see Masschaele, "Market Rights in Thirteenth-Century England."

35. *History of the Goldsmiths' Company*, 222–23.

36. *History of the Goldsmiths' Company*, 223.

37. *History of the Goldsmiths' Company*, 223.

38. See, for example, *Memorials*, 226–27, 239, 243, 246, 278, 348. The documents in this work are extracted from the *London Letter-Books*, whose calendars postdate the *Memorials* and therefore do not give full records of any of the documents contained in it. See also *Calendar of Plea and Memoranda Rolls, 1323–1364*, 39.

39. *Memorials*, 155.

40. *Memorials*, 155.

41. *Memorials*, 153–54. In the skinners' case we have on record the petition that similarly requests the charter "for the common profit and for the commonalty of the Realm." *Records of the Skinners of London*, 27–30; *History of the Drapers of London*, 1:206–07.

42. *Memorials*, 166.

43. *Memorials*, 179.

44. *Memorials*, 221.

45. *Memorials*, 227.

46. *Memorials*, 245.

47. In addition to those already mentioned, see *Liber custumarum*, 2:83, 129; *Liber albus*, 1:313, 327; *Calendar of Letter-Book D*, 271; *Calendar of Letter-Book E*, 87; *Calendar of*

Letter-Book F, 197; *Calendar of Letter-Book H,* 37; *Memorials,* 120, 145, 197, 216, 219, 235, 239, 241, 242–43, 258, 277, 280–81, 292–94, 301, 322, 341, 348–49, 354, 360, 361, 364, 391–92, 394, 401–2, 403, 406, 439–41, 541, 568, 569, 573, 625. This list is exemplary, not exhaustive. The idea of an association of those with common interests often predates the enrollment of formal ordinances. For examples, see Veale, "Mistery and Fraternity in Thirteenth-Century London," 241, 245.

48. In addition to many cases included in the previous list, see, for example, *Liber custumarum,* 2:80; *Memorials,* 218, 247, 372, 394, 438, 546–47, 559, 563.

49. Arnold Fitz-Thedmar (attrib.), *Chronicles of the Mayors and Sheriffs of London,* 104.

50. Arnold Fitz-Thedmar (attrib.), *Chronicles of the Mayors and Sheriffs of London,* 104.

51. *Calendar of Plea and Memoranda Rolls, 1323–64,* 122. The affair was quite drawn out and continues on 122, 127, and 129. Another version of the same events from the *Letter-Books* appears in *Memorials,* 210–11.

52. *Calendar of Letter-Book F,* 96.

53. *Calendar of Plea and Memoranda Rolls, 1323–64,* 103–4.

54. *Memorials,* 156.

55. *Memorials,* 156. The repercussions continue in *Memorials,* 156–62.

56. For a brief but lively summary of feuding guilds see Unwin, *Gilds and Companies of London,* 81.

57. The drapers' charter is from 1364. See *History of the Drapers of London,* 1:204–6.

58. *Calendar of Letter-Book E,* 297–98. For a detailed discussion of the various functions and activities of burellers, see Consitt, *London Weavers' Company,* 30–32.

59. *Calendar of Early Mayors' Court Rolls,* 106–7.

60. *Memorials,* 540.

61. *Calendar of Letter-Book G,* 295; *Calendar of Plea and Memoranda Rolls, 1323–64,* 229–30.

62. See, for example, *Calendar of Plea and Memoranda Rolls, 1323–64,* 238–40; *Liber custumarum,* 2:80–81; *Memorials,* 156–62.

63. *Memorials,* 567.

64. *Memorials,* 567.

65. *Calendar of Letter-Book D,* 271; *Memorials,* 529–30; *Liber custumarum,* 2:101–4.

66. *Calendar of Letter-Book D,* 272, 273.

67. Gratian, *Decretum,* D. 10 d.p.c. 6 and C. 15 q. 3 d.p.c. 4 (*Corpus iuris canonici,* 1:col. 20, col. 752); X 5.32.1 (*Corpus iuris canonici,* 2:cols. 843–44). For an overview of the Roman legal understanding of such associations, see Epstein, *Wage Labor and Guilds,* 10–18, 20–24. On the medieval legal understanding of guilds, see Black, *Guilds and Civil Society,* 14–26.

68. Dig. 3.4.1; 47.22.1–3.

69. Michaud-Quantin, *Universitas,* 221.

70. For Hugolinus see Black, *Guilds and Civil Society,* 16; Accursius, *Glossa ordinaria,* to Dig. 3.4.1 (1:col. 404); Innocent IV, *Commentaria super libros decretalium,* to 1.31.3 (f. 148r).

71. Innocent IV, *Commentaria super libros decretalium,* 5.31.14 (f. 526r); translated Black, *Guilds and Civil Society,* 17.

72. See, for example, Thomas Aquinas, *Summa,* 2–2.57.1 (*Opera omnia* [Léonine ed.], 9:3–4).

73. Bartolus of Sassoferrato, *Commentaries on the Digest,* on 47.22.4, quoted in Black, *Guilds and Civil Society,* 17–18.

74. Consitt, *London Weavers' Company,* 22–25, 182–87. See also *Liber custumarum,* 2:416–24.

75. On the history of the Bakers' Company see Thrupp, *History of the Bakers of London,* 1–40.

76. *Memorials*, 90, 121.

77. *Memorials*, 38–39, 71–72, 119, 119–20, 121, 122, 122–23.

78. *Memorials*, 498.

79. *Memorials*, 181.

80. *Liber albus*, 1:361–62 (313–14).

81. *Calendar of Plea and Memoranda Rolls, 1323–64*, 108.

82. *Calendar of Plea and Memoranda Rolls, 1323–64*, 159–60, 211.

83. See, for example, *Calendar of Early Mayors' Court Rolls*, 1–2, 92, 157–58.

84. *Memorials*, 363, 375.

85. *Memorials*, 163; the whole case is 162–65.

86. *"Boke" of the Ordinances of the Carpenters of London*, 7–10; Alford and Barker, *History of the Carpenters' Company*, 16–17.

87. *Memorials*, 232–34.

88. *Calendar of Plea and Memoranda Rolls, 1323–64*, 197.

89. *Calendar of Plea and Memoranda Rolls, 1323–64*, 251.

90. "But greet harm was it, as it thoughte me, / That on his shyne a mormal hadde he. / For blankmanger, that made he with the beste." (*General Prologue*, 385–87).

91. *Liber albus*, 1:376 (325).

92. *Memorials*, 219–220. See also, for example, *Memorials*, 244–45, *Calendar of Letter-Book F*, 99, 100, 116, 195, *Liber albus*, 1:385–86, 467–68.

93. *Codex* 3.13.7 (*Corpus iuris civilis*, 12:279).

94. *Memorials*, 266–67.

95. For the cordwainers, see *Memorials*, 420; *Calendar of Letter-Book E*, 118; *Calendar of Letter-Book H*, 23. For the skinners, see *Calendar of Letter-Book G*, 274; *Calendar of Plea and Memoranda Rolls, 1323–64*, 209; *Calendar of Letter-Book H*, 29, 161. For the pouch-makers, see *Calendar of Plea and Memoranda Rolls, 1323–64*, 108. For the goldsmiths, see *Calendar of Plea and Memoranda Rolls, 1323–64*, 242–43; Prideaux, *Memorials of the Gold-smiths' Company*, 1:1, 4, 6, 8, 11, 16.

96. *Memorials*, 341.

97. *London Lickpenny*, ed. Hammond, 63. All further references are by line number to this edition.

98. Green, "Medieval Literature and Law," 418.

99. Chism, "Robin Hood," 19.

Conclusion

1. There is some debate over the proper names of some of these figures. I follow the conventional attribution in Starn, *Ambrogio Lorenzetti*, 53. Quentin Skinner, reading the image against its inscription, has argued that the throned figure is not Common Good but "a symbolic representation of the type of magistracy by means of which a body of citizens can alone hope to create or attain an ideal of the common good, and hence obtain the blessings of peace." Skinner, *Visions of Politics*, 2:80.

2. Translation from Skinner, *Visions of Politics*, 2:96.

3. Although the consensus has been that the fresco's virtues are Aristotelian, Quentin Skinner has argued that it instead expresses Republican, prehumanist ideals. See Skinner, "Ambrogio Lorenzetti," 1–56, and his revised version of the argument in Skinner, *Visions of Politics*, 2:39–92.

4. Fowler, *Literary Character*, esp. 1–31.

5. The distinctive bell tower also appears in contemporary illuminated manuscripts. See, for example, the view of Siena from the Book of the Censi, reproduced in Starn, *Ambrogio Lorenzetti*, 11.

WORKS CITED

Manuscripts

Paris, Bibliothèque Nationale, lat. 14524 (Robert of Courson, *Summa*)
Vatican City, Biblioteca Apostolica, Borghese 328 (Guido Terreni, commentary on the *Nicomachean Ethics*).

Primary Sources

Abelard, Peter. *In annuntiatione Beatae Virginis Mariae.* Sermon 1. In *PL.* 178:cols. 379–88.
Accursius. *Corpus iuris civilis Iustinianei, cum commentariis Accursii.* 6 vols. Orléans: Ex typographia Steph. Gamoneti, 1625.
Albert the Great. *Commentarii in IV sententarium.* In *Opera omnia* (Paris ed.). Vols. 29–30.
———. *Ethica* (Second Commentary). In *Opera omnia* (Paris ed.). Vol. 7.
———. *Opera omnia.* Ed. Auguste Borgnet. 38 vols. Paris: Vivès, 1890–95.
———. *Opera omnia.* Ed. Bernhard Geyer et al. 37 vols. Münster: Monasterii Westfalorum in aedibus Aschendorff, 1951–79.
———. *Super III sententiarum.* In *Opera omnia* (Paris ed.). Vol. 28.
———. *Super ethica* (First Commentary). In *Opera omnia* (Münster ed.). Vol. 14.
Alexander of Alessandria. *Un traité de morale économique au xive siècle.* Ed. A.-M. Hamelin. Analecta mediaevalia Namurcensia 14. Louvain: Éditions Nauwelaerts, 1962.
Alexander of Hales. *Summa theologica.* Ed. Bernhard Klumper et al. 4 vols. Quaracchi: Ex typographia collegii S. Bonaventurae, 1924–48.
An Alphabet of Tales. Ed. Mary Macleod Banks. Early English Text Society Original Series 126 and 127. Repr. in one volume. Millwood, N.Y.: Kraus Reprint, 1987.
Ambrose. *De officiis ministrorum.* Ed. Maurice Testard. In *CCSL.* Vol. 15.
Andreae, Johannes. *Summa de sponsalibus et matrimoniis.* Rome, 1485.
Antonino of Florence. *Summa theologica in quattuor partes distributa.* 4 vols. Verona: Ex typographia seminarii, apud Augustinum Carattonium, 1740–41. Repr. Graz: Akademische Druck- und Verlagsanstalt, 1959.
Antonius de Butrio. *In sextum decretalium volumen commentaria.* Turin: Bottega d'Erasmo, 1967.

Aquinas, Thomas. *Commentaria in X libros ethicorum ad Nicomachum.* In *Opera omnia* (Parma ed.). 21:1–363.
——. *Commentary on Aristotle's* Nicomachean Ethics. Trans. C. I. Litzinger. Notre Dame, Ind.: Dumb Ox Books, 1993.
——. *In quattuor libros sententiarum.* In *Opera omnia* (Busa ed.). Vol. 1.
——. *Opera omnia.* 25 vols. Parma: Tipis Petri Fiaccadori, 1852–73. Repr. New York: Musurgia, 1948–50.
——. *Opera omnia.* Leonine edition. 48 vols. to date. Rome: Ex typographia polyglotta s.c. de propaganda fide, 1882–.
——. *S. Thomae Aquinatis opera omnia.* Ed. Roberto Busa. 7 vols. Stuttgart-Bad Cannstatt: Frommann-Holzboog, 1980.
——. *Summa theologiae.* In *Opera omnia* (Leonine ed.). Vols. 4–12.
——. *Summa theologica.* Trans. Fathers of the English Dominican Province. 5 vols. New York: Benziger Brothers, 1948; repr. Allen, Tex.: Christian Classics, 1981.
Aristotle. *Aristoteles Latinus: Ethica Nicomachea; translatio Roberti Grosseteste Lincolniensis, recensio recognita.* Ed. R.-A. Gauthier. In *Aristoteles Latinus* 26.1–3, fasc. 4. Leiden-Brussels: E. J. Brill–Desclée de Brouwer, 1973.
——. *Aristoteles Latinus: Politica (Libri I–II).* Ed. Pierre Michaud-Quantin. In *Aristoteles Latinus* 29.1. Bruges-Paris: Desclée de Brouwer, 1961.
——. *The Nicomachean Ethics.* Trans. Terence Irwin. Indianapolis, Ind.: Hackett Publishing, 1985.
——. *The Nicomachean Ethics.* Trans. David Ross. Oxford: Oxford University Press, 1992.
——. *The Politics.* Trans. Carnes Lord. Chicago: University of Chicago Press, 1984.
Augustine. *Concerning the City of God against the Pagans.* Trans. Henry Bettenson. New York: Penguin Classics, 1984.
——. *De civitate dei.* Ed. Bernard Dombart and Alphonse Kalb. In *CCSL.* Vols. 47–49.
——. *Enarrationes in Psalmos.* Ed. Eligius Dekkers and J. Fraipont. In *CCSL.* Vols. 38–40.
Azo. *Lectura super codicem.* Preface by Angelo Converso. Paris, 1577. Repr. Turin: Ex officina Erasmiana, 1966.
——. *Summa Azonis super IX libros codicis.* Venice: Apud Franciscum Bindonum, 1566.
Babrius and Phaedrus. Ed. and trans. Ben Edwin Perry. Cambridge: Harvard University Press, 1965.
Bartholomew of Exeter. *Poenitentiale.* Ed. Adrian Morey. In *Bartholomew of Exeter, Bishop and Canonist: A Study in the Twelfth Century,* by Adrian Morey, 175–300. Cambridge: Cambridge University Press, 1937.
Bernardino of Siena. *Opera omnia.* Ed. College of St. Bonaventure. 9 vols. Quaracchi-Florence, 1950–65.
——. *Quadragesimale de Evangelio aeterno.* In *Opera omnia.* Vols. 3–5.
Boccaccio, Giovanni. *Famous Women.* Ed. and trans. Virginia Brown. Cambridge: Harvard University Press, 2001.
The "Boke" of the Ordinances of the Brotherhood of Carpenters of London 7: Edward III (1333). Ed. Charles Welch. London: Worshipful Co. of Carpenters, 1912.
Bonaventure. *De perfectione evangelica.* In *Opera omnia.* Vol. 5.

——. *Opera omnia.* 11 vols. Quaracchi: Ex typographia collegii S. Bonaventurae, 1882–1902.

Buridan, John. *Questiones super decem libros ethicorum Aristotelis ad Nicomachum.* Paris, 1513.

Calendar of Early Mayors' Court Rolls. Ed. A. H. Thomas. Cambridge: Cambridge University Press, 1924.

Calendar of Letter-Books of the City of London, A-L. 11 vols. London: John Edward Francis, 1899–1912.

Calendar of Plea and Memoranda Rolls, 1323–1364. Ed. A. H. Thomas. Cambridge: Cambridge University Press, 1926.

Cassiodorus. *Expositio psalmorum.* Ed. Marcus Adriaen. In *CCSL.* Vols. 97–98.

Caxton's Aesop. Ed. R. T. Lenaghan. Cambridge: Harvard University Press, 1967.

Chaucer, Geoffrey. *The Riverside Chaucer.* Ed. Larry D. Benson et al. 3rd ed. Boston: Houghton Mifflin, 1987.

Corpus iuris canonici. Ed. Emil Friedberg. 2 vols. Leipzig: Tauchnitz, 1879–81. Repr. Union, N.J.: Lawbook Exchange, 2000.

Corpus iuris civilis. Ed. S. P. Scott. 17 vols. Cincinnati: Central Trust Co., 1932; repr. New York: AMS, 1973.

Decrees of the Ecumenical Councils. Ed. Norman P. Tanner. 2 vols. Washington, D.C.: Georgetown University Press, 1990.

Decretales Gregorii IX (Liber extra). In *Corpus iuris canonici,* 2:cols. 1–928.

The Digest of Justinian. Latin text ed. Theodor Mommsen with the aid of Paul Krueger. English trans. Alan Watson. 4 vols. Philadelphia: University of Pennsylvania Press, 1985.

Douay Rheims Holy Bible. Rockford, Ill.: Tan Books, 2000.

Durandus of Saint-Pourçain. *In Petri Lombardi sententias theologicas commentariorum libri IIII.* Venice: Ex officina Gasparis Bindoni, 1586.

The Early History of the Goldsmiths' Company, 1327–1509. Ed. and trans. Thomas F. Reddaway. London: Edward Arnold, 1975.

Fasciculus Morum: A Fourteenth-Century Preacher's Handbook. Ed. and trans. Siegfried Wenzel. University Park: Pennsylvania State University Press, 1989.

Fitz-Thedmar, Arnold (attrib.). *Chronicles of the Mayors and Sheriffs of London, A.D. 1188 to A.D. 1274.* Ed. and trans. Henry Thomas Riley. London: Trübner and Co., 1863.

Francis of Meyronnes. *In libros sententiarum.* Venice, 1520. Repr. Frankfurt am Main: Minerva, 1966.

Giles of Lessines. *De usuris in communi et de usurarum in contractibus* (falsely attributed to Thomas Aquinas). In Thomas Aquinas, *Opera omnia* (Parma ed.). 17:413–36.

Giles of Rome. *De ecclesiastica potestate.* Ed. Richard Scholz. Weimar: Böhlaus, 1929. Repr. Aalen: Scientia, 1961.

——. *De regimine principum libri III.* Ed. Hieronymus Samaritanius. Rome: Apud Bartholomaeum Zannettum, 1607.

——. *On Ecclesiastical Power.* Trans. R. W. Dyson. Dover, N.H.: Boydell Press, 1986.

Godfrey of Fontaines. *Les quodlibet cinq, six, et sept de Godefroid de Fontaines.* Ed. Maurice de Wulf and Jean Hoffmans. In *Les philosophes belges: Textes et études.* 15 vols. Louvain: Institut supérieur de philosophie de l'Université, 1904–37. Vol. 3.

Godfrey of Trani. *Summa super titulis decretalium.* Lyon, 1519. Repr. Aalen: Scientia, 1968.

Gower, John. *The Complete Works of John Gower.* Ed. G. C. Macaulay. 4 vols. Oxford: Clarendon Press, 1899–1902.

———. *The Confessio Amantis.* In *The Complete Works of John Gower.* Vol. 2.

Gratian. *Decretum.* In *Corpus iuris canonici,* ed. Emil Friedberg. 2 vols. Leipzig: Tauchnitz, 1879–81. Repr. Union, N.J.: Lawbook Exchange, 2000. Vol. 1.

———. *Gratian: The Treatise on Laws with the Ordinary Gloss.* Trans. Augustine Thompson and James Gordley. Washington, D.C.: Catholic University of America Press, 1993.

Guillaume de Lorris and Jean de Meun. *Le roman de la rose.* Ed. Félix Lecoy. 3 vols. Paris: H. Champion, 1973–76.

Hammond, Eleanor Prescott, ed. *English Verse between Chaucer and Surrey.* New York: Octagon Books, 1965.

Henry of Ghent. *Quodlibet 1.* Ed. Raymond Macken. In *Opera omnia,* vol. 5.

———. *Opera omnia.* Vols. 1, 2, 5, 6, 10, 11, 13, 14, 16–18, 27–29, 36 published to date. Leuven-Leiden: Leuven University Press–E. J. Brill, 1979–.

Henryson, Robert. *The Poems of Robert Henryson.* Ed. Denton Fox. Oxford: Clarendon Press, 1981.

The History of the Worshipful Company of the Drapers of London. Ed. and trans. A. H. Johnson. 2 vols. Oxford: Clarendon Press, 1914–22.

Hostiensis. *Summa aurea.* Preface by Oreste Vighetti. Venice, 1574. Repr. Turin: Bottega d'Erasmo, 1963.

Hugh of St. Victor. *Quaestiones in epistolas Pauli.* In *PL.* 175:cols. 431–633.

Huguccio. *Summa decretorum.* Ed. J. Roman. In *Revue historique de droit francais et étranger* 27 (1903): 745–805.

Innocent IV. *Commentaria super libros quinque decretalium.* Frankfurt am Main, 1570.

John of Bassolis. *In quartum sententiarum opus.* Paris, 1517.

John of Erfurt. *Die Summa confessorum des Johannes von Erfurt.* Ed. Norbert Brieskorn. 3 vols. Frankfurt am Main: Peter D. Lang, 1980–81.

Justinian's Institutes. Ed. Paul Krueger. Trans. Peter Birks and Grant McLeod. Ithaca: Cornell University Press, 1987.

Lay Folks' Catechism. Ed. Thomas Frederick Simmons and Henry Edward Nolloth. Early English Text Society Original Series 118. London: Kegan Paul, 1901.

Liber albus. In *Munimenta Gildhallae Londoniensis.* Vol. 1.

Liber albus: The White Book of the City of London. Comp. John Carpenter and Richard Whitington, trans. Henry Thomas Riley. London: Richard Griffin and Co., 1861.

Liber custumarum. In *Munimenta Gildhallae Londoniensis.* Vol. 2.

Liber sextus decretalium Domini Bonifacii Papae VIII. In *Corpus iuris canonici.* 2:cols. 933–1124.

Livy. *From the Founding of the City: Books Three and Four.* Trans. B. O. Foster. Cambridge: Harvard University Press, 1967.

London Lickpenny. In *English Verse between Chaucer and Surrey,* ed. Hammond. New York: Octagon Books, 1965.

Lydgate, John. *The Minor Poems of John Lydgate, Part II: Secular Poems.* Ed. Henry Noble MacCracken. Early English Text Society Original Series 192. London: Oxford University Press, 1934.

Memorials of London and London Life in the XIIIth, XIVth, and XVth Centuries. Ed. and trans. Henry Thomas Riley. London: Longman and Co., 1868.

Mirk, John. *Instructions for Parish Priests.* Ed. Gillis Kristensson. Lund: CWK Gleerup, 1974.

Munimenta Gildhallae Londoniensis. Ed. Henry Thomas Riley. 3 vols. in 4. *Rerum Britannicarum medii aevi scriptores (Rolls Series)* 12. London: Longman and Co., 1859–62.

Odofredus. *Lectura codicis.* Lyon, 1552.

Olivi, Peter. *Tractatus de emptione et venditione.* In *La mercatura e la formazione del prezzo nella riflessione teologica medioevale,* by Amleto Spicciani, 253–70. Rome: Accademia Nazionale dei Lincei, 1977.

Oresme, Nicholas. *The "De moneta" of Nicholas Oresme and English Mint Documents.* Ed. and trans. Charles Johnson. London: Thomas Nelson and Sons, 1956.

Paston Letters: A.D. 1422–1509. Ed. James Gairdner. 6 vols. London: Chatto and Windus, 1904.

Paucapalea. *Summa über des Decretum Gratiani.* Ed. Johann Friedrich von Schulte. Aalen: Scientia, 1965.

Peter Lombard. *Sententiae.* In *PL.* 192:cols. 519–964.

Peter of Poitiers. *Sententiarum libri quinque.* In *PL.* 211:cols. 789–1280.

Peter of Tarentaise. *In quattuor libros sententiarum commentaria.* 2 vols. Toulouse, 1649–52. Repr. Farnborough, Hants., England: Gregg Press, 1964.

Peter the Chanter. *Summa de sacramentis et animae consiliis.* Ed. Jean-Albert Dugauquier. I, II, III (1), III (2a), III (2b). Analecta mediaevalia Namurcensia, 4, 7, 11, 16, 21. Louvain: Éditions Nauwelaerts, 1954–.

Les philosophes belges: Textes et études. 15 vols. Louvain: Institut supérieur de philosophie de l'Université, 1904–37.

Placentinus. *Summa codicis.* Preface by Francesco Calasso. Mainz, 1536. Repr. Turin: Bottega d'Erasmo, 1962.

Prideaux, Walter Sherbourne. *Memorials of the Goldsmiths' Company: Being Gleanings from Their Records between the Years 1335 and 1815.* 2 vols. London: Eyre and Spottiswoode, 1896–97.

Raymond of Peñafort. *Summa de poenitentia et matrimonio, cum glossis Ioannis de Friburgo.* Rome, 1603. Repr. Farnborough, Hants., England: Gregg Press, 1967.

Records of the Skinners of London. Ed. John James Lambert. London: Worshipful Co. of Skinners, 1933.

Remigio of Florence. *Contra falsos ecclesie professores.* Ed. Filippo Tamburini, preface by Charles T. Davis. Rome: Libreria Editrice della Pontificia Università Lateranense, 1981.

Rerum Britannicarum medii aevi scriptores (Rolls Series). 251 vols. London: Longman and Co., 1858–96.

Richard of Middleton. *Super quatuor libros sententiarum Petri Lombardi.* Ed. Lodovico Silvestri. 4 vols. Brescia, 1591. Repr. Frankfurt am Main: Minerva, 1963.

Robert of Flamborough. *Liber poenitentialis: A Critical Edition with Introduction and Notes.* Ed. J. J. Francis Firth. Toronto: Pontifical Institute of Mediaeval Studies, 1971.

Roland of Cremona. *Summae Magistri Rolandi Cremonensis O. P. liber tercius.* Ed. Aloysius Cortesi. Monumenta Bergomensia 7. Bergamo: Edizione "Monumenta Bergomensia," 1962.

Rolandus. *Die Summa Magistri Rolandi nachmals Papstes Alexander III.* Ed. Friedrich Thaner. Innsbruck: Wagner, 1874.

Rufinus. *Die Summa decretorum des magister Rufinus.* Ed. Heinrich Singer. Paderborn: Ferdinand Schöningh Verlag, 1902.

Saint Erkenwald. Ed. Clifford Peterson. Philadelphia: University of Pennsylvania Press, 1977.

St. Erkenwald. Ed. Israel Gollancz. Select Early English Poems 4. London: Oxford University Press, 1922.

St Erkenwald. Ed. Ruth Morse. Cambridge: D. S. Brewer, 1975.

The Saint of London: The Life and Miracles of St. Erkenwald. Ed. and trans. Gordon Whatley. Binghamton, N.Y.: State University of New York, Center for Medieval and Early Renaissance Studies, 1989.

Scotus, John Duns. *Political and Economic Philosophy: Latin Text and English Translation.* Ed. and trans. Allan B. Wolter. New York: Franciscan Institute, 2001.

Spicciani, Amleto. *La mercatura e la formazione del prezzo nella riflessione teologica medioevale.* Rome: Accademia Nazionale dei Lincei, 1977.

Stephen of Tournai. *Die Summa des Stephanus Tornacensis über das Decretum Gratiani.* Ed. Johann Friedrich von Schulte. Giessen: Emil Roth Verlag, 1891.

Tertullian. *De idololatria.* Ed. A. Reifferscheid and G. Wissowa. In *CCSL.* 2:1098–1124.

Thomas of Chobham. *Summa confessorum.* Ed. F. Broomfield. Louvain: Éditions Nauwelaerts, 1968.

William of Auxerre. *Summa aurea.* Ed. Jean Ribaillier et al. 7 vols. Paris-Rome: Éditions du Centre national de la recherche scientifique–editiones collegii S. Bonaventurae ad Claras Aquas, 1980–87.

William of Rennes. *Glossa.* Erroneously ascribed to John of Freiburg. In *Summa de poenitentia et matrimonio, cum glossis Ioannis de Friburgo,* by Raymond of Peñafort. Rome, 1603. Repr. Farnborough, Hants., England: Gregg Press, 1967.

Secondary Sources

Adams, Robert. "The Concept of Debt in the *Shipman's Tale.*" *Studies in the Age of Chaucer* 6 (1984): 85–102.

Alford, B. W. E., and T. C. Barker. *A History of the Carpenters' Company.* London: George Allen and Unwin, 1968.

Archer, Rowena E., ed. *Crown, Government, and People in the Fifteenth Century.* New York: St. Martin's Press, 1995.

Babbitt, Susan M. "Oresme's *Livre de Politiques* and the France of Charles V." *Transactions of the American Philosophical Society* 75 (1985): 1–158.

Baker, Donald C. "A Crux in Chaucer's *Franklin's Tale:* Dorigen's Complaint." *Journal of English and Germanic Philology* 60 (1961): 56–64.

Baldwin, John W. *Masters, Princes, and Merchants: The Social Views of Peter the Chanter and His Circle.* 2 vols. Princeton: Princeton University Press, 1970.

——. *The Medieval Theories of the Just Price: Romanists, Canonists, and Theologians in the Twelfth and Thirteenth Centuries. Transactions of the American Philosophical Society* 49, pt. 4. Philadelphia, 1959.

——. *The Scholastic Culture of the Middle Ages, 1000–1300.* Lexington, Mass.: D. C. Heath, 1971.

Barber, William J. *A History of Economic Thought.* New York: Penguin, 1967.

Barron, Caroline M. "London 1300–1540." In *Cambridge Urban History of Britain,* ed. Palliser, 395–440.

———. "The London Middle English Guild Certificates of 1388–89." *Nottingham Mediaeval Studies* 39 (1995): 108–18.

———. "Ralph Holland and the London Radicals, 1438–44." In *English Medieval Town,* ed. Holt and Rosser, 160–83.

———. *Revolt in London: 11th to 15th June 1381.* London: Museum of London, 1981.

Baxandall, Michael. "Art, Society, and the Bouguer Principle." *Representations* 12 (1985): 32–43.

Benson, C. David. "O Moral Henryson." In *Fifteenth-Century Studies,* ed. Yeager, 215–35.

Biller, Peter. *The Measure of Multitude: Population in Medieval Thought.* Oxford: Oxford University Press, 2000.

Black, Antony. *Guilds and Civil Society in European Political Thought from the Twelfth Century to the Present.* Ithaca: Cornell University Press, 1984.

———. "The Individual and Society." In *Cambridge History of Medieval Political Thought,* ed. Burns, 588–606.

Blaug, Mark, ed. *Aristotle (384–322 B.C.).* Aldershot: Edward Elgar Publishing, 1991.

———. *The History of Economic Thought.* Aldershot: Edward Elgar, 1990.

Bloch, R. Howard. "Chaucer's Maiden's Head: The *Physician's Tale* and the Poetics of Virginity." *Representations* 28 (1989): 113–34.

Bolton, J. L. *The Medieval English Economy, 1150–1500.* London: Dent, 1980.

Boyle, Leonard E. "The *Oculus Sacerdotis* and Some Other Works of William of Pagula." *Transactions of the Royal Historical Society,* 5th ser., 5 (1955): 81–110.

———. "The Summa for Confessors as a Genre, and Its Religious Intent." In *Pursuit of Holiness,* ed. Trinkaus, 126–30.

Brewer, Derek. "Towards a Chaucerian Poetic." *Proceedings of the British Academy* 60 (1974): 219–52.

———, ed. *Chaucer and Chaucerians: Critical Studies in Middle English Literature.* London: Thomas Nelson and Sons, 1966.

———. *Writers and Their Background: Chaucer.* Athens: Ohio University Press, 1975.

Bridrey, Émile. *La théorie de la monnaie au XIVe siècle.* Paris: V. Giard et E. Brière, 1906.

Britnell, R. H., and B. M. S. Campbell, ed. *A Commercialising Economy: England 1086–1300.* Manchester: Manchester University Press, 1995.

Brooke, Christopher N. L. "The Earliest Times to 1485." In *A History of St Paul's Cathedral,* ed. Matthews and Atkins, 1–99.

———. *The Medieval Idea of Marriage.* Oxford: Oxford University Press, 1989.

Brown, Emerson, Jr. "What Is Chaucer Doing with the Physician and His Tale?" *Philological Quarterly* 60 (1981): 129–49.

Brown, William H., Jr. "Chaucer, Livy, and Bersuire: The Roman Materials in the *Physician's Tale.*" In *On Language,* ed. Duncan-Rose and Vennemann, 39–51.

Brundage, James. *Law, Sex, and Christian Society in Medieval Europe.* Chicago: University of Chicago Press, 1987.

———. *Medieval Canon Law.* New York: Longman, 1995.

Burke, Kenneth. *The Rhetoric of Religion: Studies in Logology.* Berkeley: University of California Press, 1970.

Burns, J. H. *The Cambridge History of Medieval Political Thought c. 350–c. 1450.* Cambridge: Cambridge University Press, 1988.

Cannon, Christopher. *The Making of Chaucer's English: A Study of Words.* Cambridge: Cambridge University Press, 1998.

Chism, Christine. *Alliterative Revivals.* Philadelphia: University of Pennsylvania Press, 2002.

———. "Robin Hood: Thinking Globally, Acting Locally in Fifteenth-Century Ballads." In *Letter of the Law,* ed. Steiner and Barrington, 12–39.

Clark, Elaine. "The Decision to Marry in Thirteenth- and Fourteenth-Century Norfolk." *Mediaeval Studies* 49 (1987): 496–516.

Clark, John. "Trinovantum—the Evolution of a Legend." *Journal of Medieval History* 7 (1981): 135–51.

Coghill, Nevill. "Chaucer's Narrative Art in the *Canterbury Tales.*" In *Chaucer and Chaucerians,* ed. Brewer, 114–39.

Consitt, Frances. *The London Weavers' Company.* Vol. 1, *From the Twelfth Century to the Close of the Sixteenth Century.* Oxford: Clarendon Press, 1933.

Cooper, Helen. *Oxford Guides to Chaucer:* The Canterbury Tales. Oxford: Oxford University Press, 1989.

———, ed. *Nation, Court and Culture: New Essays in Fifteenth-Century English Poetry.* Dublin: Four Courts Press, 2001.

Cornet, Denise. "Les éléments historiques des IVe et VIe 'quodlibets' de Gerard d'Abbeville." *Mélanges d'archéologie et d'histoire* 58 (1941–46): 178–205.

Davies, Brian. *The Thought of Thomas Aquinas.* Oxford: Clarendon Press, 1992.

Davies, Matthew. "The Tailors of London: Corporate Charity in the Late Medieval Town." In *Crown, Government and People,* ed. Archer, 161–90.

Debby, Nirit Ben-Aryeh. "War and Peace: The Description of Ambrogio Lorenzetti's Frescoes in Saint Bernardino's Siena Sermons." *Renaissance Studies* 15 (2001): 272–86.

Delany, Sheila. "Politics and the Paralysis of Poetic Imagination in the *Physician's Tale.*" *Studies in the Age of Chaucer* 3 (1981): 47–60.

De Roover, Raymond. "The Concept of the Just Price: Theory and Practice." *Journal of Economic History* 18 (1958): 418–34.

———. *La pensée économique des scolastiques: Doctrines et méthodes.* Montreal: Institut d'études médiévales, 1971.

———. *San Bernardino of Siena and Sant' Antonino of Florence: The Two Great Economic Thinkers of the Middle Ages.* Boston: Kress Library of Business and Economics, 1967.

Dictionnaire de théologie catholique. Ed. Alfred Vacant et al. 15 vols. Paris: Letouzey et Ané, 1899–1950.

Donahue, Charles, Jr. "The Canon Law on the Formation of Marriage and Social Practice in the Later Middle Ages." *Journal of Family History* 8 (1983): 144–58.

———. "The Case of the Man Who Fell into the Tiber: The Roman Law of Marriage at the Time of the Glossators." *American Journal of Legal History* 22 (1978): 1–53.

———. "'Clandestine' Marriage in the Later Middle Ages: A Reply." *Law and History Review* 10 (1992): 315–22.

———. "The Policy of Alexander the Third's Consent Theory of Marriage." In *Pro-*

ceedings of the Fourth International Congress of Medieval Canon Law, ed. Kuttner, 251–81.

Donaldson, E. Talbot, ed. *Chaucer's Poetry.* New York: Ronald Press, 1958.

Duncan-Rose, Caroline, and Theo Vennemann, ed. *On Language: Rhetorica, Phono-logica, Syntactica; A Festschrift for Robert P. Stockwell from His Friends and Colleagues.* London: Routledge, 1988.

Dunne, Tom, ed. *The Writer as Witness: Literature as Historical Evidence.* Cork: Cork University Press, 1987.

Ebin, Lois. *John Lydgate.* Boston: Twayne, 1985.

The Encyclopedia of the Social Sciences. Ed. E. R. Seligman. 15 vols. New York: Macmillan, 1930–35.

Epstein, Steven A. "The Theory and Practice of the Just Wage." *Journal of Medieval History* 17 (1991): 53–69.

——. *Wage Labor and Guilds in Medieval Europe.* Chapel Hill: University of North Carolina Press, 1991.

Evans-Jones, Robin, and Geoffrey MacCormack. "Obligations." In *Companion to Justinian's Institutes,* ed. Metzger, 127–207.

Finch, Andrew J. "Parental Authority and the Problem of Clandestine Marriage in the Later Middle Ages." *Law and History Review* 8 (1990): 189–205.

Fletcher, Angus. "The Sentencing of Virginia in the *Physician's Tale.*" *Chaucer Review* 34 (2000): 300–308.

Fowler, Elizabeth. *Literary Character: The Human Figure in Early English Writing.* Ithaca: Cornell University Press, 2003.

Fox, Denton. "Henryson's *Fables.*" *English Literary History* 29 (1962): 337–56.

Frantzen, Allen J. "*St. Erkenwald* and the Raising of Lazarus." *Mediaevalia* 7 (1981): 157–71.

Freedman, Paul. *Images of the Medieval Peasant.* Stanford: Stanford University Press, 1999.

Frugoni, Chiara. *Pietro and Ambrogio Lorenzetti.* Florence: Scala Books, distributed by Harper and Row, 1988.

Ganim, John M. "Double Entry in Chaucer's *Shipman's Tale:* Chaucer and Bookkeeping before Pacioli." *Chaucer Review* 30 (1996): 294–305.

Gardner, John. *The Poetry of Chaucer.* Carbondale: Southern Illinois University Press, 1977.

Garland, Peter B. *The Definition of Sacrament according to Saint Thomas.* Ottawa: University of Ottawa Press, 1959.

Gilchrist, John. *The Church and Economic Activity in the Middle Ages.* New York: St. Martin's Press, 1969.

Gordon, Barry. *Economic Analysis before Adam Smith: Hesiod to Lessius.* New York: Barnes and Noble, 1975.

Grady, Frank. "*Piers Plowman, St. Erkenwald,* and the Rule of Exceptional Salvations." *Yearbook of Langland Studies* 6 (1992): 63–88.

——. "*St. Erkenwald* and the Merciless Parliament." *Studies in the Age of Chaucer* 22 (2000): 179–211.

Gray, Douglas. *Robert Henryson.* Leiden: E. J. Brill, 1979.

Green, Richard Firth. *A Crisis of Truth: Literature and Law in Ricardian England.* Philadelphia: University of Pennsylvania Press, 1999.

——. "Medieval Literature and Law." In *Cambridge History of Medieval English Literature*, ed. Wallace, 407–31.

Hahn, Thomas. "Money, Sexuality, Wordplay, and Context in the *Shipman's Tale*." In *Chaucer in the Eighties*, ed. Wasserman and Blanch, 235–49.

Hanna, Ralph. "Alliterative Poetry." In *Cambridge History of Medieval English Literature*, ed. Wallace, 488–512.

Harbert, Bruce. "Chaucer and the Latin Classics." In *Writers and Their Background*, ed. Brewer, 137–53.

Helmholz, R. H. *Canon Law and English Common Law*. London: Selden Society, 1983.

——. *Marriage Litigation in Medieval England*. Cambridge: Cambridge University Press, 1974.

Hervieux, Léopold. *Les fabulistes latins depuis le siècle d'Auguste jusqu'à la fin du moyen âge*. 5 vols. Paris: Firmin-Dido, 1883–99.

Hirsh, John C. "Modern Times: The Discourse of the *Physician's Tale*." *Chaucer Review* 27 (1993): 387–95.

Holt, Richard, and Gervase Rosser, ed. *The English Medieval Town: A Reader in English Urban History, 1200–1540*. London: Longman, 1990.

Homans, George. *English Villagers of the Thirteenth Century*. Cambridge: Harvard University Press, 1942.

Hoy, Michael, and Michael Stevens. *Chaucer's Major Tales*. London: Norton Bailey, 1969. Repr. New York: Schocken Books, 1983.

Hunt, E. K. *History of Economic Thought: A Critical Perspective*. Updated 2nd ed. Armonk, N.Y.: M. E. Sharpe, 2002.

Jordan, Mark D. "Theology and Philosophy." In *Cambridge Companion to Aquinas*, ed. Kretzmann and Stump, 232–51.

Kaye, Joel. *Economy and Nature in the Fourteenth Century: Money, Market Exchange, and the Emergence of Scientific Thought*. Cambridge: Cambridge University Press, 1998.

Kempshall, M. S. *The Common Good in Late Medieval Political Thought*. Oxford: Clarendon Press, 1999.

Kretzmann, Norman, ed. *The Cambridge History of Later Medieval Philosophy*. Cambridge: Cambridge University Press, 1982.

Kretzmann, Norman, and Eleonore Stump, ed. *The Cambridge Companion to Aquinas*. Cambridge: Cambridge University Press, 1993.

Kuttner, Stephan. "Pierre de Roissy and Robert of Flamborough." *Traditio* 2 (1944): 492–99.

——. "Raymond of Peñafort as Editor: The 'decretales' and 'constitutiones' of Gregory IX." *Bulletin of Medieval Canon Law* 12 (1982): 65–80.

——. "Some Considerations on the Role of Secular Law and Institutions in the History of Canon Law." In his *Studies in the History of Medieval Canon Law*, essay 6.

——. *Studies in the History of Medieval Canon Law*. Aldershot: Variorum, 1990.

——, ed. *Proceedings of the Fourth International Congress of Medieval Canon Law*. Vatican City: Biblioteca Apostolica Vaticana, 1976.

Langholm, Odd. *Economics in the Medieval Schools*. Leiden: E. J. Brill, 1992.

——. *The Legacy of Scholasticism in Economic Thought: Antecedents of Choice and Power*. Cambridge: Cambridge University Press, 1998.

——. *Price and Value in the Aristotelian Tradition*. Bergen: Universitetsforlaget, 1979.

——. *Wealth and Money in the Aristotelian Tradition*. Bergen: Universitetsforlaget, 1983.

Le Bras, Gabriel. "Mariage: La doctrine du mariage chez les théologiens et les canonists depuis l'an mille." In *Dictionnaire de théologie catholique*, 9:cols. 2123–2317.

Lee, Brian S. "The Position and Purpose of the *Physician's Tale*." *Chaucer Review* 22 (1987): 141–60.

Le Goff, Jacques. *Time, Work, and Culture in the Middle Ages*. Trans. Arthur Goldhammer. Chicago: University of Chicago Press, 1980.

Little, Lester. *Religious Poverty and the Profit Economy in Medieval Europe*. Ithaca: Cornell University Press, 1978.

Lomperis, Linda. "Unruly Bodies and Ruling Practices: Chaucer's *Physician's Tale* as Socially Symbolic Act." In *Feminist Approaches to the Body*, ed. Lomperis and Stanbury, 21–37.

Lomperis, Linda, and Sarah Stanbury, ed. *Feminist Approaches to the Body in Medieval Literature*. Philadelphia: University of Pennsylvania Press, 1993.

Maitland, Frederic William. *See* Pollock, Frederick.

Mann, Jill. *Geoffrey Chaucer*. Atlantic Highlands, N.J.: Humanities Press, 1991.

Masschaele, James. "Market Rights in Thirteenth-Century England." *English Historical Review* 107 (1992): 78–89.

Mate, Mavis. "Monetary Policies in England, 1272–1307." *British Numismatic Journal* 41 (1972): 34–79.

Matthews, W. R., and W. M. Atkins, ed. *A History of St Paul's Cathedral*. London: John Barker, 1957.

Mayhew, Nicholas. "Modeling Medieval Monetisation." In *A Commercialising Economy*, ed. Britnell and Campbell, 55–77.

McAlindon, T. "Hagiography into Art: A Study of *St. Erkenwald*." *Studies in Philology* 67 (1970): 472–94.

McSheffrey, Shannon. "'I will never have none ayenst my faders will': Consent and the Making of Marriage in the Late Medieval Diocese of London." In *Women, Marriage, and Family*, ed. Rousseau and Rosenthal, 153–74.

——, ed. *Love and Marriage in Late Medieval London*. Kalamazoo, Mich.: Medieval Institute Publications, 1995.

Meikle, S. "Aristotle and Exchange Value." In *Aristotle*, ed. Blaug, 195–220.

Metzger, Ernest, ed. *A Companion to Justinian's Institutes*. Ithaca: Cornell University Press, 1999.

Meunier, Louis Francis. *Essai sur la vie et les ouvrages de Nicole Oresme*. Paris: Typographie Ch. Lahure, 1857.

Meyer-Lee, Robert J. "Hoccleve and the Apprehension of Money." *Exemplaria* 13 (2001): 173–214.

Michaud-Quantin, Pierre. *Universitas: Expressions du mouvement communautaire dans le Moyen-Age latin*. Paris: J. Vrin, 1970.

Middle English Dictionary. Ed. Hans Kurath and Sherman M. Kuhn. Ann Arbor: University of Michigan Press, 1952–2001.

Middleton, Anne. "The *Physician's Tale* and Love's Martyrs: 'Ensamples Mo Than Ten' as a Method in the *Canterbury Tales*." *Chaucer Review* 8 (1973): 9–32.

Miller, Edward, and John Hatcher. *Medieval England: Towns, Commerce and Crafts, 1086–1348*. London: Longman, 1995.

The MIT Dictionary of Modern Economics. Ed. David W. Pearce. 3rd ed. Cambridge: MIT Press, 1986.

Morey, Adrian. *Bartholomew of Exeter, Bishop and Canonist: A Study in the Twelfth Century.* Cambridge: Cambridge University Press, 1937.

Murray, Jacqueline. "Individualism and Consensual Marriage: Some Evidence from Medieval England." In *Women, Marriage, and Family,* ed. Rousseau and Rosenthal, 121–51.

Muscatine, Charles. *Poetry and Crisis in the Age of Chaucer.* Notre Dame, Ind.: University of Notre Dame Press, 1972.

Nelson, Benjamin. *The Idea of Usury: From Tribal Brotherhood to Universal Otherhood.* 2nd ed. Chicago: University of Chicago Press, 1969.

Newman, Barbara. *God and the Goddesses: Vision, Poetry, and Belief in the Middle Ages.* Philadelphia: University of Pennsylvania Press, 2003.

Nightingale, Pamela. "Capitalists, Crafts, and Constitutional Change in Late Fourteenth-Century London." *Past and Present* 124 (1989): 3–35.

——. *A Medieval Mercantile Community: The Grocers' Company and the Politics and Trade of London, 1000–1485.* New Haven: Yale University Press, 1995.

Nissé, Ruth. "'A Coroun Ful Riche': The Rule of History in *St. Erkenwald.*" *English Literary History* 65 (1998): 277–95.

Noonan, John T., Jr. "Gratian Slept Here: The Changing Identity of the Father of the Systematic Study of Canon Law." *Traditio* 35 (1979): 145–72.

——. "Marital Affection in the Canonists." *Studia Gratiana* 12 (1967): 479–509.

——. *The Scholastic Analysis of Usury.* Cambridge: Harvard University Press, 1957.

——. "Who Was Rolandus?" In *Law, Church, and Society,* ed. Pennington and Somerville, 21–48.

Norman, Diana. *Painting in Late Medieval and Renaissance Siena (1260–1555).* New Haven: Yale University Press, 2003.

Nussbaum, Frederick L. *A History of the Economic Institutions of Modern Europe.* New York: F. S. Crofts, 1933.

O'Donnell, J. Reginald, ed. *Essays in Honour of Anton Charles Pegis.* Toronto: Pontifical Institute of Mediaeval Studies, 1974.

O'Meara, Thomas Franklin. *Thomas Aquinas, Theologian.* Notre Dame, Ind.: University of Notre Dame Press, 1997.

Oser, Jacob, and Stanley L. Bruce. *The Evolution of Economic Thought.* 4th ed. New York: Harcourt Brace Jovanovich, 1988.

Otter, Monika. "'New Werke': *St. Erkenwald,* St. Albans, and the Medieval Sense of the Past." *Journal of Medieval and Renaissance Studies* 24 (1994): 387–414.

Owst, G. R. *Literature and Pulpit in Medieval England: A Neglected Chapter in the History of English Letters and of the English People.* 2nd ed. New York: Barnes and Noble, 1961.

Palliser, D. M., ed. *The Cambridge Urban History of Britain.* Vol. 1, *600–1540.* Cambridge: Cambridge University Press, 2000.

Patterson, Lee. *Chaucer and the Subject of History.* Madison: University of Wisconsin Press, 1991.

Pearsall, Derek. *The Canterbury Tales.* London: Unwin, 1985.

——. *John Lydgate.* London: Routledge and Kegan Paul, 1970.

——. *The Life of Geoffrey Chaucer.* Oxford: Blackwell, 1992.

Pederson, Frederik. "Did the Medieval Laity Know the Canon Law Rules on Marriage? Some Evidence from Fourteenth-Century York Cause Papers." *Mediaeval Studies* 56 (1994): 111–52.

Pelikan, Jaroslav. *The Christian Tradition: A History of the Development of Doctrine.* Vol. 3, *The Growth of Medieval Theology (600–1300).* Chicago: University of Chicago Press, 1978.

Pennington, Kenneth, and Robert Somerville, ed. *Law, Church, and Society: Essays in Honor of Stephan Kuttner.* Philadelphia: University of Pennsylvania Press, 1977.

Petronella, Vincent F. "*St. Erkenwald:* Style as the Vehicle for Meaning." *Journal of English and Germanic Philology* 66 (1967): 532–40.

Pinto de Oliveira, Carlos-Josaphat, ed. *Ordo sapientiae et amoris: Image et message de saint Thomas d'Aquin à travers les récentes études historiques, herméneutiques, et doctrinales.* Fribourg: Éditions universitaires, 1993.

Pirenne, Henri. *Histoire économique de l'Occident médiéval.* Bruges: Desclée de Brouwer, 1951.

Pollock, Frederick, and Frederic William Maitland. *The History of English Law before the Time of Edward I.* 2 vols. Cambridge: Cambridge University Press, 1968.

Poos, L. R. "The Heavy-Handed Marriage Counsellor: Regulating Marriage in Some Later-Medieval English Local Ecclesiastical-Court Jurisdictions." *American Journal of Legal History* 39 (1995): 291–309.

Powell, Marianne. Fabula Docet: *Studies in the Background and Interpretation of Henryson's Morall Fabillis.* Odense: Odense University Press, 1983.

Quillet, Jeannine. "Community, Council and Representation." In *Cambridge History of Medieval Political Thought,* ed. Burns, 520–72.

Rashdall, Hastings. *The Universities of Europe in the Middle Ages.* Rev. and ed. F. M. Powicke and A. B. Emden. 3 vols. Oxford: Oxford University Press, 1936.

Resnick, Irven M. "Marriage in Medieval Culture: Consent Theory and the Case of Joseph and Mary." *Church History* 69 (2000): 350–71.

Reynolds, Susan. *Kingdoms and Communities in Western Europe, 900–1300.* 2nd ed. Oxford: Clarendon Press, 1997.

Rima, Ingrid Hahne. *Development of Economic Analysis.* 5th ed. New York: Routledge, 1991.

Robertson, D. W., Jr. "The Physician's Comic Tale." *Chaucer Review* 23 (1988): 129–39.

———. *A Preface to Chaucer: Studies in Medieval Perspectives.* Princeton: Princeton University Press, 1962.

Roney, Lois. "*Winner and Waster*'s 'Wyse Wordes': Teaching Economics and Nationalism in Fourteenth-Century England." *Speculum* 69 (1994): 1070–1100.

Rosser, Gervase. "Crafts, Guilds, and the Negotiation of Work in the Medieval Town." *Past and Present* 154 (1997): 3–31.

Roth, Guy. *The Origin of Economic Ideas.* 2nd ed. Dobbs Ferry, N.Y.: Sheridan House, 1988.

Rousseau, Constance M., and Joel T. Rosenthal, ed. *Women, Marriage, and Family in Medieval Christendom.* Kalamazoo, Mich.: Medieval Institute Publications, 1998.

Rubin, Miri. *Charity and Community in Medieval Cambridge.* Cambridge: Cambridge University Press, 1987.

Salter, Elizabeth. *Fourteenth-Century English Poetry: Contexts and Readings.* Oxford: Clarendon Press, 1983.

Scattergood, John. "The *Libelle of Englyshe Polycye:* The Nation and Its Place." In *Nation, Court and Culture,* ed. Cooper, 28–49.

———. *The Lost Tradition: Essays on Middle English Alliterative Poetry.* Dublin: Four Courts Press, 1990.

———. "*Winner and Waster* and the Mid-Fourteenth-Century Economy." In *Writer as Witness,* ed. Dunne, 39–57.

Sheehan, Michael M. "Choice of Marriage Partner in the Middle Ages: Development and Mode of Application of a Theory of Marriage." *Studies in Medieval and Renaissance History* 1 (1978): 1–33.

———. "The Formation and Stability of Marriage in Fourteenth-Century England: Evidence of an Ely Register." *Mediaeval Studies* 33 (1971): 228–63.

———. "Marriage and Family in English Conciliar and Synodal Legislation." In *Essays in Honour of Anton Charles Pegis,* ed. O'Donnell, 205–14.

———. "Marriage Theory and Practice in the Conciliar Legislation and Diocesan Statutes of Medieval England." *Mediaeval Studies* 40 (1978): 408–60.

Silverman, Albert H. "Sex and Money in Chaucer's *Shipman's Tale.*" *Philological Quarterly* 32 (1953): 329–36.

Skinner, Quentin. "Ambrogio Lorenzetti's *Buon Governo* Frescoes: Two Old Questions, Two New Answers." *Journal of the Warburg and Courtauld Institutes* 62 (1999): 1–28.

———. *Visions of Politics.* 3 vols. Cambridge: Cambridge University Press, 2002.

Smith, D. Vance. *Arts of Possession: The Middle English Household Imaginary.* Minneapolis: University of Minnesota Press, 2003.

Smith, J. A. Clarence. *Medieval Law Teachers and Writers: Civilian and Canonist.* Ottawa: University of Ottawa Press, 1975.

Sombart, Werner. "Capitalism." In *Encyclopedia of the Social Sciences.* 3:195–208.

Soudek, Josef. "Aristotle's Theory of Exchange: An Inquiry into the Origin of Economic Analysis." In *Aristotle,* ed. Blaug, 11–41.

Spufford, Peter. *Money and Its Use in Medieval Europe.* Cambridge: Cambridge University Press, 1988.

———. *Power and Profit: The Merchant in Medieval Europe.* New York: Thames and Hudson, 2002.

Starn, Randolph. *Ambrogio Lorenzetti: The Palazzo Pubblico, Siena.* New York: George Braziller, 1994.

Stein, Peter. *Roman Law in European History.* Cambridge: Cambridge University Press, 1999.

Steiner, Emily, and Candace Barrington, ed. *The Letter of the Law: Legal Practice and Literary Production in Medieval England.* Ithaca: Cornell University Press, 1999.

Stevenson, Kenneth. *Nuptial Blessing: A Study of Christian Marriage Rites.* New York: Oxford University Press, 1983.

Strohm, Paul. *England's Empty Throne: Usurpation and the Language of Legitimation, 1399–1422.* New Haven: Yale University Press, 1998.

———. *Hochon's Arrow: The Social Imagination of Fourteenth-Century Texts.* Princeton: Princeton University Press, 1992.

——. *Social Chaucer.* Cambridge: Harvard University Press, 1989.

Sutton, Anne F. "The Silent Years of London Guild History before 1300: The Case of the Mercers." *Historical Research* 71 (1998): 121–41.

Tatlock, John. *The Development and Chronology of Chaucer's Works.* Gloucester, Mass.: Peter Smith, 1963.

Tentler, Thomas N. "Response and *Retractatio.*" In *Pursuit of Holiness,* ed. Trinkaus, 131–37.

——. "The Summa for Confessors as an Instrument of Social Control." In *Pursuit of Holiness,* ed. Trinkaus, 103–26.

Thrupp, Sylvia L. *The Merchant Class of Medieval London.* Ann Arbor: University of Michigan Press, 1948.

——. *A Short History of the Worshipful Company of Bakers of London.* Croyden: Galleon Press, 1933.

Tierney, Brian. *The Crisis of Church and State, 1050–1300.* Medieval Academy Reprints for Teaching. Toronto: University of Toronto Press, 1988.

Torrell, Jean-Pierre. *Saint Thomas Aquinas.* Vol. 1, *The Person and His Work.* Trans. Robert Royal. Washington, D.C.: Catholic University Press of America, 1996.

Trigg, Stephanie. "The Rhetoric of Excess in *Winner and Waster.*" *Yearbook of Langland Studies* 3 (1989): 91–108.

Trinkaus, Charles, ed. *The Pursuit of Holiness in Late Medieval and Renaissance Religion.* Leiden: E. J. Brill, 1974.

Ullmann, Walter. *Principles of Government and Politics in the Middle Ages.* London: Methuen, 1961.

Unwin, George. *The Gilds and Companies of London.* London: Methuen, 1908.

Van Caenegem, R. C. *The Birth of the English Common Law.* 2nd ed. Cambridge: Cambridge University Press, 1988.

Veale, Elspeth. "The 'Great Twelve': Mistery and Fraternity in Thirteenth-Century London." *Historical Research* 64 (1991): 237–63.

Walker, Sue Sheridan. "Free Consent and Marriage of Feudal Wards in Medieval England." *Journal of Medieval History* 8 (1982): 123–34.

Wallace, David. *Chaucerian Polity: Absolutist Lineages and Associational Forms in England and Italy.* Stanford: Stanford University Press, 1997.

——, ed. *The Cambridge History of Medieval English Literature.* Cambridge: Cambridge University Press, 1999.

Walsh, Liam G. "The Divine and the Human in St. Thomas's Theology of Sacraments." In *Ordo sapientiae et amoris,* ed. Pinto de Oliveira, 321–52.

Wasserman, Julian N., and Robert J. Blanch, ed. *Chaucer in the Eighties.* Syracuse, N.Y.: Syracuse University Press, 1986.

Whatley, Gordon. "Heathens and Saints: *St. Erkenwald* in Its Legendary Context." *Speculum* 61 (1986): 330–63.

——. "The Middle English *St. Erkenwald* and Its Liturgical Context." *Mediaevalia* 8 (1982): 277–306.

Wieland, Georg. "The Reception and Interpretation of Aristotle's *Ethics.*" In *The Cambridge History of Later Medieval Philosophy,* ed. Kretzmann, 657–72.

Williams, Gwyn A. *Medieval London: From Commune to Capital.* London: Athlone Press, 1963.

Winroth, Anders. *The Making of Gratian's* Decretum. Cambridge: Cambridge University Press, 2000.

Wood, Diana. *Medieval Economic Thought*. Cambridge: Cambridge University Press, 2002.

Yeager, Robert F., ed. *Fifteenth-Century Studies: Recent Essays*. Hamden, Conn.: Archon Books, 1984.

INDEX